Obsessions of a Showwoman

The Performance Worlds of
Marisa Carnesky

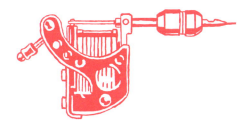

Edited by Eirini Kartsaki

intellect
Bristol, UK / Chicago, USA

First published in the UK in 2024 by
Intellect, The Mill, Parnall Road, Fishponds, Bristol, BS16 3JG, UK

First published in the USA in 2024 by
Intellect, The University of Chicago Press, 1427 E. 60th Street,
Chicago, IL 60637, USA

Copyright © 2024 Intellect Ltd

All rights reserved. No part of this publication may be reproduced,
stored in a retrieval system or transmitted, in any form or by
any means, electronic, mechanical, photocopying, recording or
otherwise, without written permission.

Chapter 'Weird Women' by Eirini Kartsaki is published
under the Creative Commons licence CC BY 4.0
(https://creativecommons.org/licenses/by/4.0/)

A catalogue record for this book is available from the British Library.

Copy editor: MPS Limited
Design and illustrations: David Caines
Cover image: Marisa Carnesky, *Tattooed Lady*, Manuel Vason Studio, 2011. © Manuel Vason
Frontispiece: Marisa Carnesky, *Carnesky's Ghost Train*, 2004. © Alastair Muir
Production manager: Debora Nicosia

Paperback ISBN 978-1-8359-501-4
ePDF ISBN 978-1-83595-012-8
ePUB ISBN 978-1-83595-011-1

Printed and bound by Short Run

To find out about all our publications, please visit our website.
There you can subscribe to our e-newsletter, browse or download our current
catalogue and buy any titles that are in print.

This book is dedicated to Showwomen past and present, who create incredible shows, but may not have been recognised or remembered for how important they are. Her show must go on.

Contents

Foreword Dominic Johnson 10

Introduction: Marisa Carnesky – Sorceress, Radical School Mistress, Showwoman
Eirini Kartsaki 13

Finding Marisa Carnesky

A Showwoman of a Certain Rage: Marisa Carnesky's Bleeding Spectacular
Josephine Machon 20

Ballad of the Bloody Pearl Daniel Oliver 44

Spectacle, Patriarchy, and Ghost Trains Paloma Faith and Marisa Carnesky 46

Finding Marisa Carnesky Liz Aggiss 51

The Cosmos of Showwomen

Marisa Carnesky, Showwoman Roberta Mock 58

Earth as Genderqueer Showwoman
Annie Sprinkle, Beth Stevens, and Marisa Carnesky 91

Conquering the World with Hoops Marawa 105

The Making of a Future Showwoman Empress Stah 110

Conjuring the Weird

Weird Women Eirini Kartsaki 146

Their Phantasmagorical Appearances
Tai Shani, Geneva Foster Gluck, and Marisa Carnesky 169

Penny Slot Somnambulist Rachel Zerihan 179

Shape Changing: The Metamorphosis of a Showwoman Vanessa Toulmin 183

Magic Blood, Mysterious Blades, and Women Who Show

Incredible Bleeding Women I
Rhyannon Styles, Livia Kojo Alour,
Veronica Thompson, and Marisa Carnesky 218

Showwomen Who Risk It All
Lucifire, Lalla Morte, Miss Behave, and Marisa Carnesky 228

Incredible Bleeding Women II
Nao Nagai, H Plewis, and Marisa Carnesky 239

Her Spectacular Entrances Marisa Carnesky 245

Radical Bodies of Work

From the Finishing School of Marisa Carnesky: Lessons in Doing It Together
Phoebe Patey-Ferguson 274

Finding Power in Pathos Alex Lyons 290

The Coven Amy Ridler 294

The Department of Feminist Conversations in Dialogue
with Marisa Carnesky's Live Archive
Mary Paterson and Maddy Costa for the Department of Feminist Conversations 298

Afterword: The Showwoman's Carriage Giulia Palladini 316

Contributors 322

Figures 333

Acknowledgements 337

She casts the circle and invites the audience in

She is the Showwoman,
The Showwoman,
The Showwoman

Foreword

Dominic Johnson

Many of the writers in this book begin with their own memory of encountering Marisa Carnesky for the first time. The experience of finding and beholding her tends to be foundational. In my first encounter, I inserted a coin in the fortune-telling slot machine between her legs, and in return, aged 23, I was gifted a future. This was her *Penny Slot Somnambulist*, in 2003, and Carnesky was already the stuff of performance folklore: as a Dragon Lady, a punk priestess flayed alive at Torture Garden, and a muse of The Divine David, but mostly for spear-heading London's neo-burlesque revival, sometimes as Lady Muck, in strip joints or performance venues. Carnesky's was a raw burlesque, neither tasteful, blushing, nor refined, but voluptuous, ornate, esoteric, phantasmagorical. She co-created a scene that sought to resemble Visconti's *The Damned*, relocated from interwar Berlin to the backstreets of 1990s Shoreditch, then an area still seedy, rubbish-strewn and tinged with violence.

I don't remember what future she granted me that night, but I remember feeling the encounter was portentous. She looked like a heady mix of Russ Meyer vixen, Hollywood Babylon femme fatale, Barnum and Bailey erotic attraction, pagan witch. Tattooed and oiled, coiled like a snake behind glass, she was all bosom and dragon-inked back and ass, with jet-black curls of hair dripping down over painted face. I admired her extremity, her esotericism, her solicitude, her taking a *nom de guerre*.

Carnesky's first full production was *Jewess Tattooess* (2001), which I saw at Riverside Studios in 2003. Twenty years later, I remember Carnesky tattooing a Star of David into her thigh, and the loud buzzing of the needle as everyone winced. I remember her posing in a blood-red sequinned gown and tasselled headdress, saying 'The Whore of Babylon is on vacation!', and a woman loudly standing up and shouting from the audience, 'This is bullshit' – a heart-stopping pause – and Carnesky unfazed but for a knowing smile. It was thrilling to see that heresy still smarts. I remember a video of Carnesky, vertically mirrored so we see her third eye, as if hers is the all-seeing cycloptic vision of a judging godhead. Hers were scenes of succour and sorcery, torment and triumph, of wounds that bleed red-black glycerine and real blood, and tricks of light and movement.

Carnesky's 'obsessions', which are so comprehensively tracked in this book, are not simply personal or private fixations writ large as art. Rather, her practice as an artist, both carnal and carnivalesque, brings together two key propositions. First, Carnesky has always been committed to putting her own body to the fore in her performances: as topic, thematic resource, canvas, and raw material. As such, Carnesky has always sought to show how the body is inevitably and necessarily particularized: when we see her body – adorned, manipulated, screened, or splayed – it calls into being, or condenses and allegorizes, her own experiences as a woman, a Jewish person, a diasporic subject (at several generational removes), and, latterly, as older; and, too, her other erstwhile selves, including as a sexual dissident, witch, heretic, self-made freak, carnival barker, and Showwoman. Second, Carnesky proposes that performance art emerges from, intersects with, and belongs to a history of esoteric, marginal, cultic, and obscure practices at the margins of cultural legitimacy. We live in a time when performance art tends to be appropriated, betrayed, and defanged by institutions of art that rewrite it as a form that is not necessarily or even usefully oppositional or disruptive. Carnesky shows that the difficult, strange, numinous, or occulted parts of performance art undergird its history, and so constitute the backbone of its volatile present.

Carnesky wears upon her sleeve a highly developed taste and ardour for the odd, the arcane, and the severe. Performance art's spell, in the mode in which she casts it, summons a promiscuous and often unremarked history of weirdness and wonder: everything in *Apocalypse Culture*; anything carny, like the lion-faced boys, human pincushions, palmists and prestidigitators in *Jay's Journal of Anomalies*, or the teratological children of Katherine Dunn's *Geek Love*; the erotic arts, particularly its historic mistresses, like Josephine Baker, Bettie Page, and Tura Satana; speakeasy soothsayers from Lydia Lunch to Vali Myers, the Witch of Positano; revolutionary 'super nova whore artivists' (in Beth Stephens' wonderfully lurid phrase), like Cosey Fanni Tutti, Terence Sellers, Scarlot Harlot, Veronica Vera, and Annie Sprinkle; the Magic Castle and anyone associated, the kitschier (and glitchier) the stage magic the better; the history of British magick (with a K), from the 'Great Beast' Aleister Crowley to Austin Osman Spare, by way of the latter day postpunk mystics, Genesis and Paula P-Orridge, Psychic TV, and the Temple of Psychic Youth; and scenes of horror and splendour in *Rosemary's Baby* and Żuławski's *Possession* and anything by Argento or Jodorowsky.

In an alarmingly beautiful scene in her ensemble production *Dr Carnesky's Incredible Bleeding Woman* (2018), she crouches in a bath of blood, driving herself back and forth, moving her hands through the gore so that it cascades over her body. In such an image, she belongs to a legitimate matrilineal history of body-based, action-oriented feminist performance art. At the same time, setting it in what recalls a haunted Victorian workhouse washroom, she also stages pitch-perfect B-movie body horror, as if a scene of mortification were salvaged from *Suspiria*'s cutting-room floor.

Carnesky's compulsion to stage both the serious facts of embodiment and performance's demeaned or negated histories makes sense of her consistent attraction to stage magic, one of the more strictly demeaned genres of the popular arts. In its rigorously choreographed illusions, stage magic is fundamentally Janus-faced: it says that what you see is what you see, while at the same time assuring us that what we see must be far from as it is. Bodies and personae in Carnesky's performances play this same game of chicanery and revelation, whether they explore systemic injustices (modern slavery, sex trafficking, forced migration, the Holocaust) or, as in later works, more intimate experiences of beauty, conviction, and suffering. Through the smoke and mirrors, Carnesky always stages a very human conflict between the frank reality and banality of bodies, and the sacred fact of the individual's own experience.

Underneath the kitsch ornamentation, and between the sleights of hand, Carnesky has a cold, clear truth to bare in her performances: the knowledge of what it means to feel different, to live in exile, to be feared or reviled, to make a family or a tribe for oneself, to survive, to love somebody, to risk being seen as crazy, to be betrayed, to grow older, to lose one's faith, to lose loved ones, to disappear.

Introduction: Marisa Carnesky – Sorceress, Radical School Mistress, Showwoman

Eirini Kartsaki

Marisa Carnesky is an indomitable sorceress, an eccentric magicienne, a Showwoman. She is a spectacular deviant, a transgressor and an empress, part-deer, part-owl, part-tarot card reader (Figure 49, p.189). Carnesky's significant innovations include her unique style of neo-burlesque in the 1990s or 'grotesque burlesque', which *Time Out* credited her for inventing (Braid in Mock 2022: 46). Through performances, such as *The Grotesque Burlesque Revue* at the Raymond Revue Bar in Soho (1997), or *Lady Muck and her Burlesque Revue* (1995–96), or *Carnesky's Ghost Train* (2004–14), Carnesky innovates and invents form. With the latter, she creates an unprecedented, immersive, all-encompassing experience, which 'haunt[s] the borders of art and entertainment' and makes her one of the pioneers of immersive theatrical spectacle in the United Kingdom (Carnesky Website 2023).

Carnesky experiments with scale, form, genre. She marries experimental body art with high-end illusions, live art with alternative cabaret. She is interested in disrupting, disturbing, and shedding light. As a sorceress, she examines the symptoms of our diseased time and investigates a cure. She performs comical stripteases that sexually transgress, and that open a dialogue about sex and body positivity. She invites us to encounter the monster within ourselves in the bizarre, grotesque, overly sexual, hybrid creatures she performs; hers is an invitation to meet our weirdness with reverence and wonder. Her unique approach comprises a fearlessness that is evident in bringing together modes and practices that are often worlds apart. Carnesky makes accessible to wider audiences niche performance and body art practices such as body modification or live tattooing. She daringly blends different styles to create a spectacular elixir that entices and seduces. From her early work with The Dragon Ladies in the 1990s, her one-to-one performance *Penny Slot Somnambulist* (2000–03), to the full-scale solo *Jewess Tattooess* (1999–2002), *The Girl From Nowhere* (2003) or the multisensory *Tarot Drome*

(2012), Carnesky's performances function like a pharmakon, a potion or concoction whose aim is to help us see ourselves more clearly: as devilish beasts, the receivers of our foretold, inescapable future, as outsiders far from home, displaced, uprooted, wondering what it would mean to belong. Ultimately, seeing ourselves in this way, in the provisional community of an audience, participating in menstrual rituals, understanding our place in the world, as individuals, outsiders or those who do not fit in, is part of the sorcery of Carnesky and our cure. Our cure in fact has to do with community itself, the community of being part of Carnesky's bold and multifaceted experiential performance experiments. From this place, we look with wonder at what we have learnt in this journey. And it has been rich, and fulsome, and its gifts abundant.

When reading this book, you will experience the sorceress conjuring the spirits of historical women artists whose influence has been overshadowed. You may sense her divination in identifying compelling questions about marginalized experiences, bodies in perpetual transformation, bodies that are faltering, failing, but not apologizing; desiring bodies, wanting to exist in transformation and in loss; bodies that hold the weight of others that preceded them; that are in perpetual state of conflict: a tattooed Jewish woman, a body that menstruates but does not reproduce, a body that does not menstruate but follows the cycles of the sun and the moon. This conjuress' gifts include seductiveness, generosity, and an ability to hold space for difficult questions and painful experiences. In essence, this sorceress' elixir shows us that transformation is not only an illusion; it takes effort, but when it happens, we can finally see clearly who we have become.

In recent years, Carnesky's work has been preoccupied with accounting for marginalized experiences of women artists with extraordinary skills who have been written out of the historical canon. These are women who appeared in the 1930s and 1940s within the contexts of the entertainment industry, such as Lulu Adams, one of the earliest female clowns, who topped the bill at Bertram Mills Circus; or Marjorie Dare, who rode the Wall of Death, accompanied by one of her many big cats who took their place in the side car; or Koringa, the legendary alligator hypnotist, who climbed ladders of swords, wore the mark of the French Resistance on her forehead and used her mesmeric skills to support the British army behind enemy lines, once drawing huge audiences, now all but invisible to history. In her most recent show *Showwomen* (2022), alongside other women with extraordinary skills, Carnesky speaks clearly about her own identity as an artist, maker, and collaborator:

I am not the greatest showman because I am not a man. I am not a showgirl and I am not a showboy. My name is Marisa Carnesky and I am a Showwoman, with two WWs in the middle, one for the show and one for the woman. [...] Traditionally the proprietress of working-class popular entertainments, she is the boss. She runs the show. Her showwomanly spectacle is different to the showman's, because as a former showgirl she really knows how to collaborate. Most importantly her vision is not about exploiting difference. Because she is different. She is showing herself. Because she wants to. [...]. Her perspective might be the immigrant, the witch, the daredevil, the activist [...]. She has always been here, sometimes she is obscured – she often appears in wartime, she is subversive, she is spectacular and she makes covert actions for radical change using her incredible talents in circus and variety. She makes herstory, she makes new visions of spectacular matriarchal utopias. She is the Showwoman, the Showwoman, the Showwoman.
(*Showwomen* Script 2022)

Carnesky is a Showwoman. She has abandoned her earlier title of showgirl and argues that we should finally allow the showgirl to graduate into adulthood. This is Carnesky's most vital, recent contribution to the worlds between entertainment, theatre, and performance. Carnesky's forceful and spirited presence advocates for an existence of independence, collaboration, and care. This book is an urgent gesture to introduce 'Showwoman' into the theatrical vernacular, and to let go of the limitations of the showgirl and the oppressive conditions of working under the showman.

Carnesky has aspired to be the tattooed avant-garde and queer version of Jewish grand dames such as Sylvia Young or Anna Scher who have led renowned London schools and influenced generations of actors and theatre-makers (Carnesky in Patey-Ferguson, in this volume). Alongside her full-scale productions, rigorous research and development periods and alternative cabaret acts, Carnesky is a Radical School Mistress, as she has been educating future generations of artists with her Finishing School since 2008. As Phoebe Patey-Ferguson and Alex Lyons attest in this book, Carnesky's key principles include doing everything together (an expansion of the more often encountered DIY), constructing moments of wonder, being truthful to oneself, pushing boundaries, and finding power in pathos. This Radical School Mistress has encouraged her students to draw on political and personal beliefs and convictions, confront issues with openness and vulnerability in order to find within the context of cabaret or spectacle what feels truthful and authentic. Ultimately, she has empowered her students to discover that their voice is loud and that it matters. Carnesky has done the same for many of the artists she has collaborated with over the years. This book is another such collaboration with a vibrant group of artists, including Annie Sprinkle and Beth Stephens, Empress Stah, Veronica Thompson, Rhyannon Styles, and others. The book gives a platform to artists to recount their remarkable journeys and Carnesky's part in who they are today. For instance, Paloma Faith and Tai Shani, who met Carnesky in the early stages of their career, explain the compelling role that their participation in *Carnesky's Ghost Train* has played in their lives and work.

Obsessions of a Showwoman is structured around these three themes: sorcery; performance as a radical school; and showwomanry. The book offers contrasting textures and counterpoints in the form of different types of writing: short memory pieces by Liz Aggiss, Marawa, Vanessa Toulmin, and Amy Ridler, who give accounts of their first encounters with Carnesky; conversations with artists who have participated in Carnesky's work over the years (such as Livia Kojo Alour, Lucifire, H Plewis, Nao Nagai, Lalla Morte, Miss Behave, Geneva Foster Gluck), chapters by theorists and historians of theatre and performance, which rigorously frame the key preoccupations in Carnesky's work (Roberta Mock, Josephine Machon, Eirini Kartsaki), and shorter texts that account for single performance instances (Daniel Oliver, Rachel Zerihan). The Department of Feminist Conversations (Maddy Costa and Mary Paterson in this instance) opens a dialogue with Carnesky's *Live Archive* on disappearance and remains. Finally, the book is exquisitely enveloped by the words of Dominic Johnson and Giulia Palladini. Mostly, this book opens the floor for a dialogue with and about Showwomen around the globe, whose existence and contributions confirm the urgent need to reconsider and radically change the language we currently use. Showwomen are women who take the lead, work for themselves, collaborate with others, women who have come into their own power and own the show; women who lead strange dance troupes or pop bands, who do weird shows about menstrual rituals and occult magick; women that ultimately rejoice at the thought of a world that resembles a feminist, matriarchal utopia.

In this book, this fairground ride, you will encounter fabulous aerial dancers, curious hair hangers, and spectacular sword swallowers. You will come across dangerous acts of fire, peculiar ghosts, menstruating rivers, and tattooed dragons that come alive in their contact with your skin. You will encounter the Whore of Babylon, Lilith the Demon, the Tattooess, and the disgraced Jewess. You will also see *mezuzahs* in places where *mezuzahs* should not go, gravity being defied and women covered in blood in esoteric rituals. Ghosts and spirits will accompany you on this ride. You will be kept relatively safe.

Bibliography

Carnesky, M. (2022), *Showwomen Script*, Jackson's Lane, 16–18 June, unpublished, Marisa Carnesky archival material.

Carnesky Productions Website (2023), available at https://carnesky.com. Accessed 31 January 2023.

Mock, R. (2020), 'Marisa Carnesky, Showwoman', in M. Chatzichristodoulou (ed.), *Live Art in the UK: Contemporary Performances of Precarity*, London: Methuen Drama, pp. 45–67.

Finding Marisa Carnesky

A Showwoman of a Certain Rage: Marisa Carnesky's Bleeding Spectacular

Josephine Machon

Introduction

Let me tell you a tale, where we'll follow a trail, which begins at London's BAC, in its former falling down glory, with a Ph.D. and a conversation at a bar, to a studio and its curios, a catalogue of public work to another Ph.D. Here hangs a tale and a trail, of the here and the now and the when and the how and the why we met.

Marisa Carnesky and I first met in 1999 at Battersea Arts Centre (BAC), on the cusp of the new millennium, a point where we were both professionally coming of age within the field of experiential performance practice. She generously agreed to be a case study for my Ph.D., so there was a rewarding symmetry felt as her supervisor, twenty years later, when she received her doctorate. In retracing this journey, recapitulating an appreciation of certain works along the way (see Machon 2012, 2013), it is easy to chart Carnesky's key 'performance-rituals' of passage, from *Jewess Tattooess* (1999–2002), aboard *Carnesky's Ghost Train* (2004–14) to alight at *Dr Carnesky's Incredible Bleeding Woman* (2015–19). *Jewess Tattooess* and *Ghost Train* are defining works that expose signature aesthetics unique to Carnesky's Showwomanry; a prioritization of the body as subject and object of performance; a marking of time and temporality in process, theme, and durational experience; the use of magic, spectacle, illusion, and horror in the form and formulae of her process; and the persistent presence of blood.

Carnesky excavates personal histories as the source of her performance material. She underpins this with rigorous research into wider cultural and historical contexts so that it expands beyond herself and her subjects to tap into shared experience. She then defamiliarizes these stories, makes them strange, through metaphor and magic, using theatrical form to convey difficult subject matter. In so doing, she foregrounds how the body creates its own language, which communicates polyphonically, viscerally, *showing* how the personal, cultural, social, and political are always an intertwined narrative. My emphasis here on 'showing' draws attention to Carnesky's evolving celebration of what it is to be a 'Showwoman', her own self-coined term, 'with two WWs in the middle, one for the show and one for the woman' (Carnesky 2022). Not a showgirl, at the beck and call of the male maestro but a self-managed, employee-paying businesswoman and artiste. Carnesky's Showwoman revels in the multifarious meanings encompassed by the 'show'. It incorporates the showiness of *showing off* and *showing out*, a sparkling spectacular that applauds expertise. In Carnesky's work, this aspect of 'the show' is an artful nod to the knowing-show of the meta in the metatheatrical, self-consciously referencing the conventions of performance. It also includes the commitment involved in producing the work, where *the show must go on*. Here, glitter and glamour bolsters the artistry and the art that comes from the challenge and toil of making work.

Carnesky's Showwoman has been born out of a progressive understanding of how *showing* corresponds to demonstration, comprising the testing of a hypothesis and also embracing a feminist gestic style, where lived social circumstances and experiences are bound up in the performer's body as much as they are manufactured in a character's action and attitudes. Following Elin Diamond's reinvigoration of Bertolt Brecht's 'gestus' through feminist critique, where an implied/received social attitude of performance is made visible to the audience, primarily through the gendered body: 'to read a gesture, a line of dialogue, or a tableau gesturally is to draw into analysis the author's history, the play's production conditions, and the historical gender and class conditions through which stage action might be read' (Diamond 1997: xiv). Here then, a Showwoman's actions always speak louder than words. Furthermore, as *Dr Carnesky's Incredible Bleeding Woman* illustrates, a demonstration for the Showwoman is *showing up*, becoming an activist through these actions, using art and collectivity to rage against the regime. The working out of these gestic possibilities, in concept and content, returns to the body at every stage as an embodied act of defiance. Correspondingly, Carnesky's work equally honours expressionist roots in arts practice, where the body shows itself to reveal multilayered depths about what it is to be human, influenced by her training in contemporary dance (see Machon 2011: 126). Carnesky reinvents storytelling modes through theatrical techniques and augmentations that morph the body, transforming its fleshliness via costume, contortion, digital and magical illusion, and circus daredevilry.

Carnesky's body of work is an interdisciplinary mashup, with dramaturgical and aesthetic influences drawn from European film, live art, burlesque, cabaret, circus, classical ballet, folk dance, modern dance, and magic shows. She develops each project through an iterative process, editing and finessing with each presentation to an audience, responding to the spaces and collaborators for which and with whom each show is developed. Consequently, there is an active shapeshifting quality to the dramaturgy of each show that allows the work to evolve while maintaining its thematic backbone. The visual and physical imagery in her work is boldly thought through in rich tableaux from initial concept to eventual production. Some time at the beginning of this century, I met Marisa in a curio-filled shared artist's space where she showed me paintings that revealed her phantasmagoric imaginings for what would become *Ghost Train*, evidencing how she 'write[s] the story visually first' (Carnesky in Machon 2011: 129). Two images that remain in my mind's eye are of a mesmerizing face with Medusa-like tresses that reached to the edges of the paper, and another of women's bodies piled up and spewing out of a trailer. I mention this not only to highlight how this memory has remained but also to show how then, as now, the interchange between Carnesky's visual concept and consequent scriptwriting is underpinned by embodied, dreamscape thinking. Carnesky collaborates with filmmakers, illusionists, animatronic experts, and scenographic designers familiar with reinventing architectural spaces, to realize these decadent ideas and stories. Spectacle has been there all along:

> I was brought up with a really strong sense of the holocaust […] images of piles of bodies, it is a spectacle of the macabre, it's of epic proportions. I am interested in big, bold, symbolic things, which is kind of cultural. If you're Catholic or Muslim or Jewish you've been brought up with large symbolic meanings, reading stories about rivers running with blood, it sticks in your mind. I love a bit of ritual […] I do genre hop and I do make strange shows that explore current experiences, but I have to do it through a lens of dreamy, nostalgic otherworldliness because that's what makes me feel moved.
> (Carnesky in Machon 2011: 130)

Carnesky was among the early pioneers of the noughties who experimented with a new take on the immersive form, before this term was being used to describe such work. From an intimate, close-up magical encounter with a sword-in-doll-house-box trick and disappearing human-sized insect produced for BAC's attic; a rite of passage, where she materialized in a Victorian horse-drawn hearse for her audience, who then travelled with her through the streets of Soho to lay her burlesque Carny persona to

Figure 1: Marisa Carnesky, backstage at The Vauxhall Tavern, 1998. London. © Ruth Bayer

Figure 2: Marisa Carnesky, *Lady Muck*, Hackney Marshes, 1995. London. © Ruth Bayer

rest; the full-scale touring Victorian ghost-train, which travelled from Brick Lane across the land to come to rest as a permanent fixture of Blackpool promenade; to *Tarot Drome*, a bizarre underground bazaar in the Old Vic Tunnels at Waterloo, which toured around UK festivals; and to Cirque De Jules Verne in France. A desire to experiment with site and audience interaction is key to this. Also unmistakeable is the cinematic strain that runs through her work indicating a kinship with the likes of Punchdrunk and Shunt, a generation that owes as much to film (especially the horror and thriller genre) as it does to the live art and physical theatres of the late twentieth century.

Carnesky's interest and expertise in illusion and magic tricks have been deployed through each new production. These skills are used not solely for the pizzazz of it but as an artistic intervention, as a performance mechanism and metaphor that exploits the *unheimlich* ('unhomely', uncanny or eerie) quality of magic. It enables the fantastical *showing* of stories and experiences that have, historically, been bound up with the unimaginable and unrepresentable. Trickery and illusion are used as a theatrical device by which the ineffable is conveyed and amplified, artifice becoming art. Stage magic and spectacle in Carnesky's work feed a taste for that epic-macabre in audience entertainment, while her carefully researched artistic application returns magic to its roots, in ritualized practice.

With this signature approach and aesthetic in mind, I'll now take you on that promised ride, to illustrate and unpack these tropes and tricks of her trade. Traversing the key thematic concerns that connect one show to the next, as well as *showing* how, with each new project, Carnesky's work has morphed through time to see her, as Showwoman extraordinaire, come of (r)age.

So, let's start with the tale of the serpent's tail. With its bloody trail through needles and blood to a sequin pyre, we'll trace a signature style from performances past to performances present and performances yet to come.

A Carny Is Born – *Jewess Tattooess*

To be honest, the Carny was born a while before this within the Dragon Ladies troupe in the mid-1990s but, arguably, she came into her own, found her singular Carnyesque/Carnesky voice, through *Jewess Tattooess*. This Carny was the progenitor of the Showwoman, Carnesky's first full-length solo show version. This production marked the iterative process for developing a concept that would return across her body of work. This show foregrounded the body as source, sight, site, and cite of performance.[1] With each iteration across 1999–2002, *Jewess Tattooess* juxtaposed live performance with otherworldly film installations, drawing on the aesthetic of early-cinematic spectacle, nostalgic, balalaika-fuelled folklore, and gothic fairy tale.

The original script was a prismatic mixture of Yiddish, carnival vernacular, cautionary-tale idiom, Hebrew scripture, extensive archival research, and playful, burlesque banter. This was a distinctive writing style that would reappear through to *Dr Carnesky's Incredible Bleeding Woman* and answered Hélène Cixous' call to, 'write yourself: your body must make itself heard' (1993: 97).[2] It also speaks to the mission of Cixous's '*Juifemme*', 'Jewoman' (1991: 3–5). The *juifemme* rewrites the Torah through her own experience and her lived rage, sighting/siting/citing desire and the divine within the body. Correspondingly, Carnesky's visceral-verbal writing enabled the audience to *feel* the intellectual ideas being playfully constructed and worked out as they were delivered alongside the visual/physical action and illusions that comprised the show. Exclusive to this project, Carnesky incorporated the live scarring of her own flesh with a tattooist's needle to score, in every sense of the word, a central theme of the work. With *Jewess Tattooess* Carnesky conceived a 'Jewwoman–Showwoman'. While Cixous' *juifemme* phonetically plays on '*j'ouis femme*' ('I am woman'), I intentionally incorporate the two WWs here, emphasizing, 'I am Showwoman'. Carnesky's Jewwoman–Showwoman offered a resistant body in performance, an unruly body reinventing performance disciplines, an explicit body that was transgressive in traditional performance terms, and a full-back-to-thigh dragon-tattooed body that resisted conforming on a cultural level.

... body and blood

Jewess Tattooess examined and exposed how inherited cultural trauma as much as sex-gendered politics are embodied. Carnesky self-consciously took herself, her history and inheritance, and spun a tale from it rendering herself abject-subject and site of performance. Like her influences from feminist performance art, such as Karen Finley and Annie Sprinkle, Carnesky demonstrated how her body as *the show* – the source and stage – became a site of potential rather than a fixed given. Her body as a complex blend of highly charged mappings – physiological, sexual, historical, social, and political.

Playing on cultural iconography around body and blood, Carnesky rewrote folk rituals by exploiting the visceral imagery of cautionary tales, artfully subverted by contemporary references. The mythologized needle that pricks to draw red blood is continually remarked: 'Grandma's needle glowed. Lulla awoke in a trance and became enchanted by it', declares the silent film tableaux projected on the screen (Carnesky 1999). The original production began with a soundscore of ethereal, childlike singing against discordant chords and the buzz of the tattooist's needle, instantly establishing an unsettling atmosphere. A low, red light comes up on the kneeling, rocking Carnesky who slowly brings her arm up to reveal that she is employing a heavy, automatic, tattooist's needle, in a disquieting darning action akin to a traditional needle and thread. Later, a short, stylized sequence *en pointe* signified fairy-tale feet forced to bleed and feel pain until death. The suggestion of the naked foot against the *pointe*, jabbing into the floor, conveyed hidden bruised and bleeding ballerina feet, or the 'pins-and-needles' brought on by the wearing of these torturous slippers. In the Copenhagen production, Carnesky extended this image by dressing her naked body in block-heeled, leather shoes, which the audience gradually became aware were oozing fake blood (2001). When Carnesky removed these shoes, she imprinted the stage, made of pages of the Torah, with dark, bloody footprints.

In this way, her dancing body became spectacle. The ballet, performed by Carnesky's pubescent character 'Lulla', was stilted, imposed on and impeding her feet, not moving with the body but hard against it. This dance was then remarked, when Carnesky performed the tease of 'The Tattooed Lady', reve(a)lling in a semi-naked-sequin-clad-nipple-tasselled new form. Lulla, having come of carny age, had shed her outer skin and was allowing the painted body to speak a new movement language, coiling its now brightly coloured dragon tail. The dance of this body was moving in a way that was natural to it, following its undulating curves and rhythmical gyrations, rather than in angry opposition to it. Playing with the trope of the striptease, knowingly she bent over, as if to reveal her genitals in full yet instead she slid her hand between her legs, simultaneously hiding herself and finding herself, explicit exploration, owning, claiming, performing in true Showwoman style. In contrast to the restrictive ballet, this was an unconstrained writ(h)ing of the body. Slippery and serpentine, the striptease as a self-referential gesture of showtime technique played on the metaphor of a serpent shedding its skin, reminding the audience that this skin was her original skin, integral to the mover and the movement, the two inseparable. As a clear performance ritual, this dance represented the passage from one state to another, chrysalis and catalyst, marking the journey from girl to woman, innocent to experienced. Always multilayered with dual personalities, always representing that which is fluid(s), both secreting and secret, the Carny body and Carnesky's body performed itself. Carnesky *showed* the (con)fusions of experience, absorbed by and emanating from her tattooed and tabooed body, within this tale-tail-telling.

... the body under the lens

Carnesky plays further on embodying the revealed and concealed through various disguises throughout the performance. She used film to accentuate and reflect back on the live body conveying its own history. Depicting Grandmother, Rabbi and Serpentina (a 'Siamese Tattooed Carny Creature'), the film characters were invented from Carnesky's face and body inverted or doubled, augmented by hair-buns, beard, and make up, kaleidoscopically turned in and reflected back upon itself to create uncanny resemblances and strange mythical creatures. To a vibratory buzzing soundtrack of the tattooist's needle the Rabbi harangues, 'how can you claim the tattoo as a mark of freedom when for us it meant so much suffering' (Carnesky 1999). With this personal blow to Carnesky, the full force of recent Jewish history, Jews tattooed with their concentration camp number, is felt in the body of the audience, marking a collective memory that is carved in social history. In the Copenhagen production, this idea was emphasized by the addition of a bittersweet sequence, delivered in an unsettling monotone, a story of a sailor who tattoos over the concentration camp number of a prostitute with the image of a rose (Carnesky 2001).

The interplay of Carnesky's filmed body alongside her fleshly body emphasized resistant readings of identity. The film sequences exposed Carnesky's stage show alter-egos and highlighted the explicit showing of spectacle as a carnivalesque exhibition. A particular incarn(y)ation was Serpentina, announced by overtly theatrical silent film subtitles; 'See the human exhibit, an oddity extraordinaire, a creature from your strangest dreams, born with the second sight! A rarest of beauties. Alive!' (Carnesky 1999). Creat(ur)ed from Carnesky's dragon-tattooed torso, doubled by a mirror-image, a two-torsoed being, formed from the same hips, upper bodies holding each other in its own arms. The duality of this creature was further emphasized by the twofold delivery of speech, a vocal play with a sultry, seductive American, Deep South Sideshow drawl. Carnesky's voice overlaid on itself, two different tonal qualities, one always slightly behind the other, with a repetition of words within the speech; 'I am the tattooed soothsayer. Dragon lady, dragon lady, Serpentina, Serpentina. Read my skin, watch my lips, lips. My complexion tells a story' (1999).[3] Serpentina later morphed, the

Figure 3: Marisa Carnesky, *Jewess Tattooess*, studio shot, 2000. London. © Manuel Vason

two-headed body became joined at the breasts, hanging like udders on a mythical chimera. The arms, also suspended, writhed, and punctuated the speech, the hair lusciously falling, accentuated the femininity of this creature. Here, the doubled, filmed Carny-Creature called the live Carny to herself, in a tri-personal display of the multilayered self, calling Carnesky playing Lulla playing the Tattooed Lady to them as 'a shameless bird of passage' (Carnesky 1999), a passage that highlighted a body that is continuously evolving, metamorphosing.

... marking time

For the final act of *Jewess Tattooess*, marking this ongoing passage of time, Carnesky turned a camera onto herself to relay her live body onto the screen. Magnified through this lens, she performed a live scarring of a Star of David on her thigh with the heavy tattooist's needle. In this instance, Carnesky's fleshly body most powerfully became both site and sight of performance as it merged with the set and forced itself under the audience's microscopic gaze. In the screened close-up, the audience could see the shadow of those stars that had been drawn in earlier shows on the thigh and, in later iterations, around her navel, the traces of previous performances on her body tallying and telling yet another bodily story that had been written on her flesh. A ritualized act of marking this moment moved her body from sight/site to cite of performance. In marking her flesh, the searing stage image moved beyond the gaze to cite itself in this spectator's consciousness. Each Star of David, etched into her thigh, remained present and presented throughout the passage of the run, the trace of previous performances in her flesh, and in embodied memory in my subsequent recall. In Copenhagen, following this live scarring, Carnesky inserted two *mezuzahs* into her vagina before inserting herself back into the manuscript entrance she emerged from at the start (2001).[4] This ritualized double insertion, into entrance and exit, became a performance ritual of burial and rebirth. It highlighted the passing of that night's show, all previous shows, as the passage of performance time within and upon her, shared with an audience, came to pass. Just as the Star of David remained scratched into her thigh, her whole body in this final, quietly insurgent insertion and iteration, like those bloodied footprints before it, left its mark on the Torah fragments after she had left the stage.

... sequins and spectacle

Carnesky exploited the spectacle of live performance in a metatheatrical demonstration of the show's artifice, a Showwomanly show of explicit role play. Accompanied by sideshow music, she entered as the Tattooed Lady, costumed in a sequined burlesque outfit. In this altered state, she stared at the audience, for the first time acknowledging them, playing with them, forcing direct participation as part of the 'act': 'if you want riches to come into your life, you must tell people about my show', as she reminded the audience of the dates of following performances (1999). This jesting highlights notions of the 'real' self and the performative self, reflexively referencing the performance artist who uses autobiographical detail as material for her work; Carnesky in the role as Lulla, in the role as the Carny/Tattooed Lady, also playing 'out of role' as the actual auteur of the performance yet doing this self-referentially in the role as 'cabaret Carnesky'. She repeatedly refers to the idea of being the object of the gaze (as performer and as a woman), being on show, an exposed body that delivers lines as explicit as her naked body; 'I'm always a performance in your eyes', 'read my limbs', 'skin that sings', 'I rewrite my sex on my skin' (1999).

This play with the theatrical is inherent to Carnesky's Jewwoman-Showwoman. It is meta-theatre, a disciplined and deliberately staged gestic performance within a performance. The shapeshifting form of *Jewess Tattooess*, from the original to the latter productions, reduced speech in favour of the body speaking for itself, showing rather than telling. The verbal play was distilled into edited references to previous performance narratives. In the final performances, Carnesky retold certain sequences that had been previously performed as reveries, verbally retracing the production history. Mirroring Carnesky's physical body, it encapsulated, demonstrated, the continual rewriting of this body of work.

Equally theatrical and metamorphic, the set design gradually altered from venue to venue, mutated further during each performance through physical interaction with the structural design. In the final run, Carnesky's bandage-bound head and body painfully emerged from that lit Star of David (slow-faded up on the stage, to illuminate those printed pages of the Torah) leaving a gash across this set as she pulled herself, wholly bandage-bound from it, as if rebirthing herself. She removed these slowly, ritualistically, to reveal her tattooed body, *showing* itself, unbound. The double insertion, along with the bloodied footsteps which had imprinted her body upon the already imprinted Hebrew text, combined with the live-feed scarring of her own flesh writ large as a backdrop, ensured her body merged with the space as site/sight/cite of performance.

This emphasis on the theatrical, on *the show* within the show, underscored its gestic potential, with Carnesky self-referentially demonstrating her body as live(d), culturally inscribed, and politically charged. 'Live(d)' here emphasizes how performing and perceiving bodies in experiential performance are charged by the sensual aesthetic and energies of the piece in a live and ongoing present. It also denotes how feminist performance reveals lived histories and shared experiences. It encompasses the fact that the human body is always a 'lived' being (physiological, social, cultural, historical, political, etc.), where experiential aesthetics intentionally tap into this in form and content to expose these *lived* narratives, silently, statuesquely, representing the political charge of feminist rage.

This is best illustrated by the final sequence in the first iteration of *Jewess Tattooess* (1999). Carnesky sheds her sequin skin to stand naked, tattooed. The flame-red, twinkling costume is rolled up to represent a fire. By using the costume as the pyre in this way, symbolizing a phoenix from theatrical flames, Carnesky drew attention to the destroying of the Carny self, making way for a new, multilayered self, compounding images of metamorphosis, ownership, and rebirth. *Jewess Tattooess* ended with the

Figure 4: Marisa Carnesky, installation inside *Carnesky's Ghost Train*, 2010. Blackpool Promenade. © Jo Duck

line, 'like the tide, I reinvent myself [...] it's something in my blood', exposing ideas of multiple identities, ancestry, and the tattooist's ink, all of which remain a visible/hidden bodily presence. It foresees the future Carnesky as Impresario, standing silently by her Ghost Train, a beckoning placard questioning, 'What are the Politicians Doing about our Disappeared Daughters?' (2004–08); it foretells her re-birth as Dr Carnesky, orating at her lectern, new blood ready to seep.

And so to the ride on that train with its haunted tracks, where mothers cry, daughters vanish and women silently rail.
To trail our tale across those railing tracks is to tell of tricks and technology and trains caught in time.

A Ghost Train Is Caught

I experienced *Carnesky's Ghost Train* in its first and possibly purest iteration at East London's Brick Lane in 2004, joining an audience that queued to buy a ticket for the journey on a sunny afternoon amidst the bustle of the weekend crowd. An immersive and sensational (in all senses of the word) experience, this ghost train accentuated the spectral as much as the spectacular. It adapted a traditional touring ghost-train ride ('I wanted to use the most experimental, experiential, ridiculous thing that I could'), into an interdisciplinary artwork with 'visual and magic illusions; visual and sound installations; dance, theatre, film' using 'digital, video and special effects [...] fairy-tales and folklore' to push 'boundaries of tied geography and the body' (Carnesky qtd in Machon 2012: 114). Its original version was an homage to the ghost train, not pastiche. Custom built with 50 metres of bespoke track, employing an ensemble cast of aerialists, contortionists, performance artists, and Showwomen, it played with the multifarious possibilities of haunting the imagination that the form offered when employed as an artistic intervention.

... caught in time

This train ride was about time, duration, and marking time. Temporal play, as a performance rite, came into effect in a variety of ways. The train journey itself made present the play across historical time in its narratives. On embarking, the passenger was made to feel like a young child, combining a sense of excitement with the sensation of trepidation. The rifle-wielding-fishnets-wearing Guard's barked orders, followed by the unfolding horrors of the journey, evoked stories of *Kindertransport*, trains full of Jewish children fleeing for their lives, leaving homes, parents, and heartlands. Structurally and allegorically, this ride encapsulated the possibilities of being betwixt and between. Just as *Carnesky's Ghost Train* settled between the borders of art and fairground ride, poetry, and politics, the histories it revealed were of those forced to flee, to remain neither here nor there in time and geography. The train itself was narratively between borders, a 'Night Train' (even if you rode it during the day) with a journey set during the hours of slumber and a plot that ran between one station and the next. This train was figuratively liminal as it ferried its passengers between waking and sleeping, life and death, the imagined and the unimaginable, in an indeterminate state established by the eeriness of the journey and the limbo realm of the lives it marked. A ludic in-between time. Carnivalesque fairground time.

Via ghostly voiceover and a series of illusions and tableaux vivant *Carnesky's Ghost Train* told a story of three daughters who escaped from their war-ravaged town in the thick of night, stowing away on a train, only to disappear forever. The daughters had boarded a ghost train – this ghost train – sent by spirits to haunt a broken world. Though hung on this phantom tale, it was the more chilling narratives of displaced women from recent history that came to the forefront. Each revolution presented images of female bodies, chained up, contorted, dismembered body parts reaching out, calling out. Through drawing attention to artifice within the visual stories presented, the multilayered form exposed the true horrors of the subject matter at the heart of the work, *showing* rather than telling, communicating its rage through the *felt* as much as the seen. For those that attended to the images presented in conjunction with its kinaesthetic and audio underscoring, the experience went well beyond surface entertainment to confront stories that addressed deracination, enforced migration and sex trafficking. It found wordless forms that bowed to the unrepresentability of the experiences on show. Primarily, this was aroused physiologically by the rollercoaster locomotion. This train had its own choreographed rhythm, swerve and sway, that tantalized when slowing down to capture moments before snapping out of this, tugging back heads as it pulled away. It accentuated the fairground rhythms and rumbles of foreboding and fear, wonder, and delight, while eerily contrasting these with the illusionist's stilled rhythms that held the unexpected and the otherworldly. The combined experience gave form to disorientation, foregrounding what is felt by individuals compelled by circumstances beyond their control to flee their homeland. Senses displaced by the experience of the ride become a *felt* metaphor for the social dislocation that enforced migration causes.

... illusion and artifice

Women's stories of being disappeared, whether captured for the sex trade, or through migration, fleeing countries and cultures under political duress, were told through a range of theatrical devices. The acrobatics of the aerialist, that burlesque Guard, revolved above and alongside in an equally disorientating fashion. Her locomotion echoed the rolling of the train, pulling focus, making stomachs roll as eyes followed the rotations of her flight in this nightmarish scenario. The visceral images with which the audience was bombarded included live evocations and faked effigies of mutilated women, angrily ghastly variations on 'the woman cut in two'. Similarly, the live, female contortionists forced into almost inhuman positions, suggestive of women forced into unbearable compromise. These performers were Showwomen extraordinaire, trained by Carnesky in stylized horror-film poses, 1930s German expressionist dance, and Victorian illusion techniques, bringing with them backgrounds in Butoh or burlesque. This hybridized aesthetic added to the disquieting quality of the ride, producing a variety of attitudes that represented a decadent 'dance of death'. Mannequin art positioned alongside the sensual, human bodies of performers were disconcerting, giving physical form to embodied disembodiment. In the Blackpool version, waxwork bodies disturbed perceptions of what was real, unreal, alive, or dead. These illusionary techniques played tricks with the seen and unseen, conjuring bodies that were absent in their presence.

'Pepper's Ghosts' and 'Amphitrites' accentuated this, offering a magical play on the feeling of time suspended, as they accompanied passengers with their absent-presence on this journey. Pepper's Ghost is an illusory effect that uses plate glass and lighting techniques to make humans appear, metamorphose, and vanish. An Amphitrite is a variation of this, conjured in floating form, as if ethereally rotating in air or within the depths of waters. In *Carnesky's Ghost Train*, Carnesky provided the female form of the Amphitrite, a watery apparition enwrapped in her own burnished auburn tresses (that painted image from the studio made manifest in unearthly form). The image in turn enraptured the passenger, enigmatically swirling alongside and above, a lost soul, held in time, before slowly evaporating, dematerializing, almost there then gone. The Amphitrite and Pepper's Ghosts served as both metaphor and manifestation, a visceral-virtual materialization of the lives and stories of women lost across borders and in time, victims of forced migration and human trafficking. Like memory suspended at the point at which a person is forced to flee, they were neither here nor there, neither of one place nor another. These apparitions were crucial to the haunting quality of the immersive experience; quintessentially *unheimlich* evocations of disappeared women worn into a collective visual psyche, whether from fairy tales or newsreels. Those images and sensations remain as I recall the experience, held in memory in an equivalent manner to the diaphanous way they hovered in the work.

Now the rail turns to rage and Show(woman)ing your age; speaks with wit(ches) and wisdom, of courage and conjuring, of Medusas and Magic(k) and Menstruactivism.

A Showwoman Comes of (R)age

> I'm not interested in reviving old variety for its own sake. I'm particularly interested in […] using those spectacular and popular forms to explore cultural politics that I'm living through, which is what differentiates my work from practice that just revives the act for the skill itself. What I think is important is where performance traditions meet socio-political discussion, like the history of feminist performance and criticism, complicated ideas about the times we live in that fuse politics and sexual identity […]. I like things that have a popular aesthetic but the subjects I deal with are not necessarily popular subjects […] a lot of magic performance [is] about women having violence enacted upon them as a fetishised act of illusion and I wanted to turn the tables.
> (Carnesky qtd in Machon 2011: 125–27)

Where once Carnesky described herself as 'a showbiz hack' (in Machon 2011: 129), she has now confidently delineated a Showwoman's discourse, theorized through her productions and/as scholarly practice. Her work has progressively marched towards its rightful place in the academy, contributing to queer feminist activism. In this respect, she joins a lineage of women practitioners that engage with rage, on a socio-cultural and political level as much as a driving force in creative methodology and artistic output. *Dr Carnesky's Incredible Bleeding Woman* (2015–19), a lecture spectacle, showed its audience alternative visions of womanhood, a living Showwommanifesto. Here, Showwomen redefined themselves through sensational performance rituals, expressing a revolutionary and authoritative position to ideology, politics, and power. These Showwomen were present, presenting and presented to us, a range of ages, diverse bodies, some with wombs, some without, some who menstruate, some who do not. The research and development for the project played, knowingly, on academic methods for collecting scientific data on menstrual synchronicity, reworking these as

theatrical tropes in the analysis and dissemination of findings. This approach became a theme to inform the investigative workshops, and an idea to subvert regarding de-medicalizing menstrual cycles. As the show itself demonstrated, the development of menstrual rituals through performance acts was achieved by elevating artefacts, materials, and activities through considered theatrical form. It made the mundanity of menstruation marvellous, through story, setting, sequins, and silk, along with gravity-defying techniques.

... synchronising time, suspending time

As prevalent as the fake blood, crimson lipstick, gold lamé, and shimmering sequins were distillation, repetition, revelation, and the slowing of time in all of the rituals presented in this production. A sincere respect for the ritual within the performance underscored the seriousness of the work and its message. Marking her own performance ritual, the audience watched, along with Dr Carnesky, a film of Carnesky naked in what looked like a Victorian infirmary ceramic bath, full of fake blood. The choreography of the bathing allowed for a respectful intimacy, while the unadorned retelling of the accompanying context ensured artifice became art.[5] The bath connoted

Figure 5: Marisa Carnesky, lecture from *Dr Carnesky's Incredible Bleeding Woman*, Soho Theatre, 2015. London. © Ruth Bayer

the Mikveh (baths used for ritual immersion in Judaism to achieve ritual purity, particularly for women after menstruation or childbirth), as much as it became a visual representation of the several miscarriages Carnesky had experienced since the project had begun.

Time was then slowed by Carnesky's keynote delivery, recalling Serpentina, the Tattooed Soothsayer, the rhythms, repetitions, and metaphors of her Carny ancestor; 'shedding shedding shedding the skin/the inner skin the blood skin [...] secret shedding blood skin forbidden blood within' (2018). The Virgin Mary projected behind her, in 'divine blue drapery', the lights shifted to a blood-red wash as Dr Carnesky's voice mutated, became mythic, a deific Medusa, writing her own experience while her speech raged against the cultural cleansing of woman across the centuries through Judeo-Christian iconography and patriarchal religious teachings. She gave a monstrous voice to the feminist rage that is bound up in what it is to be subjugated by the body and bodily function alone. She resisted this through subversion, celebrating 'the uterine renewal that comes with the serpent's dark moon. The slimy loss of skin, when the moon turns thin and the night sky darkens [...] the dirty red cycles of the planet and the female body' and poetically underscored the connections of the natural cycles of women with ecofeminist thought.

Throughout this speech, Carnesky ceremonially pulled hidden drawstrings in her Virgin-Mary-blue-stocking professorial dress. As the speech drew to a close, her outfit had been drawn open, morphed to reveal blood-red sequins clawed across it. In a spectacular show, the dress had theatrically bled to reveal Carnesky, carny-esque, as the Mother of all Menstruants, Showwoman Extraordinaire, manifesting 'The Incredible Bleeding Woman' in costumed form (Carnesky 2018). The whole stage image, in a beautiful bloody spectacle, echoed Cixous's promise, 'You only have to look at the Medusa straight on to see her. And she's not deadly. She's beautiful and she's laughing' (1976: 885) and reverberated with Andrea Juno and Vivian Vale's call to feminist arms:

> Reflective of the systematic destruction of matriarchal history by the patriarchy, the Medusa expresses *anger* [...] rage, embodied by seething snakes that turned men into stone [...] anger can be a source of power, strength and clarity as well as a *creative* force [...] rage that can be channelled. [...] Anger can spark and re-invigorate; it can bring hope and energy back into our lives and mobilize politically against the status quo.
> (1999: 5, emphasis original)[6]

Dr Carnesky's Incredible Bleeding Woman is the decadent-descendent of *Jewess Tattooess* and *Ghost Train*, evolved through a collaborative research context. The understanding of collective ritual and personal catharsis was *shown* in the show as much as it was told, a marvellous act of gestic feminism. As with *Jewess Tattooess* and *Ghost Train*, by using the body as medium – concept, canvas, and conduit – Carnesky and her Menstruants *showed* how the living body is inextricably linked with the political, the social, the cultural, and the ideological. The work exposed systems of patriarchy throughout recent history and provided an experiential discourse of resistance, with an attitude and actions that contribute to its overturning. It was through attending to lived challenges and potentials in live performance practice that these Showwomen demonstrated the 'livedly' (and, lividly) political. By *showing* these rituals to us, marked by reverential rhythms, wrapped in wit and wisdom, these Showwomen elaborated a feminist thesis of menstrual empowerment. Their rituals became an invitation to shape individual or collective performative actions. The closing, rallying cry to reimagine the future through a queered, feminist-defined philosophy and practice was an affective form of intersectional activism. It confronted and challenged what it is to show up as a woman, questioning both personal and societal expectations and attitudes in the act.

Recasting menstruating women as the ultimate Showwomen, this show offered a theatrical reclamation of witchcraft. No longer cast as barren, aged hag, the witch here was returned to her rightful place of venerable sage *because of age*, witch as magician. Much feminist theory has reclaimed the witch, 'crone', 'hag', as a sagacious phase of post-(or non)-maternal, menopausal femalehood. This reclamation subverts the patriarchal agenda that discredits female knowledge and experience, renders it as other when it exists for itself and without deference to whiteness, straightness, or maleness.[7] It exposes the ways in which 'the witch' is a status that has been culturally ascribed, through embodied and economic inequalities. It resists the racialized and sexualized fear that has been applied to the witch, beyond literature, by institutional authorities and as violent action throughout history and through to the present day. Reflecting this, by resisting the notion of the corrupt coven, the synchronicity of Carnesky's troupe of Showwomen celebrated the activist potential of collective consciousness.

The knowing-show of this show nods to its righteous anger, harnesses it, directs it into creative, proactive energy. The rendering of lived narratives as a bloodied, magical spectacle, foregrounded the objectified and abjectified politicization of bodies marked and maligned as other by patriarchal systems. In contributing to the feminist activism

around the politics of menstruation, highlighting the ageing and alt-fertile female body as part of this, it directly connected to the recent surge in activism by Gen X women, no longer accepting silence around older women's bodies and health.[8] It contributed to the fight to elaborate and energize menopause matters as an urgent health and welfare matter, and equally as a space for reclaimed female authority.

And so, to the end of this tale and its serpentine t(r)ail
through Metaphor, Metamorphosis and Magic
to alight at Showing you(R)age as a Showwoman Sage,
See! How she owns and commands her next stage.

Long Live Being Lividly Live

In retracing the trail of Carnesky's work, *Dr Carnesky's Incredible Bleeding Woman* trails a blaze for the menopausal Showwoman. Like *Jewess Tattooess* and *Ghost Train* before it, it wove imagery and conventions from high and low culture within a theatrical spectacle that produced heightened moments of performance ritual. This show was

Figure 6: Marisa Carnesky, introducing *Carnesky's Showwomxn Sideshow Spectacular*, Smithfield Grand Avenue, 2023. London. © Ruth Bayer

thesis wrapped in spectacle. It offered a critique of what it is to be a woman, defined by a body and by its powers of menstruation; what it is to have a womb, what it is to have cycles, to menstruate or not, to conceive, to miscarry or give birth, to menstruate no more. It is vital to a broader performance practice that makes visible and makes space for the dawning of a new (r)age of the menopausal woman.

Dr Carnesky's Incredible Bleeding Woman reve(a)lled in the multifarious resonances encompassed in the 'show'. Its showiness was a bejewelled showing off of expertise; yet, through the theatrics and fun, it was the sincerity of the message within the artistry that came through. Personal challenges and shared experience were wrought through dramaturgical discipline to show the art and activism that might emerge when the show must go on. To extract an apposite metaphor, Carnesky's Showwomen also plugged into ideas that resonate with 'the show'; the plug of mucus from the cervix that comes away as hard labour is activated and an outcome is delivered. Here, *showing* as demonstration allowed spectacular actions to speak louder than words, where *showing up* led to collective activism. In testing the parameters of performance-manifestation as performance-manifesto, the more serious message of this show signalled how a queer-feminist rage might contribute to an ecofeminist future, where the cycles of the human body are recognized as, and respectful of, cycles of nature. In a society where #MeToo, Times Up, and Bloody Good Period have galvanized a shift in public thinking, Carnesky's final, tongue-in-cheek call to matriarchal arms is not so far-fetched, given the project saw to the formation of 'Menstronauts', a direct-action movement.[9] Since 2016, the Menstronauts have held workshops, joined women's marches on parliament and continue to meet in person and via social media.

Like a true Showwoman, Carnesky's history of practice through the last three decades might be seen to correspond to acts. She's marching proactively into this next act, expanding the reach of Carnesky's Radical Cabaret School through her BA in Contemporary and Popular Performance, delivered in collaboration with Tramshed at Rose Bruford College. Here she will facilitate a new generation of showmakers to blaze their own trail as Dr Marisa Carnesky, mentor and maestro. In tandem with the rise of Carnesky's Showwoman extraordinaire in this third act, and the 'new, matriarchal utopias' planned for future productions (Carnesky 2022), I predict the glorious, energizing rage of the Menopausal Menstronaut, abundant in her wisdoms, and all embracing in her glorification of those who identify as (R)Aging Showwoman, loud, proud, and bloody spectacular.

Bibliography

Ahmed, S. (2017), *Living a Feminist Life*, Durham and London: Duke University Press.

Anzaldua, G. (1987), *Borderlands/La Frontera: The New Mestiza*, San Francisco: Aunt Lute Books.

Bates, L. (2022), *Fix the System, Not the Women*, London: Simon & Schuster Ltd.

Carnesky, M. (1999), 'Concept, writer, designer, performer'. *Jewess Tattooess*, Films by Alison Murray. Soundtrack, Dave Knight with specially commissioned tracks by Katherine Gifford & James Johnson. Tattoos and set, Alex Binnie. London, BAC, 21 October and ICA, 9 December.

Carnesky, M. (2001), 'Concept, writer, designer, performer', *Jewess Tattooess*, Copenhagen: Kanon Halleh, 18 January.

Carnesky, M. (2004–08), 'Concept, writer, director, designer, deviser, performer', *Carnesky's Ghost Train*, Brick Lane, London, UK.

Carnesky, M. (2008–14), 'Concept, writer, director, designer, deviser', *Carnesky's Ghost Train*, Blackpool, England, UK.

Carnesky, M. (2018), 'Concept, co-deviser, writer', *Dr. Carnesky's Incredible Bleeding Woman*, Southend-on-Sea, Metal, and London, The Institute of Archeology, National Theatre Studios (2015–17), London: Soho Theatre, 19–24 November.

Carnesky, M. (2022), 'Concept, co-deviser, writer, producer', *Showwomen*, London: Jackson's Place, 16 June.

Chemeley, S. (2018), *Rage Becomes Her: The Power of Women's Anger*, London: Atria Books.

Cixous, H. (1976), 'The laugh of the Medusa', *Signs* (trans. K. Cohen and P. Cohen), vol. 1, no. 4 (Summer), Chicago: University of Chicago Press, pp. 875–93.

Cixous, H. (1991), *Coming to Writing and Other Essays*. Introductory essay by Susan Rubin Suleiman (ed. D. Jenson, trans. S. Cornell, D. Jenson, A. Liddle, and S. Sellers), Cambridge, MA: Harvard University Press.

Cixous, H. (1993), *The Newly Born Woman*. With Catherine Clément (trans. B. Wing), Minneapolis, MN: University of Minnesota Press.

Cixous, H. (2011), *Hemlock: Old Women in Bloom* (trans. B. Bie Brahic), Cambridge: Polity Press.

Cixous, H. (2012), *Eve Escapes: Ruins and Life* (trans. P. Kamuf), Cambridge: Polity Press.

Cornet, W. (2022), 'Ghana: Accused of witchcraft, hundreds of women banished to camps', *France24*, First broadcast, 24 January, available at https://www.youtube.com/watch?v=UzmXXWPIAXU. Accessed 13 June 2022.

Diamond, E. (1997), *Unmaking Mimesis: Essays on Feminism and Theater*, London: Routledge.

Gore, A. (2017), *We Were Witches*, New York: Feminist Press.

Greer, G. (2019), *The Change – Women, Ageing and the Menopause*, London: Bloomsbury.

hooks, b. (2000), *Feminism is for Everybody: Passionate Politics*, Cambridge, MA: South End Press.

Juno, A. and Vale V. (eds) (1999), *Re/Search #13: Angry Women – New Edition*, New York: Juno Books.

Kwatra, A. (2012), *Condemned without Trial: Women and Witchcraft in Ghana*, London: ActionAid International.

Levy, D. (2019), *The Cost of Living*, London: Penguin.

Levy, D. (2021), *Real Estate*, London: Penguin.

Lorde, A. (2000), *The Collected Poems of Audre Lorde*, New York and London: Norton.

Lorde, A. (2019), *Sister Outsider*, London: Penguin Classics.

Machon, J. (2011), *(Syn)aesthetics: Redefining Visceral Performance*, Basingstoke and New York: Palgrave Macmillan.

Machon, J. (2012), 'Experiential identities in the work of Marisa Carnesky', in S. Broadhurst and J. Machon (eds), *Identity, Performance and Technology: Practices of Empowerment, Embodiment and Technicity*, Basingstoke and New York: Palgrave Macmillan, pp. 111-25.

Machon, J. (2013), 'Immersed in illusion, haunted by history: Marisa Carnesky's *Ghost Train*', in S. Munt and O. Jenzen (eds), *The Ashgate Research Companion to Sociocultural Studies of the Paranormal*, London: Ashgate, pp. 241-54.

Moran, C. (2020), *More than a Woman*, London: Ebury Press.

Segal, L. (2014), *Out of Time: The Pleasures and Perils of Ageing.* Introduction by Elaine Showalter. London and New York: Verso.

Shaw, J., Fletcher-Watson, B., and Ahmadzadeh, A. (eds) (2022), *Dangerous Women: Fifty Reflections on Women, Power and Identity*, London: Unbound.

Traister, R. (2018), *Good and Mad: The Revolutionary Power of Women's Anger*, London: Simon & Schuster Ltd.

Notes

1. See Machon 2011 (23–24) regarding the body as sight/site/cite, where 'cite' denotes that which refers back to a source in form, which in turn 'marks' itself within immediate perception, so is automatically referred back to in any subsequent recall in audience interpretation.

2. Cixous' *écriture feminine* or 'writing the body' is both a sensual writing practice and an analytical tool. It is 'insurgent' and offers 'another way of knowing' and 'producing' where 'the huge resources of the unconscious … burst out'. *Écriture féminine* breaks down rigid oppositions (especially of feminine/masculine) to take pleasure in the slippage in-between, a fluid, expansive space of making/interpreting 'where each one is always far more than one', embracing difference, ambiguity, slippage, and transgression in the making of work and the making of meaning from that work (Cixous 1993: 84–97). To write the body is to blend 'personal history … with the history of all women' with 'national and world history' (1976: 882).

3. Notably, Cixous' *juifemme* shares a linguistic style with Carnesky's Carny and Serpentina;

> To fight against the law that says, 'Thou shalt not make unto thee any graven image, nor any likeness of anything that is in Heaven above or that is in the earth beneath, or that is in the water under the earth'. Against the decree of blindness, I have often lost my sight; and I will never finish fashioning the graven image for myself. My writing watches. Eyes closed. You want to have. You want everything. But having is forbidden to human beings. Having everything. And for woman, it's even forbidden to hope to have everything a human being can have … In me is the word of blood, which will not cease before my end (1991: 3–5).

4. *Mezuzahs* are fragments of parchment inscribed with Hebrew text, encased and placed on doorposts – entrances and exits – as an amulet of protection.

5. As with each of the Menstruants' rituals, the dramaturgically disciplined testimony resonated with bell hooks thinking around, 'the confessional moment as a transformative moment, a moment of *performance* where you might step out of the fixed identity in which you were seen, and reveal other aspects of the self […] as part of an overall project of *more fully becoming who you are*' (Juno and Vale 1999: 80, emphasis original).

6. Juno and Vale's *Angry Women* collection, emblazoned with Medusa's face on its front cover, incorporates a rich array of interviews with leading artists from performance, including the forementioned Finley and Sprinkle, and writer-philosophers such as bell hooks and Kathy Acker. Other feminists who have directly explored female anger, its sociocultural implications, and its political potential include Ahmed (2017), Bates (2022), Chemeley (2018), Lorde (2019), Shaw et al. (2022), or Traister (2018).

7. See, for example, Anzaldúa, Gore, Greer (2019: 389–410), Lorde (2000: 78, 124, 134, 141, and especially 234), and Moran (259–70). For current evidence on the continued patriarchal violence directed at 'the witch', see Anjali Kwatra's 2012 report and Wassim Cornet's 2022 broadcast on the witch camps in Ghana.

8. Menopause and its associated rage are theorized in Greer's *The Change* (2019), while broader feminist examinations of mid-late-life and its ramifications for women include writings by de Beauvoir (1996), Cixous (1991, 2011, 2012), hooks (2000), Levy (2019, 2021), or Segal (2014). A menopause discourse now burgeons across popular culture, with an abridged overview including Dr Nighat Arif's TikTok videos, Dr Shahzadia Harper's Facebook lives, Dr Louise Newson's 'The Menopause Doctor' podcast, or the Webnetwork 'Rock my Menopause', from the Primary Care Women's Health Forum, which educate on women's health and menopause, including transgender experience; Kirsty Wark's *Menopause and Me* (BBC, 2017), Mariella Frostrup's *The Truth About the Menopause* (BBC, 2018), and Davina McCall's *Sex, Myths and the Menopause* (Channel 4: 2021); books such as those by India Knight, Christa de Souza, or Sandra Tsing Yeo are matched by populist podcasts and social media enterprises, including Karen Arthur's *Menopause Whilst Black*, Sam Baker's *The Shift*, Omisade Burney-Scott's *Black Girl's Guide to Surviving Menopause*, or Rachel Weiss' *Menopause Cafes*.

9. See https://metoomvmt.org, https://timesupnow.org, www.bloodygoodperiod.com, and https://www.facebook.com/groups/menstronauts/.

Ballad of the Bloody Pearl

Daniel Oliver

Marisa Carnesky appeared (as Marisa Carr) in a documentary called *XXXTripping* on Channel 4 in the United Kingdom in 1998. The documentary was about sex, death, magic, transgressive art, and underground culture and included short sections from her performance with the Dragon Ladies, entitled 'Ballad of the Bloody Pearl'. I saw it when I was about seventeen, after getting home drunk from my favourite pub and putting the telly on. I lived in a small town in the countryside in South West England and spent a lot of time in that pub. It was about three houses down from my home. There was not much else to do.

I am watching it again now. It is out of focus, or the TV reception was bad, or the VHS was old, or something happened that I don't understand to do with resolution when I transferred it to YouTube. In the background, there is one of those party curtains made of strips of gold tinsel foil. Carnesky appears in front of the curtain. A sort of off-balance circus trapeze music plays. This is the first glittery, showy moment in a documentary full of scratchy edits, woozy focus, shaky camera handling, and an overall sense of stylistic fidelity to the rawness and resistance of the ideas, aesthetics, and behaviours of the artists and writers interviewed. Alan Moore was in it, and Genesis P-Orridge, and a bunch of transgressive filmmakers and performance artists from New York.

The top half of Carnesky's body, including her face and head, is covered in a thin layer of latex decorated with sailor tattoos. A black skirt is long at the back but split open from just below her crotch in the front. She wears stockings. At one point, she has a wig of black curly hair. Later, she looks bald, except for two plaited bunches which poke out from the latex on either side of her head. She pulls a pearl necklace out from the latex near her temples, so it appears to come from beneath her skin. She plays with the necklace, handling and looking at it with a mix of doll-like vacancy, erotic desire, and maternal tenderness. The pearls are pushed into her red knickers which come down slightly, exposing the top of her pubes. She rubs them between her legs then whooshes them outwards and upwards.

I remember my favourite pub as rude and lawless and dangerous and also as a safe haven on the edge of a small judgy town and also as a magical place and as a mundane place and as euphoric and also a bit sad and as a place where you could sort of do what you wanted but where you might also get hurt bad for not much reason at all. There were a lot of fun drugs and fun weirdos and some not-fun people that beat up fun drug users and weirdos and a landlord who wore a top hat and was known to be the hardest man in town. Me and my friends were some of the weirdos and we were skinny and arty and the landlord liked that and told us to come to him if anyone caused us any trouble for being weirdos. Often, when trouble did kick off in the pub, he would shout out from the bar 'if anyone is going to fight, they have to fight me', and that would usually calm things down. When I used to go there, I imagined it would always be there and that I would always be able to and need to go there and that there was nowhere else like it and that there was no one else like me and the other weirdos who frequented it and that there was no other really hard people like the landlord, who I could go to if anyone caused me any trouble for being a weirdo. The pub is gone now – it was knocked down about twenty years ago.

Getting home from there and seeing Carnesky's performance had a big impact on seventeen-year-old me. A sort of thinky horny teeny magical mess of an impact. Just like the pub, it felt unexpectedly homely, and also like a glimpse into a world I wanted to escape to and create more of. I showed it to my mum and dad so that they might better understand what I meant when I said I wanted to be a performance artist when I grew up.

Spectacle, Patriarchy, and Ghost Trains

Paloma Faith and Marisa Carnesky

Marisa Carnesky: Can you talk about your early days in performance and cabaret, including working with me and how this has influenced your style and vision?

Paloma Faith: As a kid, I idolized my older cousin, who had a massive crush on Marilyn Monroe; all the posters on her bedroom wall in Italy were of Marilyn. I looked up to her and she looked up to Marilyn. That kind of vintage style was always something that I gravitated towards, even as a little girl. Then I trained as a dancer and in theatre, and I was already embedded in that vintage way of dressing, but I had not met anybody else who did. When I was working behind the bar in Shoreditch dressed up as a glamorous young pinup, a vampire came in.

MC: A real vampire?

PF: A real vampire, and his name is David Piper.

MC: Oh, yes, he is a real vampire [laughing].

PF: He told me that he was compère for a night called Whoopee Club. When I went there to watch, I thought that it was an amalgamation of all the things I loved. I came from a performance, contemporary dance, and physical theatre background. I was really interested in artists like Franko B and Pina Bausch, who pushed boundaries. This was around the time you and I met when burlesque was very niche and not many people were into it. Not many people were searching for the types of performers that were doing that kind of work, like Penny Arcade in New York.

MC: In New York, when I went to clubs like Jackie 60 in the early 90s, performance artists, like Penny Arcade and amazing drag performers, like Kiki and Herb, were crossing over with performers dressing up and doing burlesque. Whereas in England, it was very niche.

PF: I resented it at the beginning of my music career, when I was constantly being called a burlesque performer, because I was a performance artist. You and I met on the bus and it was a meeting of kindred spirits. We started doing various workshops and I already was having glimpses of what I was interested in, but I had never met anybody who could open the door to me, which you did, by exposing me to a whole world of people like me. It turns out there is a whole tribe, and we are all pushing boundaries. I think that probably meeting you and working at Agent Provocateur were the two most pivotal and influential times. Working at Agent Provocateur influenced me, as I was very much at the helm of meeting people who used fetish as an escape and a place to be understood. I found it amazing having first hand a sort of Nan Goldin experience of meeting people who were somehow searching for their place within humanity and dealing with the constraints of social expectation. These were all the things I wanted to explore and still explore as an artist, what it is about the human condition that is universal.

When we were on the *Ghost Train*, people just walked past and got on it, thinking that it was a ghost train; in a way, the elitism of high-end art was challenged, and the work was made accessible. This is also why I ended up wanting to act and make music because these are the most accessible art forms. There have been times during my career when I have erred more on the commercial side in order to create a platform that exposes me to more people, but never have I lost my conceptual backbone.

MC: Yes, amazing. What lovely things you say. I wanted to ask you, when you create, when you have a new song or an album, I imagine that you have a vision. What comes first, is it the vision or the music?

PF: I tend to trust my subconscious; I write the music without being constrained by an idea or concept. Because when I do that, sometimes the music can be contrived. It is usually an amalgamation of what I am going through emotionally, plus whatever books I have read, films I have seen, and art that I have been exposed to or gravitated towards at the time. Then I start to try and figure out what the thread is by overseeing it, once it is all written.

Figure 7: Paloma Faith, New York. 2023. © Ryan Muir

MC: It is interesting to know that the song comes first, and the visuals after. You have this commitment to things being spectacular, as do I.

PF: I love the spectacle because in order to tap into real feelings, I need to go to extremes; understated and mediocre is not really something that I have ever been interested in. We cannot get to the truth of anything unless we go to the extremes. In order to find the middle, you have to swing in between. I think spectacle is escapism and stems from trauma response. When I look back at the ways that I escaped from childhood, it was all make-believe.

MC: That is so interesting. I have never thought of spectacle as a trauma response. You are very theatrical; you are very rich and colourful.

PF: It is war paint as well, though, isn't it? We are all inherently vulnerable and those are the subjects that we are talking about. In order to have the confidence to do that, spectacle needs to happen. Whenever people come up to me in the street and say, 'could I have a picture with you?' I always say, 'I am sorry I don't have any make-up on'.

MC: Yes. True, true. I have been so proud and thrilled by you being political, talking about your experiences with childbirth and your support of socialist ideas. I just wondered if you could reflect on how your politics fuses with your art in that way.

PF: Unfortunately, we live in an era where people are very apathetic politically. I think it is irresponsible to have a platform and not use it to influence in a positive way. My platform can be used to promote moral good. I talk about kindness, and I will have someone like [political commentator] Owen Jones on my album or on tour with me because he represents a lot of what I stand for. I feel proud that I have the ability to do that. Being silent is not an option for me. I was born on picket lines and anti-Thatcher marches. But then, on the other hand, I feel very restrained in what I choose to say and not to say. I have to maintain the platform because it is counterintuitive to alienate people and then have no voice whatsoever. I think it is always a fine line.

MC: I like that you tread that line because you could easily choose to say nothing. Recently, you have been speaking out about your experiences of childbirth, and you were talking about your IVF experience and postpartum depression. A lot of women in your position would not take that platform. I did a slightly more controversial underground art version with my menstrual show. You know, we are Showwomen.

PF: I have come through the vehicle of the music business, and, like many industries, it is significantly run by white powerful men. I have been in many meetings with a male management representative and the person has not looked at me once and my manager has had to say, 'ask Paloma'. It is interesting to me what happened during the time of the #MeToo campaign. It is really important that people understand that it has been like climbing up an ice scotch with a pickaxe; even at age 41, I have never directed one of my videos and I have asked and pitched so many times. I genuinely think that this would not have happened to a male artist. But I also do not bite the hand that feeds me.

There have been a lot of men in my career who have really championed me and really pushed for me; I would not have a career if they had not. But this is still a patriarchy. The cogs are run by men and that is not about to change, and it probably will not for a long time. I know that only 6 per cent of commercial music that is successful is authored by women. I am just as political, creative, and neurotic as I was in the early days. But now it is just different. I am writing a book about female identity. I think it is important to recognise that most women artists that you are writing about have worked and progressed within a patriarchal construct.

MC: Yes, it is true. It is very true. Thank you very much.

Finding Marisa Carnesky

Liz Aggiss

I am on a memory quest. It's Brighton. It's 1990. I meet a woman who is on the wrong journey. And she knows it. She is named Marisa Carr. And we all know names are just the beginning of the journey. She doesn't know what her route is, but she needs to remove herself p.d.q. from the one she is on. The one where she is training to be a dancer, to interpret other choreographers' ideas, to rein in her body and render it useful to others, and to make her mark as a contemporary dance maker. The very thought of it! She is studying at a London conservatoire. She might explode or disappear as a future feminist icon if she stays a moment longer. Her sense says it's no sense. She is being hampered by no(n)sense. She is clambering up a ladder and falling down a snake. We talk. She intrigues me. Her head is cluttered with black curls and ideas. Her body is disembodied. Her anxious forehead: her listening self: her questioning other. I decide I want her on my team. She is half qualified with her unqualified other half framed formally, and awkwardly, as visual art. But let's put that to one side. She has wit, intellect, focus, passion, drive, and ambition. She knows she wants 'another something', but not what that 'a n other something' is. I spot a woman whose political body requires nurturing. She is in it for the long haul. She is talking like a live artist, though live arts are yet to be re-invented. I catch hold of my responsibilities. Brace Brace Brace. Here, she can (em)brace her current dislocation and channel her ambition and call to action. She has come to the right place, her next new home. She will learn how to walk forwards, look sideways, check the back-ways, and avoid trip hazards. She is so close she can smell it. She is a political animal finding her feminist feet. She has caught a whiff of her buried showwoman. She has caught the scent of her identity. What's in a name? I will over-ride the institutional system and welcome her into the body of the visual performance 'kirk'. Her cohort of 'chosen others' are remarkably adept and able to push their personal envelopes and change the template to suit their destinies. She will belong here. I am but a conduit. I provide the framework tailored to individual needs. I offer a critique to 'hold' the space. None of us has a rulebook. We are all just trying to frame our own creative journey. I just happen to be wearing the tutor cloak at the University of Brighton. She just happens to be pulling on her student coat. And so, it begins.

To contextualize my 'voice' within the body of this text, I am Liz Aggiss, often referred to as lizaggiss, all one-word lowercase, and I, like Marisa Carnesky (nee Carr), am an artist academic. Since those early tutor/student days, our parallel trajectories and artistic paths have often delightfully crossed, which statement transitions neatly to this next written intervention with questions; 'How was Carnesky's work shaped within this formative student context?' and, 'What artistic dialogues can shed light at the end of this tunnel?'

I feel a memory coming in. Don't quote me it's over 30 years ago. *It's a cabaret piece. There's a cabinet stuffed with shoes. The door hangs open. It's a visual performance. I'm thinking of shoes taken from Holocaust victims and piled high. I hear shattering glass. Kristallnacht? This solo is raw and awkward, fierce, and unashamed. I think she's scuffling with the tower of shoes. That's all. I don't have any more memory detail. I just know Marisa Carr is in the building.*

And back to the present. How do Carnesky's and Aggiss' paths cross?

Liz Aggiss cut her feet in cabaret settings, pubs, and clubs as choreographer/performer in The Wild Wigglers (1980–86), then into black box theatres as director/choreographer/performer for Divas Dance Theatre (1986–97), which briefly featured Carnesky as company member, and then onto solo works and Performance Lectures (1997–future). For the past 40 years, Aggiss has been re(de)fining her own brand of performance, dodging categorization, and being classifiably unclassifiable, and like Carnesky they both occupy a queasy fit as un-disciplined artists slipping between the floorboards of disciplines. Their work challenges cultural norms and opens up new perspectives on gender, and their defiant formidable paths have enabled both women to be presented within a broad soup of live art, vaudeville, WOW, queer, contemporary, and dance theatre festivals.

I feel another memory coming in. *She's wearing a transparent travel storage garment bag. She's hung herself on a curtain rail. Suffocated, squashed, hidden yet visible. A survivor. I'm thinking concentration camps and women hiding their babies on clothes pegs. Hanging one life,*

Figure 8: Liz Aggiss, *Slap and Tickle*, 2017. © Jo Murray

one hope, on one peg to sustain lineage. Such dark thoughts. Don't quote me. My memory may be skewed. It's over 30 years ago.

Then, the language of performance discourse was rusty, needed some cranking up. We are all now better informed. These next words are those we wanted to adopt but couldn't since we were not yet able to say we were artists. Now, we are both here on the same page as artists. Ka Boom! Back of the net!

And this is the page which states that both Carnesky and Aggiss, as critically acclaimed artists, share a common dialogue, though as a mature artist lizaggiss is the 'grand dame of anarchic dance' or 'enfant terrible of the bus pass generation', and Carnesky has yet to reach this latter version of herself. As feminist artists, both Carnesky and Aggiss are uncompromising and are committed to the power of their voices and politics. Popular culture and music hall define how both use the stage space, the 'apron', and cross the fourth wall to 'act out and act up', to revise attitudes and preconceptions about female visibility and de-familiarize the homogenized notions and codings of femininity. Carnesky takes it one step further and creates spectacle, using every trick in the book, making a spectacular spectacle of herself. The ultimate, unforgettable, in your face, brittle, and brash visual performance.

Don't quote me as it's over 30 years ago, but this is burnt into the back of my retina. Carr is now Carnesky. I told you there was something in a name, and a Jewess Tattooess; a double transgression, as a woman and a Jew (the Torah forbids self-decoration). She begins this journey by enduring an extreme large-scale spectacular dragon back tattoo which renders her temporarily immobile. A precursor to making large-scale site-based works? She is the sideshow. She's making her mark. Now she's inking herself live on stage. I'm not wrong, its indelibly imprinted, herstorys' history, baring flesh, scored into flesh, marking a female line on her upper leg like a stocking top, a garter of stars, merging vaudeville and identity.

Back to the artist discourse, the context and sub-texts.

In seeking to further underpin their cohesion, both Carnesky and Aggiss' work is framed by extensive contextual research that considers and uses the personal and historical as reference. From dance archives, Aggiss focuses on predominantly a pre- and inter-war lost generation of female dancers, Ausdruckstanzereins, Grotesque Dancers, and Music Hall artistes. Carnesky's research similarly considers this practice fair game, but delves further into Showwomen, recovering a lost generation from popular culture and dragging them into the twenty-first century. For both women, these unashamed, unafraid, expressive female bodies have left an indelible legacy and it is these 'cultural carriers' that feature in both their practices: for Aggiss as 'bodies recovered from the library': for Carnesky reinventing and repositioning as a new impressive scaled up art form.

I'm reliving a memory here. *I'm at Raymond Revuebar, Soho, London. I'm watching, or rather being immersed in displa(y)ced play;* Carnesky's Nightmare Chorus Line. *It's Egon Schiele meets punk Tiller Girls. It's a reimagining, a bit grubby, sarcastically sordid, tongue in cheek, out off kilter spectacle in the now washed–up former home of the 'Worlds Centre of Erotic Entertainment'. It's the underbelly of cabaret. Don't quote me. It's over 30 years ago!*

In repositioning and creating an invisible umbilical cord to 'recovered bodies', these two artists, Aggiss and Carnesky, tug on the connection that redefines '(in)visibility' as female artists and stamp their relationship and influence within contemporary feminist practice. Both artists bear homage to their lineage and embrace their dedication to researching and repositioning the under-documented history of women live artists.

Ladies and Gentlemen, I give you my friend, your friend, everybody's friend, Marissssssaaaaaaa Caaaaaaaaarnessssskkkkkyyyyy.

A final memory. *Marisa is a sideshow penny slot machine in an art gallery. She has found her Showwoman. She's lying on her side, her back side bare, posed, poised, and waiting. Her tattooed engraved body a voyeur's delight. Between her thighs a small wooden box. She waits for us to put a penny in her slot. Oooer missus. She is the entertainment. My father in his 80th year is curious as this is his first iteration of live art. He approaches her slot with his penny and slips it in. Marisa looks over her shoulder at him and prophesies his future. My father has never seen the like. He laughs like a drain and with that, my work is done.*

The Cosmos of Showwomen

Marisa Carnesky, Showwoman

Roberta Mock

My shows are always set in Showtime. Showtime is a rare experience of being right here, right now and yet not here at all. Showtime exists simultaneously in and out of reality [...]. I've been making shows as long as I can remember and I intend to carry on doing so for as long as I can.
(Carnesky 2002)

Marisa Carnesky refers to herself as a Showwoman. Neither a showgirl nor a showman – although drawing from, repudiating aspects of, and exceeding both – Showwoman is an appellation that, like most of Carnesky's work, feels like it has always existed (if only you knew where, or how, to find it).[1] She defines such a woman as either one who possesses the power of 'bombastic theatrical flair and an extraordinary skill, most likely within the worlds of "low brow" variety entertainment', or else (or in addition), one who 'manages and produces large scale spectacular shows with a great talent for creating a buzz and getting publicity in inventive and risqué ways' (Carnesky 2015). Perhaps most importantly, Showwomen 'do not work for the management or the man. Showwomen work for themselves and other people work for them' (Carnesky Productions website, n.d.).

This chapter positions Carnesky's performances to date, as she suggests, as 'work' at the intersection of aesthetic show-making and commercial show-business, in order to explore what it is that she is attempting to present and make present, how she does so, and why it matters. Her subject matter and themes have remained remarkably consistent over a 25-year period. According to Carnesky, they 'are always in the same vein but with a different emphasis: cultural identity as it lives in the unconscious, folklore, ritual, sexual performance and the politics that surround women's bodies as entertainment' (Carnesky 2012). Similarly, she has been consistently fascinated by a particular aspect of 'Showwomanry': that which uses 'the abject, the taboo and the forbidden to create spectacle and magic' (Carnesky 2015). Carnesky's is the abject described by Julia Kristeva in *Powers of Horror*: sensual, Jewish, queer, feminine, vulgar, liminal, frightening, perverse, and ambiguous. It is not a narrative, but 'a vision', one that represents a boundary or limit (Kristeva 1982: 154). According to Kristeva, the time of abjection is always double, 'of veiled infinity and the moment when revelation bursts forth' (1982: 9), resonating with Carnesky's identification of a Showtime that exists simultaneously in and out of reality.

Carnesky specializes in what Rogan Taylor (1985) called 'the Death and Resurrection Show' of traditional shamen/showmen: in re-animation, in making apparent, in the reparative conjuring of affect, in the production of *jouissance*. Waxworks, dolls, ghosts, half-remembered traditions, ancestors, mythical goddesses, archetypes, performance genealogies and repertoires, and the disappeared are brought to life in quirky, fragile, sexy, fun, political, and provocative ways. Carnesky piles genre upon genre, blurring the boundaries of live cultures. 'What I do', she told one interviewer, 'is really a mix of performance art, spectacle, circus, and experiential promenade installation theatre. Or perhaps it's easier to say that it's experimental visual theatre' (Carnesky in McLaren 2012). Even that description feels partial. Five years earlier, *Time Out* magazine credited her with the invention of 'grotesque (or carnivalesque) burlesque' in the 1990s: her edgy, political, 'high end' turns included one, for instance, in which she played Eve and removed her clothes while eating an apple that was squashed in her mouth (Baird 2007). It was Carnesky's combination of erotic entertainment and avant-garde performance that established her at the forefront of what is now recognized as feminist neo-burlesque in the United Kingdom. Occasionally, often due to the choice of venue, her 'satirical striptease' (Carnesky in Rees 2004) pushed too many buttons. In a lecture at the Union Chapel in London, for instance, she discusses the curtailing of an early performance at the same venue; she had been wearing a 'Jesus beard' and spilling red wine over her naked body (Carnesky 2013b).

One way to categorize, and hence to understand, Carnesky's amalgamation of performance cultures is as live art, described by the Live Art Development Agency (LADA) on its website as not so much 'an artform or discipline, but a cultural strategy to include *experimental processes and experiential practices* that might otherwise be excluded from established curatorial, cultural and critical frameworks' (my emphasis). *Experimental* and *experiential* are the very words Carnesky chose to categorize her practice above, and she has used them together to describe at least two of her pieces: *Carnesky's Ghost Train* (Carnesky in Machon 2012: 114) and *Carnesky's Tarot Drome* (Carnesky in Purves 2012). Indeed, she is a textbook example of an artist who has both broken with 'the traditions of the circumstance and expectations of theatre' and turned to her body as the site and material of her practice, in order to explore 'the possibilities of the "event" or "experience" of art that is live' (LADA website, n.d.).

Carnesky builds the risks inherent in her 'cultural strategy' into what drives it. When asked about her intended 'messages' in an interview with a long-standing collaborator, the photographer Manual Vason, she responded that they are less statements than a series of interrelated questions (Carnesky 2013a). Echoing Richard Schechner's 'efficacy entertainment dyad' model for performance (Schechner 2013: 79–80), Carnesky's creative enquiry circulates around the role of the political in popular entertainment and how popular forms might respond to the inclusion of radical art practices and ideas; how ritual and sexual representation might affect audiences of such a hybrid performance form; how work that is entertaining might also be transgressive; or whether it is always 'reduced' as – or to – spectacle (Carnesky 2013a). In Schechner's model, efficacious performances, which he associates with ritual, are located at one end of a continuum; entertainment – its primary purpose 'to give pleasure, to show off, to be beautiful' – is harnessed with 'performing arts' at the other end. These 'poles' are not intended as a binary and Schechner observes that any individual performance is located somewhere along this spectrum; precisely where is determined by its purpose. It is also worth noting that there are those who analyse specific forms of popular performing arts that are central to Carnesky's work – for instance, circus (Bouissac 2012: 23–26) or neo-burlesque (Aston and Harris 2013: 151) – as, or as including, ritual.

In keeping with many live art events, the form, content, and context of Carnesky's performances are inextricably imbricated in their meaning-making. Moreover, their processes of development and presentation are engaged both simultaneously and iteratively. Preferring to continuously shape a show according to response, Carnesky has claimed that she doesn't 'spend a lot of time in the rehearsal room …. I like to work it in front of the audience' (Carnesky in Machon 2009: 126).[2] Placing value on the potential for and implications of change, she has said that her

> shows change all the time in relation to the nature of different venues and audiences and my own moods and body. Live shows are full bloodied things: they remind you that you are a living, breathing, sweating entity.
> (Carnesky 2002)

Figure 9: Marisa Carnesky, excerpts from *Dr Carnesky's Incredible Bleeding Woman*, Cirque Electric, HEY! Festival, 2015. Paris. © Zoe Forget

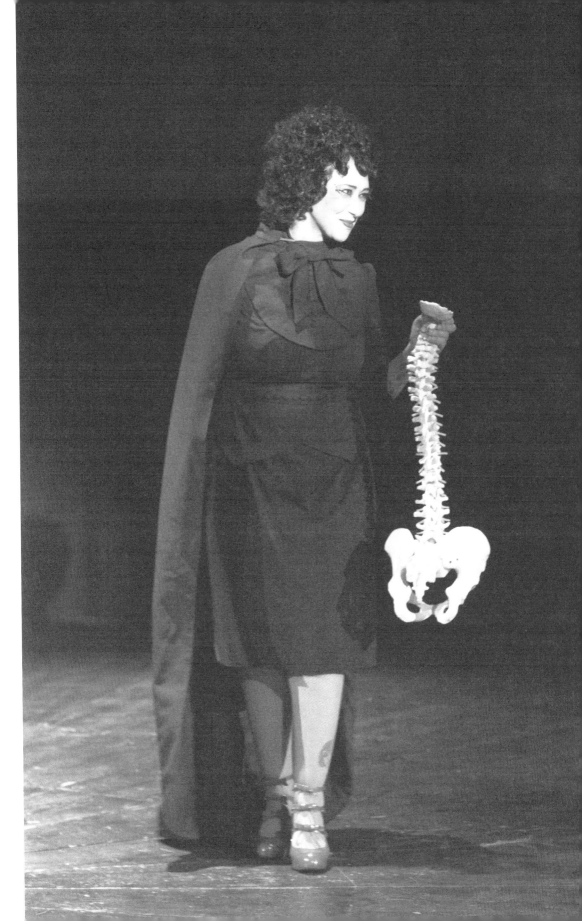

Parts of these shows can be detached – for example, performed discretely on a variety bill with other artists – or else, their visual elements repurposed for performance-to-camera; eventually, some become the kernels of new productions. Such a practice – encompassing event and technique, synchronic act, and diachronic action – more closely resembles the generation of a stand-up routine or circus production that transforms over an extended period of time while maintaining a recognizable (in this case, 'Carnesky') signature.

A Body of Work

Elizabeth Osborne and Christine Woodworth have identified a number of tropes emerging from the academic field of work studies that are relevant to analyses of theatre.

These include:

> the permeability or erasure of the boundaries between work and life; the connection between work and economic, social, or political power; the ways that labor is embodied and, in turn, how particular types of labor are inscribed on the bodies of workers over time; and the value ascribed to certain kinds of work over others.
> (Osborne and Woodworth 2015: 7)

All are apparent in Carnesky's first one-woman show, *Jewess Tattooess* (1999–2002), which examined her relationship with Jewishness, performance, gender, and the Shoah through taboos surrounding tattoos, blood, and menstruation in Judaism. With vaudevillian flourishes and employing a cabaret structure, Carnesky integrated striptease (quite literally unravelling mummy-like strips of fabric to reveal her body underneath), storytelling, gestural choreography, Jewish folk tale and flashes of Yiddish melodrama, film projection (both prerecorded, with heavy post-production, and live feeds), and 'freak show' performance staples such as 'the bed of nails'. In doing so, the mimetic and representational qualities of theatre (in particular, in Carnesky's shape-shifting performance of a number of characters, including a somnambulist alter-ego called Lulla, a rabbi and 'a Siamese Tattooed Carny Creature') were juxtaposed with elements associated with performance art – that is, actions with material consequences, the production of experience rather than narrative, and what

Josette Féral described as the appearance and disappearance of 'flows, networks and systems' (1982: 179).

It was those latter elements that, perhaps inevitably, commanded the most attention, especially Carnesky's acts of on-stage 'tattooing'. Such 'demonstrations', Féral argues, suggest paths of freedom for a body that is 'made conspicuous' and 'rendered as a *place of desire*, displacement, and fluctuation', by bringing repression 'to the surface' through and as performance (1982: 171; original emphasis). Carnesky's impetus for creating *Jewess Tattooess* was discovering that the tattoos she began accumulating as a teenager might prevent her from being buried in a consecrated Jewish cemetery with her parents.[3] In the show, Carnesky-as-rabbi on video cites the prohibition against tattooing in Leviticus (19:28) and then admonishes live Carnesky-as-Lulla: 'Your body is on loan from god [...]. You are a Jewess. Why? Why? Lulla, how can you claim a mark of freedom when this for us is a mark of suffering?' Carnesky does not pretend to have a straightforward answer. As she stated in an interview to promote early performances of *Jewess Tattooess*, her tattoos began as gendered markings of agency, bravado, 'visibility' and an affinity with 'outsider' cultures, and *not* 'as an act against the Jewish faith' (Brennan 1999). In the show, (commercial) fairground practices often replace, enhance, or supplant Judaism (as religion), if not Jewishness (as culture). Carnesky-as-Lulla recounts a dream, for instance, in which she dies and is refused burial by a rabbi; in limbo, her corpse is honoured in a carnival procession but, as the carnival is poor, her mummified tattooed skin is then displayed as a ticketed attraction.

Paradoxically, in *Jewess Tattooess*, Carnesky's tattoos mark her sexed body *as* Jewish, even – or especially – when this body is either rejected or othered from within Judaism (itself already othered by dominant cultures in the diaspora), or when its history is occluded. In one version, Carnesky tells the story of a sailor who encounters a woman wearing black leather gloves to conceal a concentration camp tattoo on her wrist which he then, in a gently erotic act, covers with a new tattoo of a flower. 'You can still see [the concentration camp number] if you look very hard', she says, before disinfecting her stomach and using a tattoo gun (but no ink) to etch a Jewish star around her navel. The live video projection behind her offers a magnified perspective and, if we look very hard, we can see the faint scars of the *magen david* made during previous performances behind the fresh welts and trickles of blood.[4] As Josephine Machon has noted, by leaving these traces on her body, Carnesky tells 'another bodily story, actually cited in her flesh' (2012: 121). During this scene, as for much of *Jewess Tattooess*, Carnesky is nude. Although she is wearing gloves, court shoes, and a hat that demurely and wittily covers her hair (in accordance with modesty codes for Jewish women), it is her already tattooed skin that acts as a costume.

As part of the process of creating *Jewess Tattooess* – influenced by images of tattooed women in the nineteenth-century sideshows as well as women associated with the Japanese gangster culture of Yakuza – Carnesky had a large dragon tattooed on her back, buttocks, and thigh by Alex Binnie. The hybridity of the dragon as a fantastic symbol, comprising elements of a variety of non-human animals, also aligned with Carnesky's sense of self as a British Jew: 'Dragons made from snake bodies and tiger claws, dog heads, bird feathers and lion manes. Dragons like the Jews are complex and contradictory, cerebral and superstitious' (Carnesky 2002). The dragon's metonymic presence is reinforced through her spoken text in the show: 'I am the tattooed soothsayer. / Dragon lady, dragon lady / Serpentina, serpentina / Read my skin, watch my lips, lips'. The lines of Carnesky's tattoo were drawn larger than usual so it could be seen clearly by audiences at a distance when she was performing onstage. Exemplifying how work produces a body-in-process in the same moment that work is produced through that body, Carnesky (2017) reflects that she is now 'living forever with a giant thickly lined dragon on my back. Sometimes I love it and embody it fully. Sometimes it feels a little grotesque/large/OTT for other aspects of my life'.

According to Steven Connor, skin cannot be considered a *part of the body* because it cannot be separated 'without taking the whole of the body with it', a body that is 'always a work in progress' (2004: 29). Skin is a porous membrane that delineates and acts as a barrier between interior and exterior corporeal horizons; tattoos, seemingly outward facing, live in skin due to the intervention of the immune system which defends the body from invaders. Skin is 'bilateral, both matter and image stuff and sign' (Connor 2004: 41). The original stage set designed by Binnie for *Jewess Tattooess*, featuring three receding proscenium arches constructed from 20-foot-high models of tattooed arms, operated in a similar way, reinforcing the synecdochical connections between skin, tattoos, Carnesky's body, playing space, this specific performance and her body of work as a whole:

> Like my work, my body is colourful and crowded. I am burning-building-destroyed- culture-fire-orange, lost-in-the-forest-anxiety-green, carnival-showman-yellow, sweet-smelling-old-lady-nearly-ghostly-lilac, hot-Mexican-pornographic-pink, ostentatious-proud-lucky-peacock-blue, difficult-

stubborn-purple and a menstrual-open-wound-dark-coagulated-red.
(Carnesky 2002)

Following the first UK tour, the scenography transformed significantly while continuing to evoke indeterminate spaces between interiority and exteriority, belonging and alterity. Gone were the outsized tattooed arms, replaced by a giant Jewish star on the floor through which Carnesky emerged and finally disappeared as if into an enormous vulva.

The star of David on the stage floor – echoing the one she was to mark on the skin at the centre of her body, around the trace of an umbilical cord – was made of dozens of sheets of paper covered with writing in Hebrew: the translated text of Carnesky's own version of a prayer that requests forgiveness for transgression, as mandated in the Torah (that is, the Jewish bible, comprising the five books of Moses or the Pentateuch). That this transgression encompasses both sexed difference and body modification is made clear through her act of walking across the text, naked and oozing (fake) blood from her high-heeled shoes, a representation of the impurity of a menstruant (or *niddah*) in Jewish law. The connections between, and gendered exclusion from, liturgy, ritual, and Hebrew text are enforced further by Carnesky's use of the *mezuzah*, which is an amulet that encases a fragment from the Torah ('Hear O Israel, the Lord our God, the Lord is one'); positioned in the doorways of Jewish homes, some kiss it (via their fingertips) in passing. Carnesky translates these thresholds and lips onto her own body. In some versions of *Jewess Tattooess*, *mezuzahs* are placed over her eyes; in others, she (also) inserts them into her vagina.

Within a religious tradition that has excluded women from text-based learning, associating them with unruly corporeal dangers (and temptations) and confining them to material and pragmatic (rather than holy and scholarly) spheres, Carnesky's carnivalesque disruptions of gendered boundaries – inserting text in body and body in a text smeared by the residue of its abjection – are not without strategic dangers. In a *Jewish Journal* interview, she explained that her show referenced and reclaimed figures like Salomé (via Jewish silent screen vamp, Theda Bara) because 'the very sexual, decorated woman is reviled in most cultures and I was looking for characters that societies have created to guide people away from them' (Carnesky in Pfefferman 2003). As Lori Hope Lefkovitz has written, while the Jewish woman's body, her fluids, and her voices 'provide bases already inscribed in the Jewish textual tradition for a theory of woman's subversive powers', there is always a risk that acts of subversion based on sexual difference will 'keep her tied to man by the energy of opposition' as well as the 'normative discourse that names her, defines her, legislates for her, and restricts her' (Lefkovitz 1995: 158–59).

Nevertheless, Jewishness offered Carnesky the opportunity to merge personal, artistic and professional identities and identifications, and the relationship between word and body was central to this operation. In an interview conducted while she was creating *Jewess Tattooess* in 1999, she announced that:

> I've changed my name. I've changed it to the name of my grandmother: Carnesky [...]. It's kind of a political thing in that all the Jews tended to Westernize their names. I'm now de-Westernizing it, going back to my Eastern European name that is my *real name*.
> (Carnesky in Bayley 2000: 348; my emphasis)

The making of this show thus not only transformed the complexion of Carnesky's body while consolidating her themes, her public image, and her stagecraft, but it also (quite literally) made her name. As one critic noted, it is a name that is 'fortuitously redolent of both carnival and the carnal' (Palmer 2004). Additionally, however, Carnesky's performing persona – indelibly linked to the name that would become her brand – is rooted in a gynelineal sense of 'realness', of matriarchal authenticity.

Prior to reclaiming the Latvian family name that had been anglicized in the 1940s, she worked under the name with which she was born. And so, it was as Marisa Carr that she organized the 1994 Smut Fest cabaret in London – during which she produced a full English breakfast from her underwear and sang 'Don't Put Your Daughter on the Stage, Mrs Worthington' while it sizzled – and later appeared in a remounted programme in a disused synagogue in New York that was filmed for HBO's *Real Sex* series (1995). It was as Marisa Carr that she posed as a 'Nice Jewish Girl' for Annie Sprinkle's deck of Pleasure Activist playing cards.[5] It was as Marisa Carr that she removed a string of Union Jack bunting from her vagina to the tune of 'God Save the Queen' in Robert Pacitti's show, *Geek* (1995), which was subsequently censored in Nottingham for 'licentious behaviour and public disorder'. In a newspaper article that doesn't mention her by name, Pacitti notes that in the circus, a geek (as opposed to a freak) is a performer who chooses to be unlike others through their own actions or behaviour. He describes Carnesky's act as a provocative metaphor for nation and belonging via the relationship between interiority and exposure: 'At the start of the performance she takes the flag from inside herself and drags it out into the open, where it is up for grabs' (Carnesky in Bayley 1995).

In the same year, Carr/Carnesky performed as part of the influential Jezebel season at the ICA in London – which also included performances by Karen Finley, Penny Arcade, Helena Goldwater, and Robbie McCauley – in a double bill with La Ribot. Prior to reappearing in *Jewess Tattooess*, the title of that performance, *Dragon Lady* (1995), was repurposed as the name of a collective she directed a few years later. With the Dragon Ladies, Carnesky produced *The Grotesque Burlesque Revue* (1997) at the Raymond Revuebar, a famous strip club in Soho (though by then in decline). In this 40-minute piece, she first appears in character as Dolly Blue, a 'comic whore' murdered by her lover, Bluebeard, before she, as Dolly, transforms into the figurehead of a ship and then finally emerges from the sea as the avenging monster, Bloody Pearl, who kills sailors with golden pearls stashed in her vagina: 'The she-thing peeled the tattooed skins off the sailors' corpses. / Creature of her own conception / Bloody Pearl, Bloody Pearl. / The outsider, the survivor' (Carnesky in Bayley 2000: 358). Carnesky wears a latex bodysuit which is covered with tattoos and features large breasts and a lurid mouth, its tongue protruding through sharp teeth and dripping with pearls, over her crotch. Palmer describes her slithering out of the same skin at the Torture Garden, a fetish club in London, at about the same time, as an act of 'giving birth to herself' in 'a sweaty, heaving mash of leatherboys' (Palmer 2004).

Carnesky was still working as a stripper then, which both informed and financially supported her other performance work, but she was already disenchanted:

> It's less fascinating now because it's exploitative, not because of the stripping because that's your personal choice but because there are no unions, no lunch hours and no showers …. And there are terrible things in the sex industry as a whole.
> (Carr/Carnesky in Brosnan 1998/2013: 92)

Haunted Borders

Carnesky marked her retirement as a stripper in 2002 by staging her own funeral on the streets of East London in a performance entitled *Carnesky's Ghost Box*.[6] As Alice Rayner has noted, ghosts 'animate our connections to the dead' via 'a certain mode of attention, a certain line of sight' and bring about a 'moment of unforgetting'. In performance, they produce 'a visible, material and affective relationship to the abstract terms of time and repetition, sameness and difference, absence and presence', thus drawing attention to the 'function of perception in world making' (Rayner 2006: xiii–xix). In *Carnesky's Ghost Box*, the artist lay in a glass casket in showgirl costuming, drawn by plumed black horses, like those she describes leading the oneiric carnival cortège in *Jewess Tattooess*. Her friends followed behind, dressed in black and carrying wreaths, accompanied by a marching band; as the procession passed the strip clubs at which she used to work, tokens of her career (such as garters and tassels) were left behind and a 'pall bearer' would draw chalk lines around them as if it was a crime scene. And then, to the amazement of onlookers, Carnesky's body magically appeared and disappeared in her casket.

This one-off performance was produced by club/performance promoter Duckie, with whom Carnesky regularly collaborated, as part of their Nightbird Season. The following year, their *C'est Barbican!* – which Carnesky devised and performed with Ursula Martinez, Chris Green, and Miss High Kick – won an Olivier award for Best Entertainment. Running for a month over the Christmas period, this event (called *C'est Vauxhall!* when originally staged on home ground) featured a showgirl-style cabaret opening and finale with synchronized shimmies and poses but revolved around close-up and interactive 'bite-sized burlesque' turns. These were ordered from a menu by audience members and paid for with 'Duckie dollars'. Dressed in a flesh-coloured body stocking to simulate nudity, Carnesky performed table-top acts with titles like 'Stilettos of Death' and 'The Woman Who Burnt Her Chicken'. Echoing audience/performer transactions in lap-dancing clubs while nostalgically looking back to the art of tease, *C'est Barbican!* was meant as 'a joke at the expense of corporate entertainment and sex entertainment' (Carnesky in Cripps 2003); Carnesky later expressed some surprise that it was ironically subsumed as the very type of corporate entertainment it was attempting to subvert. In a show that was saucy, satirical, queer, and kitsch, sex itself blinked in and out of sight like Carnesky's body in its glass coffin.

In addition to definitively marking Carnesky's professional transition away from the sex industry, ensuring that it would be 'unforgotten', *Carnesky's Ghost Box* is significant for two reasons: it is the first instance of Carnesky branding within the title of a show, as well as Carnesky's first performance collaboration with the illusionist Paul Kieve, which culminated spectacularly with *Carnesky's Ghost Train* a few years later. Described in its promotional material as 'a dark ride across haunted borders', this purpose-built, large-scale art installation/carnival attraction with state-of-the-art optical illusions, mannequins, and live performers was located first in Brick Lane, in London's East End (the historic site of immigrant communities, including Carnesky's own family a hundred years earlier), in 2004. After touring to other cities and various festivals including Glastonbury, *Carnesky's Ghost Train* began an extended residency in Blackpool (2008–14), a long-established working-class British entertainment and leisure destination. Those who experienced the juddery eleven-minute ride witnessed spectral women reaching and wailing through bars, spinning through the air in perpetual rotation, struggling to re-attach limbs or to twist their heads into forward-facing positions, falling through floors, levitating, and evaporating. Carnesky explained in the 'Foreword' to the 2004 souvenir poster/programme that:

> These are the ghosts of migrant women's journeys from Eastern Europe to Western Europe [...]. Ladies displaced between borders, stories of people suspended between two worlds. The characters in this ghost train transform themselves like magicians [*sic*] assistants, showgirls whose bodies defy natural law [...]. Magicians assistants with the supernatural ability to put themselves back together again, as displaced people have to, despite all the odds.
> (Carnesky, 2004)

In early versions of the ghost train, audience members were greeted by an armed border guard/station mistress, sternly sexy and powdered like a Weimar cabaret artiste in a tutu; in its Blackpool incarnation, she was replaced in this function by a grieving mother who is endlessly searching for her missing daughters. Our journey, like this crone's, is to a place that is 'nowhere', since 'when people are disappeared there's no closure, they don't get a funeral as there's no body to bury' (Carnesky in Machon 2009: 128). Behind its deceptively muted Victorian façade – described by the critic Lyn Gardner as 'a shabby, faded, ornate, fairground beauty, like an exquisite woman past her prime' (2004a) – the train alternately hurtles and tantalizingly stalls through a series of haunted stations. With every lap of the circuit, the vignettes and tableaux become more violent and sexually charged.

The missing link between *Jewess Tattooess* and *Carnesky's Ghost Train* is an hour-long solo show called *The Girl From Nowhere* (2003), which Carnesky made and performed (like *Carnesky's Ghost Box*) as part of the research and development for the *Ghost Train*.

According to Carnesky, *The Girl From Nowhere* continued to explore the figure of the 'illustrated lady' as a human exhibit, an outsider lifted from the nineteenth-century fairground with reference to the similarly subversive figure of the 'wandering Jew' [...] and staged the magician's assistant as a body torn between borders, to represent critical concerns in border and gender politics, and migration.[7]

The figure of the magician's assistant, simultaneously metaphor and job description, and connected to that of the 'showgirl', is central to Carnesky's body of work. As Mick Mangan has discussed, while *an* assistant is always essential to the set-up and working of magic, by the late nineteenth century the male conjurer/female assistant was already 'a showbiz cliché' and it was almost always a woman who was used for 'tricks which involved symbolic death and resurrection: being put to sleep, hypnotised, incarcerated, levitated and made to vanish in various ways' (Mangan 2010: 166). Blaire Larsen, co-producer of the 2008 documentary, *Women in Boxes*, about the relationship between magicians and their female assistants, became increasingly incensed that it was the latter who executed the majority of illusions, often taking huge physical risks, while fading into the background when the magician took the applause: 'I watched the assistants come out in these skimpy outfits and be cut in half and stabbed [...]. They're playing these victims on stage yet they ended up being the brains behind the magic – the actual magician' (Carnesky in Bruns and Zompetti 2014: 7).

The promotional material for a double bill of *Jewess Tattooess* and *The Girl From Nowhere* at the Riverside Studios in London in 2003 states that if 'the Jewess tattooess is a magician whose star of David bleeds from the urgency to speak', then 'the girl from nowhere is a sex trafficked woman'. Carnesky had clearly begun the process of revisioning herself from showgirl to Showwoman, from exploited assistant to conjurer. *The Girl From Nowhere*, set in a fairground and woven around the story of her own family's exile from Riga as well as filmed testimonies of migrant women working in the East End, seems to rehearse the back stories of the other-worldly inhabitants of *Carnesky's Ghost Train*. Among them is a young woman who is sold into prostitution when she believes she is coming to London to work as a nanny, her flowing hair nailed to a wall to prevent escape; a Roma girl who saves her Slovakian settlement and family from destruction; and a Russian stripper who makes a fortune and buys a loft apartment in London's increasingly gentrified East End. For Lyn Gardner, the show's 'ragged quirkiness' produced a tangible sense of 'past and future, the long dead and the not yet living', and made it seem 'as if the entire history of Europe's faceless, dispossessed and disappeared has been crammed into the studio' (Gardner 2003).

Some of these 'invisible people' had already begun to materialize in Carnesky's contribution to Duckie's East London promenade performance, *Blowzabellas, Drabs, Mawks and Trogmoldies* (2001),[8] for which she converted the Museum of Immigration and Diversity, once a synagogue, into the Museum of Strange Women. Here, audiences discovered women whose bodies had fused with their trades: a street seller covered with bagels, a tailor festooned with metal instruments, and a weaver who is enveloped by her long hair that merges into a loom. The latter is a figure who detaches and returns, a revenant: the promotional image for *The Girl From Nowhere* is of a floating Carnesky, wrapped only in a wild mane of auburn hair. She also appears as an ethereal Amphitrite – a Victorian illusion in which a woman somersaults gracefully in space with no visible means of support – in *Carnesky's Ghost Train*, the printed programme for which exhorts punters to 'Enter a world where the phantasmagorical collides with fragments of stories of displacement and exile'. It is a tagline that would have been equally applicable to *The Girl From Nowhere* which culminated with an illusion, created by Kieve, of a girl disappearing in a magic box. At the end of *Carnesky's Ghost Train*, all the women glimpsed from the moving carriage line up on the platform, dance, and then simply vanish: 'The light is the same, the scenery hasn't changed, the audience hasn't blinked – but what they've watched has disappeared. Not aged, not faded, just gone' (Clapp 2004).

Phantasmagorias were light and shadow shows, augmented by live sound effects, often held in atmospherically spooky settings. Introduced in Paris shortly after the French Revolution by Étienne Gaspard Robert, who billed himself as Robertson, they remained popular through the first half of the nineteenth century. Phantoms, ghosts, skeletons, and demons would materialize, distort, and disappear through tricks of projection, creating a 'nightmare world in which the boundaries of life and death dissolve' (Mangan 2007: 125). Robertson originally conceived his Phantasmagoria as a scientific exhibition that demonstrated the relationship between optics and the psyche, but embraced more lucrative and wide-reaching showmanship when it became clear that audiences in the years following The Terror 'had developed a taste for the macabre and the uncanny' (Mangan 2007: 123) which also expressed the political, religious, philosophical, and erotic undercurrents of the time.

With her phantasmagoric ghost train, Carnesky similarly became a businesswoman with an expanded audience base. It took five years to bring such an ambitious project to fruition, its opening postponed and tour dates rearranged many times while technical issues were ironed out. She raised around £500,000 to make *Carnesky's Ghost*

Train (largely from the Arts Council, NESTA, and Hellhound Productions, which is co-directed by Alison Murray, who collaborated on the films for *Jewess Tattooess*); when Blackpool Council leased the ride (at no charge), it became financially responsible for its refurbishment, illumination, maintenance, and relocation. Carnesky retained the intellectual property rights and artistic control, continuously attempting to balance her thematic concerns, aesthetic strategy, and the expectations of an accessible and popular seaside 'scare attraction'. Perceived value for money was always important. Most early reviews of *Carnesky's Ghost Train* in 2004 mentioned the cost per minute of the ride; towards the end, online customer reviews tended to focus on the extent to which they found it creepy or frightening. When it closed, Carnesky explained that the ghost train was not originally built for a ten-year run, and that 'Commercial realities, unfortunately, mean that we simply aren't able to invest what's needed in the structure and refresh the experience' (Carnesky Productions website, n.d.). The announcement also addressed the plight of cast members who would be losing their jobs as a result, drawing attention to another change that occurred in Carnesky's transition from self-employed artist to impresario: that is, in multiplying her body, Carnesky not only gestured to the historic grand-scale of people trafficking, generations of displaced women and ubiquity of refugee experience but was also able to absent herself from the work which bore her name on a daily basis. Over the course of a decade, at some point, Carnesky played almost all the roles on the ghost train, in order to create and experiment with them but also to train other performers who shadowed her; as a result, audiences would occasionally see twinned versions of characters, ghosts haunting other ghosts.

For Elaine Aston and Gerry Harris, *Carnesky's Ghost Train* deployed popular generic conventions as an act of control and repair which 're-membered' vanished and deformed bodies by reassembling them into a new and different 'whole' (2013: 187). While they are not convinced that all audiences would have recognized the intended metaphors and allusions – something borne out by the reviews of both professional critics and consumers, in different ways, throughout its run – they believe that in juxtaposing performance art and popular entertainment, pleasure and feminist politics, Carnesky trusted and enabled spectators to construct a range of intrinsically valuable personal meanings without leading them to easy 'categorical' conclusions. According to Machon, this meaning-making was fundamentally based on the corporeal experience created by the *unheimlich* (or uncanny) 'potential of artifice in its mechanical technologies and modern conjuring practice'. In particular, the moving mannequins and waxwork bodies that were 'positioned with and against the sensual, human bodies of actors and audience [made] extant the disconcerting idea of embodied disembodiment' and disturbed the 'boundary of what is real/unreal, alive/dead', seen/unseen, absent/present (Machon 2016: 250).

One of the origin stories of *Carnesky's Ghost Train* is that Carnesky was inspired by a television documentary about a gruesome discovery on a disused ghost train (Gardner 2004b; Palmer 2004): during the filming of an episode of *The Six Million Dollar Man* in 1976, an arm was knocked off a plaster and waxwork dummy of the 'hanging man', revealing a mummified human corpse inside. It is a scenario that maps more closely onto *Dystopian Wonders*, which Carnesky first presented at the Roundhouse in London during its 2010 CircusFest. In this production, audiences were led through an exhibition of cyborgian bodies (one of which had two heads) that merged live flesh with wounds and organs made of wax, silk, and embroidered felt. Carnesky performed the role of exhibition 'curator', obsessed with the glass-eyed wax saints and splayed open anatomical models in lurid colours that she proudly displays – captivated by the beauty of their still and serene faces, like sleeping Snow Whites – and convinced that, come the day of judgement, they will all come to life. Her increasingly deranged lecture eventually reveals that she is a member of a cult led by a charismatic preacher, face wrapped in bandages and played by her then-husband, Rasp Thorne. Disciples begin to perform their devotion: an aerialist glides above us on silks; a beautiful contortionist disappears into the open womb of a waxwork, making complete the type of the nineteenth-century anatomical female automata that, according to Corinna Wagner, are best characterized 'as bodies without organs' or 'empty bodies that are all exterior', which expressed disgust towards gendered biological difference (2017: 2). Carnesky-as-curator is much more solid, embedding a large (trick) knife into her forearm with some exertion before operating on a planted 'volunteer' from the audience who says she wants to live forever following the resurrection, by clamping the volunteer to a velvet-covered podium and boring into her head with an industrial electric drill.

Such mock executions, for Matt Trueman (2010), were reminders that, despite (or because of) the 'artifice and approximation', encountering a waxwork 'is to observe one's own corpse', which manufactures both the fear of disembodiment and 'the ache' of imagining being trapped in a paralysed body that is 'stripped of purpose.'[9] Carnesky, however, seemed equally if not more interested in the reverse process. In an interview just prior to the premiere of *Dystopian Wonders*, she explained that 'I'm fascinated by the

Figure 10 (overleaf): Marisa Carnesky, *Dystopian Wonders*, featuring Marawa The Amazing, Empress Stah, H Plewis, Rasp Thorne, Raphelle Boitel, Duncan De Morgan, Rebel Royale, Amber Topaz, The Roundhouse, 2010. London. © Manuel Vason

idea of the body reanimating and how – certainly for me – when you see waxworks, the thing you're most excited by is that they might come back to life' (Carnesky in Carter 2010). Echoing the promotional copy for the show, she uses the word 'Showwoman' (rather than 'curator') to describe the character she is playing – and a 'morbid' one at that – rather than her professional role as a performance-maker or artist; significantly, it is also a piece of work that does not include *Carnesky* in its title. Perhaps – in a show that, for instance, provokes reflection on Madame Tussaud's circumstances and ethical positioning as a Showwoman – Carnesky was distancing herself from a fictional narrative that might implicate her performing body in the physical and emotional manipulation of other women.

Still, *Dystopian Wonders* did bear many of the hallmarks of Carnesky's work as a Showwoman, including her hiring and championing of talented and striking burlesque, cabaret, and circus performers. It featured Marawa the Amazing, for example, who ascended a ladder made of razor-sharp swords barefoot, recreating an act popularized by Koringa, the 'only Female Fakir in the World', in the late 1930s. Made during Carnesky's Arts and Humanities Research Council (AHRC)-funded fellowship at the University of Sheffield's National Fairground Archive (2008-11), which was entitled 'Confessions of a Showwoman: Reinventing and Documenting Extraordinary Live Entertainments', *Dystopian Wonders* began the work of resurrecting a tradition of popular performance by professional women, with the aim of bringing it to wider public attention and keeping it (a)live in the haunted borderspace between archive and repertoire.

Revolutions

In 2009, Carnesky participated in the making of a tarot deck for the Spill performance festival, which featured a veritable who's who of live artists including Ron Athey, Kira O'Reilly, Franko B, and Oreet Ashery. Each card in the Major Arcana is a performance-to-camera, made collaboratively with Manuel Vason; the card chosen for Carnesky by Robert Pacitti, the Artistic Director of Spill, was Wheel of Fortune. In this image, she emerges from a wall mid-torso, pouting diffidently in a red slip (one reviewer of tarot decks described her as 'blowsy') and holding an old clock face embossed with the word 'Theatre' above her head. A red sign beneath her reads 'Please adjust your dress before leaving'. She is surrounded by maps and illegible scraps of paper and disused currency, by photographic portraits of long-dead women, by other clocks telling other times, and limp red ribbons. In promotional photos for the Blackpool version of *Carnesky's Ghost*

Train, this is the set that frames Eva, 'the Defected Disappeared Border Guard' who pleads forgiveness from her sisters for succumbing to 'misdirection' and the power of bureaucracy – that is, becoming 'tangled in red tape' (Carnesky Productions website, n.d.). The artist Anne Bean refers to performances-to-camera as 'reformations', a term that Dominic Johnson suggests 'allows for productive *infidelity* to one's achievements, towards the creation of a new work informed by one's own creative history as a generative artist' (Johnson 2015: 24; original emphasis). On the basis of this image which Carnesky made with Vason, it is possible to observe that performances-to-camera are able to subtly signal the *business* of art-making as well.

In readings of the Tarot of Marseille, Wheel of Fortune orients towards change. Because 'everything is condemned to vanish', it indicates the ending of one cycle which sets the next in motion. In addition to 'the cycle of death and rebirth in the large sense', it 'represents financial profit in folk notions' (Jodorowsky and Costa 2009: 135–37). Carnesky's embodiment of this card points towards an extended moment of professional transition for her as a performer, from the staged subject of the gaze to the body that directs the gaze on stage. In circus terms, this might be considered equivalent to adding the role of 'ringmaster' (that is, the compère who manages the performance in real time) to those of 'act' (that is, the performer) and/or 'director' (that is, the proprietor, whose name often defines the enterprise and who has overall control of production content); in traditional circus, the ringmaster has worn a red coat since the 1920s (Beadle and Könyöt 2016: 77). The colour red, so prominent in her Wheel of Fortune image, becomes increasingly significant in Carnesky's scenography (see, for instance, Figure 10, the promotional image for *Dystopian Wonders*). In tarot, it represents materiality, activity, and complex associations with blood, including both the danger of taboo and comforting warmth: that is, death when it is presented on the outside of a body, life when circulating within (Jodorowsky and Costa 2009: 70).

Participation in the Spill Tarot project inspired the making of *Carnesky's Tarot Drome* (2012). In this large-scale promenade performance, spectator participants followed their intuition through the Old Vic Tunnels beneath Waterloo station in London,[10] encountering living manifestations of the Major Arcana before eventually congregating for a rock opera that featured a choreographed archetypal constellation in capes and gold bikinis on roller skates. Prior to this high camp finale, each card repeatedly performed its own 'ritual' – Temperance (Rowan Fae) plunging in and emerging breathless from a water tank; Death (Nina Felia) caked immobile in plaster and writhing her way out of bondage – some of which were participatory and all visually spectacular, together offering audience members an alternative, three-dimensional form of tarot reading depending on one's whim and route.

Carnesky herself embodied The World, the card considered the key to the tarot's spatial and symbolic organization (echoing her credited role as the production's 'writer and director') and described in the accompanying programme brochure as 'accomplishment in the world [...]. She is the cosmic centre, fame, the universal soul and women's sex'. Wearing a slinky gold evening dress and a winged headpiece reminiscent of that associated with Hermes (the Greek trickster god of commerce, boundaries, and their transgression), she welcomed audiences to the opening set piece of the show, a *lucha libre*-style wrestling match between The Emperor and Strength: 'Seekers of the truth', she announces, 'take hold of your senses and prepare for new experiences'.

The programme note for *Carnesky's Tarot Drome* suggested that while its imagery might 'speak to your unconscious mind' and provide a 'road map to your soul', it was up to individual audience members to make what they would of the show's 'fleshy dreamscape of psychomagical phenomena'. This language of self-transformation is that of experimental film-maker Alejandro Jodorowsky, a practitioner of tarot who spent years teaching and reconstructing the original Tarot of Marseille, as well as the deviser of a therapeutic system called 'psychomagic' which aimed to heal trauma through shamanistic practices. Carnesky once cited Jodorowsky's *Santa Sangre* (1989) – which features a tattooed woman circus performer, a cult that revolves around a pool of fake holy blood, and a mannequin that acts as a psychic substitute for an armless dead woman – as her favourite film, admiring its density, bright colours, and dream-like qualities. She has said that she often imagines her shows in 'filmic terms' which she then attempts to translate to a live experience: 'I want the audience to be trapped in the fantasy to be engaged in the other world' (Carnesky in Machon 2009: 130–31). This other world stands in for what is unknown in the present and reaches back to the past in order to prepare for the future.

Like all of Carnesky's work, *Tarot Drome* emerged at least in part from personal associations. When she first started reading tarot cards as a teenage goth, she was warned against it for reasons which once again conflated Jewishness with prohibition: 'My grandmother would say that Jewish people must not go to fortune tellers, or try to contact the dead – which of course made me all the more fascinated' (Carnesky in McLaren, 2012). It is no coincidence that a crystal ball glinted from within a ghost train station, that the protagonist of *Jewess Tattooess* was a soothsayer, or that

Figure 11: Chi Chi Revolver, *Carnesky's Tarot Drome*, Old Vic Tunnels, 2012. London. © Sarah Ainslie
Figure 12: Rowan Fae, *Carnesky's Tarot Drome*, Old Vic Tunnels, 2012. London. © Sarah Ainslie

Carnesky occasionally appeared at burlesque nights (such as the Whoopee Club) and in performance installations – for example, as part of the 24-hour Bataille-inspired Visions of Excess event curated by Ron Athey and Vaginal Davis (Fierce Festival, Birmingham, 2003) and the Hayward Gallery's *Carnivalesque* touring exhibition in Brighton (see Prior 2000: 8–9) – as a nude, penny-in-the-slot fortune teller.

Even focusing only on this thematic strand, it is striking the extent to which Carnesky has experimented over the course of her career with the many 'ways in which space and design are employed by the showman', as identified by Brooks McNamara in his classic study of traditional popular scenography (1974: 16). These categorizations include booths and other itinerant arrangements of space by street and fairground performers; improvised theatres; venues for variety entertainments; spaces devoted to spectacle or special effects; processional forms; and entertainment environments, such as travelling carnivals, festivals, and amusement parks which include tent shows, waxworks, and rides. Writing mainly about theatrical forms, McNamara noted that many showmen created opportunities for, and then concentrated their money and attention on, 'trickwork, fantasy and spectacle' that attracted audience numbers (1974: 20), shaping their productions on the 'principle of variety structure in which there is no transfer of information from one act to another' (1974: 19). Indeed, it is inferred that one of the principal roles of a showman is to use their professional judgement to combine various acts or 'compartments' into a production. This too is applicable to Carnesky's practice, not only in company work like *Carnesky's Ghost Train* but also in solo shows like *Girl From Nowhere*, in which the 'transfer of information' between sections is largely cumulative and associative.

One of the key differences is that, according to McNamara, dramaturgical construction by traditional showmen was never the result of thematic consideration or attempts at coherence. Arising from this is the implication that, with the exception of spectacular set showpieces, showmen in this lineage take a fairly laissez-faire attitude to the nurturing and development of the individual acts and performers they programme within such structures. Carnesky's approach to showwomanship, by contrast, has always included (to a greater or lesser extent) the input of the other performers with whom she works, many eventually participating in more than one of her projects:

> I approach the artist and see if they are interested in collaborating with me, bringing a bit of what they do and their identity into a shared process where

we make new material together, mixing a bit of them and a bit of me under my direction.
(Carnesky 2012)

For *Carnesky's Tarot Drome*, this process included not only working individually with each of the performers to exploit their performance specialisms and public persona in their turns as an archetype but also a weekend-long, work-in-progress experiment called *Carnesky's Tarot Village* at Bestival in Dorset (2011) with students from her 'Finishing School'.

Carnesky's Finishing School (CFS), initiated in 2009, is an ad hoc series of cohort-based training opportunities in the form of evening classes, five-day or weekend workshops. In 2016, in partnership with Bethnal Green Working Men's Club, CFS had a four-month residency in the basement of Foyles' bookshop on Charing Cross Road in London, during which it also ran a pop-up cabaret venue showcasing the work of the students, alumni, and associate artists. The purpose of CFS is to 'empower people who may have no formal training or are from backgrounds or social groups that have traditionally had little access to affordable tutoring' to create their own new 'transgressive' cabaret work, launch their careers, and 'develop their own artistic languages so that they can go forth and change the world' (Carnesky in McLaren 2016).

Carnesky has said that pedagogy is 'in my blood' and that she aspires to become 'the tattooed avant-garde queer version' of the 'Jewish grande dames' of London stage schools like Sylvia Young and Anna Scher (Carnesky in Walters 2016). If, as Jacki Willson suggests, 'Showmen show us the spectacle of gendered heteronormative bodies performing in an expected way in order to induce magic and joy' (2015: 174), Carnesky's practice as a Showwoman not only recalibrates pleasure through other ways of seeing in the making of her own cultural products but also aims to develop and promote alternative expressions of bodily freedom that acknowledge positions of power and politics by new generations of performers. The singer-songwriter Paloma Faith, who was in the original cast of *Carnesky's Ghost Train*, has said that 'Marisa is the nearest thing I have to a mentor', that Carnesky taught her to be 'confident on stage' and, 'especially as a woman, that it's your job to go out there and raise hell' (Carnesky in Sturges 2009). Additionally, some Finishing School graduates go on to perform in Carnesky productions, such as the sword swallower, MisSa Blue, one of the 'menstronauts' who collaborated with Carnesky on *Dr Carnesky's Incredible Bleeding Woman*.

Dr Carnesky's Incredible Bleeding Woman (2015–19) was advertised as 'an all-out genre bending contemporary performance spectacular' that 'scrutinised, politicised and reclaimed' issues circulating around 'fertility, miscarriage, trans identities, lost ancient herstories and what it means to be "female"', while 'putting the magic back into the last unmentionable taboo: menstruation'. Influenced by the work of the Radical Anthropology Group, whose evening lectures she attended with the Dragon Ladies in the 1990s, and, in particular, its founder Chris Knight who posited a woman-centric theory of cultural origin based on menstrual cycles (Carnesky 2018), Carnesky plays 'herself' as a kooky academic anthropologist who is also a Showwoman. Central to her performance text is the story of what happened when she gathered together a group of 'menstruants' (all cabaret/live artists who may or may not actually menstruate but who identify as either female or non-binary) that met during dark moons over a period of three months at Metal, an artist space in Southend-on-Sea. Here, they participated in group devising exercises, meditation, spell casting, and discussions of their lived experiences of 'bodily transformation and change', experimenting with performance techniques to embody these experiences, and then creating new rituals in the surrounding landscape (Carnesky in Walters 2016). Like all rituals, these actions were symbolic and reiterative, creating a 'sacred' moment in time and space that simultaneously reaffirmed both individual senses of identity and communitas or shared collective consciousness.

These sited, 'private' rituals were filmed and then, if possible, refined into cabaret performances, their power reasserted 'in repeating them onstage' in a show that attempted to balance 'menstrual activism' with 'menstrual spiritualism' (Carnesky 2018). H Plewis, a member of Duckie who had been a *Ghost Train* cast member as well as a *Carnesky's Tarot Drome* collaborator, produced a red jelly rabbit made (apparently) with her own menstrual blood which she jiggles on her belly, shoves in her mouth, and smears over the stage; in later versions of the show, she is accompanied by the daughter who was conceived during the ritual-making phase of the project when Plewis created and ingested similar jellies. Wearing a dress that deconstructs itself to reveal a glittery red applique river within, Carnesky connected these live rituals and those filmed on site with a survey of mythical, art historical, and popular culture figures – Medusa, Kali, Carrie – that speak to the fear of menstruation. By harnessing its power, linked to ecological cycles and the renewal of humanity itself, and by overcoming the cultural distaste that serves to shame women's bodies, the patriarchy can be overturned: 'The Revolution will be bloody. The Revolution will be menstrual' (Carnesky 2016).

For Carnesky to refer to herself as 'doctor' in the title of this show, which was created as part of her practice-as-research (PaR) Ph.D. project at Middlesex University, was knowing, witty, and cheeky. PaR methodologies both generate new knowledges and disseminate them through acts of performance, meaning that Carnesky was effectively claiming her doctorate within the title of an essential element of her thesis that had yet to be examined. She was, of course, also alluding to a tradition of 'doctors' in popular performance: for instance, the circus of the fictional Dr Lau, in the 1935 novel by Charles G. Finney, which displayed captured mythological creatures including Medusa and a giant (male) sea serpent; or nineteenth century 'Medicine Shows' in which showmen 'doctors' peddled miraculous elixirs, or 'snake oils', interspersed with testimonials, musical acts, acrobats, or fortune telling. In the 2016 version of *Dr Carnesky's Incredible Bleeding Woman*, Carnesky describes the 'magical serpent's body' as 'a symbol of menstrual synchronicity and women's solidarity'. 'What if we could synchronise our bodies like one giant connected powerful snake?' she asks, before suggesting (with echoes of Bloody Pearl so many years earlier) that humanity could 'Rise rise rise then in a sea of menstrual anarchy!' while quickly anticipating our scepticism: 'Do you think we are selling you a snake oil?'[11] Like its title, the hybrid form of *Dr Carnesky's Incredible Bleeding Woman* was ambivalently effective within an artistic research context. Daniel Ladnar has discussed how the 'lecture performance' is able to temporally and conceptually link aesthetic and cultural forms of performance while simultaneously participating in and exploring 'the performative production and dissemination of knowledge enacted in traditional lectures' (Ladnar 2014: 16–17). As *Dr Carnesky's Incredible Bleeding Woman* demonstrates, lecture performances enable artist-scholars to revisit works that were conceived as site-specific projects (such as Rhyannon Styles' menstrual ritual at the sea's edge, the tide lapping at her screaming, balloon and tinsel-covered body), and share them with different audiences. Moreover, as 'one manifestation of a larger (research) process', they are able to 'make reference to a context whose scope exceeds its articulation in the performance event itself' (Ladnar 2014: 14).

Although Carnesky had experimented with the lecture performance format before, as in *Dystopian Wonders*, she tended to be framed more explicitly as a 'character' who is distinct from herself within a fictional narrative or setting. In her (largely) solo performance *Magic War* (2006–07), Carnesky discusses strategies for survival, the war on terror, and the ways in which magic has been used to wage war, while dressed as a glamorous sequinned Pallas Athena. While some versions featured a story arc

about a secret society trying to create a new world order, the show mainly revolved around illustrative stock magic tricks and equipment – for instance, catching a bullet in her cleavage in an homage to Jean Eugène Robert-Houdin's quashing of an Algerian insurrection in the 1850s by performing a range of magic tricks, including having a gun fired at his heart, that offered evidence of supernatural power. These often involved audience participation. Audience members were asked, for instance, to decide whether Carnesky should use her guillotine to cut off the finger of a volunteer, who had been cast as a terrorist, if this were to prevent a bomb exploding nearby; they always said yes and, even though the finger was magically saved despite the action of the blade, the routine raised serious questions about the ethics of violence, retribution, moral responsibility, and the body politic in times of war.

Although Carnesky performed some of the illusions in *Magic War* on and with her own body – such as levitating – she adamantly asserted that she was a 'magicienne' and *not* the magician's assistant. While she had signalled in *The Girl From Nowhere* that she considered the magician's assistant to be a victim of naturalized images of violence

Figure 13: Marisa Carnesky, *Dr Carnesky's Incredible Bleeding Woman*, Soho Theatre, 2016. London. © Claire Lawrie

and gendered exploitation, the process of making *Magic War* enabled Carnesky to work through and reflect upon the practical implications of combining the tropes and instruments of magic with the ownership and celebration of eroticism and one's sexed body. She described how in a very early version

> I ended up naked with a black bag over my head, on all fours, inviting people to come and cut my head off and it was awful. I just thought, it was interesting in the 90s, it felt radical to get naked and it doesn't now [...]. [I]t feels too exposing because I am always representing a version of myself [...]. I guess the more you work, the more you start to question your own practice and with *Magic War* it was about the wider idea of violence to people's bodies, not violence to women's bodies.
> (Carnesky in Machon 2009: 127)

Of all the tricks in *Magic War*, it was sawing a body in half – which Carnesky performed on other people, often men – that was loaded with the most explicit misogynistic associations. Introduced by the British illusionist, Percy Thomas Tibbles, or 'Selbit', in 1921, it has almost always involved the dismemberment of a woman in a coffin-like box; in fact, one of Selbit's first publicity stunts was to offer Christabel and Sylvia Pankhurst, leaders of the women's suffrage movement, large sums of money to be sawn in half (Mangan 2009: 164). This is why it became so important for Carnesky, not simply to control, but also to reappropriate this illusion, to alter its meaning by emphasizing how it finally symbolizes the making whole of a woman's body as much as it does violently forcing it apart. In *Dr Carnesky's Incredible Bleeding Woman*, this illusion becomes another menstrual ritual. 'Our greatest trick as Showwomen', she proclaims after sawing one of the menstruants in half, 'is that we perform an act of temporary death each month and then are miraculously resurrected' (Carnesky 2016). Perhaps even more radically, the 2018 version of the show dispensed with showing the act of dismemberment; instead, Rhyannon Styles, who is a transwoman, comes on stage in two halves (see Figure 13) and is 'reborn' when the blades are removed and the box reconjoined.

Dr Carnesky's Incredible Bleeding Woman returns, quietly but insistently, to many of the themes, questions, and motifs of *Jewess Tattooess*. The Whore of Babylon – who was so exasperated by the demonization of women's sexuality in the latter that she was said (by 'Serpentina') to be away sunbathing with her friend, the Queen of Sheba – makes an appearance as a 'mythological menstruating witch' riding her many-headed serpent off to steal sperm. Carnesky even reclaims the performance actions within *Jewess Tattoess* as menstrual rituals in the spoken text of *Dr Carnesky's Incredible Bleeding Woman*: 'As Showwomen we have dripped our menstrual blood on holy texts' (Carnesky 2016). Most extraordinarily, however, was Carnesky's own filmed ritual, screened within the latter. She is nude, in a white bathtub, in a white bathroom; we see her only from behind, her thickly lined dragon tattoo unmistakably recognizable. The tub is full of red liquid which she splashes repeatedly over her head, allowing it to run down her face and back. This is a ritual Carnesky made in response to her own miscarriages, alluding to the *mikvah* – a bath used by the *niddah* to achieve ritual purity following menstruation according to Jewish law. It is an open, haunting, moving, and generous image: a detournement of abjection.

As Julia Kristeva has observed, 'the various means of *purifying* the abject' lead to 'the catharsis par excellence called art, both on the far and near side of religion' (1982: 17). In Carnesky's case, this artistic experience 'which is rooted in the abject it utters and by the same token purifies' (Kristeva 1982: 17), has unfolded over an extended period of time, during which what has become increasingly visible is 'one of the ghosts of the theatre': that is, labour 'as an act, a process, and a creative product' (Osborne and Woodworth 2015: 4). This visibility is especially significant when she engages in performance forms – such as magic – in which labour needs to be concealed to ensure efficacy. During Carnesky's transition from showgirl to Showwoman, which was neither linear nor inevitable, she has shown how the lived experience of an individual (diasporic, secular Jewish) woman is able to foster the presentation and representation of shared, often collective, experiences of diverse women (as well as those who identify as genderqueer or non-binary and, occasionally, as men) through the making of a body of work.

This chapter is reproduced with permission from the volume *Live Art in the UK: Contemporary Performances of Precarity* (ed. M. Chatzichristodoulou).

Bibliography

Aston, E. and Harris, G. (2013), *A Good Night Out for the Girls*, Basingstoke: Palgrave Macmillan.

Baird, S. (2007), 'The A-Z of Burlesque', *Time Out*, 1 May, available at https://www.timeout.com/london/cabaret/the-a-z-of-burlesque. Accessed 1 April 2017.

Bayley, B. (2000), 'The queer carnival: Gender transgressive images in contemporary queer performance and their relationship to carnival and the grotesque', Ph.D. thesis, University of Exeter, available at http://www.brucebayley.co.uk/The_Queer_Carnival__Bruce_Bayley_2000.pdf. Accessed 6 August 2017.

Bayley, C. (1995), 'I'll be banned if I will', *The Independent*, 3 June, available at https://www.independent.co.uk/arts-entertainment/ill-be-banned-if-i-will-1584805.html. Accessed 5 May 2017.

Beadle, R. and Könyöt, D. (2016), 'The man in the red coat: Management in the circus', in P. Tait and K. Lavers (eds), *The Routledge Circus Studies Reader*, Abingdon: Routledge.

Bouissac, P. (2012), *Circus as Multimodal Discourse: Performance, Meaning, and Ritual*, New York: Bloomsbury.

Brennan, M. (1999), 'Challenge of the tattooed lady', *The Herald*, 26 November, available at http://www.heraldscotland.com/news/12204891.Challenge_of_the_tattooed_lady_Mary_Brennan_explores_Jewish_culture__faith__and_body_art_with_Marisa_Carnesky/. Accessed 4 April 2017.

Brosnan, J. (1998/2013), 'Performing the lesbian body – The new wave', in N. Rapi and M. Chowdhry (eds), *Acts of Passion: Sexuality, Gender, and Performance*, New York and London: Routledge, pp. 79–94.

Bruns, L. C. and Zompetti, J. P. (2014), 'The rhetorical goddess: A feminist perspective on women in magic', *Journal of Performance Magic*, 2:2, pp. 8–39, available at http://eprints.hud.ac.uk/id/eprint/22906/. Accessed 16 April 2018.

Carnesky, M. (2002), 'Artist statement', in M. Vason, L. Keidan, and D. Brine (eds), *Exposures*, London: Black Dog, n. p.

Carnesky, M. (2012), Email to author, 15 August.

Carnesky, M. (2013a), 'Marisa Carnesky interviewed for double exposures' (video), Manual Vason Studio, available at https://vimeo.com/82096890. Accessed 2 April 2017.

Carnesky, M. (2013b), 'Marisa Carnesky: Being a showwoman' (video), *The Lost Lectures*, available at https://lostlectures.com/talk/Showwoman/. Accessed 5 August 2017.

Carnesky, M. (2015), Email to author, 29 September.

Carnesky, M. (2016), Unpublished draft script of *Dr Carnesky's Incredible Bleeding Woman*, sent to the author by email on 16 September.

Carnesky, M. (2017), Facebook message to author, 20 April.

Carnesky, M. (2018), 'Menstruating together in theatres, tents and other unlikely locations' (video), Radical Anthropology Group, 1 May, available at http://radicalanthropologygroup.org/av/video/menstruating-together-theatres-tents-and-otherunlikely-locations. Accessed 30 December 2018.

Carnesky Productions (n.d.), *Showwomen* and *Carnesky's Ghost Train*, available at http://carnesky.com. Accessed 2 September 2015 and 1 April 2018.

Carter, I. (2010), 'Marisa Carnesky: "I'm fascinated by the idea of the waxwork body coming back to life"', *The Guardian*, 11 April, available at https://www.theguardian.com/stage/2010/apr/11/marisa-carnesky-circus-roundhouseinterview. Accessed 13 April 2010.

Clapp, S. (2004), 'A-haunting we will go', *The Observer*, 8 August, available at https://www.theguardian.com/stage/2004/aug/08/theatre2. Accessed 3 December 2018.

Connor, S. (2004), *The Book of Skin*, London: Reaktion.

Cripps, C. (2003), 'Adding insult to innuendo', *The Independent*, 3 December, available at https://www.independent.co.uk/arts-entertainment/theatre-dance/features/adding-insult-toinnuendo-80949.html. Accessed 19 August 2018.

Féral, J. (1982), 'Performance and theatricality: The subject demystified' (trans. T. Lyons), *Modern Drama*, 25:1 Spring, pp. 170–81.

Garber, M. (1999), *Symptoms of Culture*, London: Penguin.

Gardner, L. (2003), 'The Girl From Nowhere, Riverside Studios, London', *The Guardian*, 27 June, available at https://www.theguardian.com/stage/2003/jun/27/theatre.artsfeatures. Accessed 1 June 2018.

Gardner, L. (2004a), '*Carnesky's Ghost Train*, Old Truman Brewery, London', *The Guardian*, 4 August, available at https://www.theguardian.com/stage/2004/aug/04/theatre. Accessed 12 May 2016.

Gardner, L. (2004b), 'Smoke and mirrors', *The Guardian*, 4 May, available at https://www.theguardian.com/stage/2004/may/04/theatre1. Accessed 12 May 2016.

Jodorowsky, A. and Costa, M. (2009), *The Way of Tarot: The Spiritual Teacher in the Cards* (trans. Jon E. Graham), Rochester, Vermont: Destiny Books.

Johnson, D. (2015), 'Performance, photography, collaboration, revisited: A history of Manual Vason', in M. Vason and D. Evans (eds), *Double Exposures*, London & Bristol: Live Art Development Agency and Intellect Books, pp. 21–30.

Kristeva, J. (1982), *Powers of Horror: An Essay on Abjection* (trans. L. S. Roudiez), New York: Columbia University Press.

Ladnar, D. (2014), 'The lecture performance: Contexts of lecturing and performing', Ph.D. thesis, Aberystwyth University, available at http://cadair.aber.ac.uk/dspace/handle/2160/14051. Accessed 20 August 2018.

Lefkovitz, L. H. (1995), 'Eavesdropping on angels and laughing at God: Theorizing a subversive matriarchy', in T. M. Rudavsky (ed.), *Gender and Judaism: The Transformation of Tradition*, New York: New York University Press.

Live Art Development Agency (n.d.), 'What is live art?', available at http://www.thisisliveart.co.uk/about/what-is-live-art/. Accessed 1 April 2017.

Machon, J. (2009), *(Syn)aesthetics: Redefining Visceral Performance*, Basingstoke: Palgrave Macmillan.

Machon, J. (2012), 'Experiential identities in the work of Marisa Carnesky', in S. Broadhurst and J. Machon (eds), *Identity, Performance and Technology: Practices of Empowerment, Embodiment and Technicity*, Basingstoke: Palgrave Macmillan, pp. 111–25.

Machon, J. (2016), 'Immersed in illusion, haunted by history: *Marisa Carnesky's Ghost Train*', in O. Jenzen and S. R. Munt (eds), *The Ashgate Research Companion to Paranormal Cultures*, London & New York: Routledge, pp. 241–54.

Mangan, M. (2007), *Performing the Dark Arts: A Cultural History of Conjuring*, Bristol: Intellect.

Mangan, M. (2010), '"Welcome to the house of fun": Eros, Thanatos and the uncanny in grand illusions', in K. Gritzner (ed.), *Eroticism and Death in Theatre and Performance*, Hatfield: University of Hertfordshire Press, pp. 160–177.

McLaren, J. (2012), 'Interview: Marisa Carnesky talks to *Run Riot* about her much anticipated new show *Carnesky's Tarot Drome*', *Run Riot*, 19 July, available at http://www.runriot.com/articles/blogs/interview-marisa-carnesky-talks-run-riot-about-her-much-anticipatednew-show-carnesky. Accessed 1 March 2017.

McLaren, J. (2016), 'News: Carnesky's finishing school arrives in Soho', *Run Riot*, 9 September, available at http://www.run-riot.com/articles/notices/news-carnesky%E2%80%99s-finishingschool-arrives-soho. Accessed 10 December 2018.

McNamara, B. (1974), 'Scenography of popular entertainment', *The Drama Review, TDR*, 18:1, pp. 16–24.

Mock, R. (2008), 'Vaginal voyages: Performances of sexuality and the Jewish female body', in N. Abrams (ed.), *Jews & Sex*, Nottingham: Five Leaves Publications, pp. 162–176.

Osborne, E. A. and Woodworth, C. (2015), 'Introduction: The world of play in performance' in E. A. Osborne and C. Woodworth (eds), *Working in the Wings: New Perspectives on Theatre History and Labor*, Carbondale: Southern Illinois University Press, pp. 1–20.

Palmer, J. (2004), 'Expensive thrills', *New Statesman*, 14 June, available at https://www.newstatesman.com/node/159984. Accessed 1 April 2018.

Pfefferman, N. (2003), 'Staging a body of work', *Jewish Journal*, 26 September, available at https://jewishjournal.com/culture/arts/8471/. Accessed 8 April 2017.

Prior, D. M. (2000), 'Le Freak – C'est Chic', *Total Theatre*, 12:2 Summer, pp. 8–9.

Purves, L. (2012), '*Carnesky's Tarot Drome* at Old Vic Tunnels, SE1', *The Times*, 7 September, available at https://www.thetimes.co.uk/article/carneskys-tarot-drome-at-old-vic-tunnels-se1fw6hkdfm3xs. Accessed 20 March 2017.

Rayner, A. (2006), *Ghosts: Death's Double and the Phenomena of Theatre*, Minneapolis: University of Minnesota Press.

Rees, J. (2004), 'Ghost train that's a work of art', *The Telegraph*, 2 August, available at http://www.telegraph.co.uk/culture/art/3621709/Ghost-train-thats-a-work-of-art.html. Accessed 1 September 2011.

Schechner, R. (2013), *Performance Studies: An Introduction*, 3rd ed., London & New York: Routledge.

Sklaroff, L. R. (2018), *Red Hot Mama: The Life of Sophie Tucker*, Austin: University of Texas Press.

Sturges, F. (2009), 'An act of Paloma Faith', *The Independent*, 11 September, available at https://www.independent.co.uk/arts-entertainment/music/features/an-act-of-paloma-faith1785104.html. Accessed 4 December 2018.

Taylor, R. (1985), *The Death and Resurrection Show*, London: Anthony Blond.

Trueman, M. (2010), 'Guarded and susceptible', *Culture Wars*, 8 November, available at http://www.culturewars.org.uk/index.php/article/guarded_and_susceptible/. Accessed 2 December 2018.

Wagner, C. (2017), 'Replicating venus: Art, anatomy, wax models, and automata', *Interdisciplinary Studies in the Long Nineteenth Century*, available at https://ore.exeter.ac.uk/repository/handle/10871/26734. Accessed 5 December 2018.

Walters, B. (2016), 'Summon the courage: Marisa Carnesky on fighting with theatre', *Run Riot*, 17 October, available at http://www.run-riot.com/articles/blogs/summon-courage-marisa-carneskyfighting-theatre. Accessed 8 April 2017.

Willson, J. (2015), *Being Gorgeous: Feminism, Sexuality and the Pleasures of the Visual*, London: I.B. Tauris.

Notes

1. Although not a term that is often encountered, the Jewish American entertainer, Sophie Tucker (circa 1886–1966), for instance, was billed as the 'master showwoman of the times' in 1921 (Sklaroff 2018: 97), and Carnesky's definition would certainly apply to her work then.

2. Among the numerous implications for this strategy is that critics attend most new productions very early in a run, especially those that are eagerly anticipated. Many reviews of Carnesky's shows thus tend to praise their concept, polished scenography and (where relevant) her presence as a performer, but also note that they still feel unfinished. It also means that there are numerous versions of the productions discussed in this chapter; I tend to cite and describe those that I saw myself, usually at work-in-progress or premiere stages, although I saw *Dr Carnesky's Incredible Bleeding Woman* during its final run as well.

3. While there *are* some Jewish communities and burial societies that refuse to do so, it is a common misconception that religious law, or *halacha*, prohibits people who are willingly tattooed from being buried in Jewish cemeteries. Moreover, since at least the sixteenth century, rabbinical sources have made it clear that those who are involuntarily tattooed should be considered 'blameless', an interpretation that was tested and upheld following the Shoah.

4. In previous versions of *Jewess Tattooess*, Carnesky used the tattoo gun to draw a *magen david* (Star of David) on her thigh and this scene was positioned differently in the overall performance text.

5. Elsewhere I discuss Carnesky, Annie Sprinkle, and (to a lesser extent) original Smut Fest creator/organizer, Jennifer Blowdryer – separately and together – as situated within a tradition of sex-positive Jewish female performers and in relation to the *fin de siècle* stereotype of the Jewess (Mock 2008).

6. Occasionally billed at the time as *Carnesky's Burlesque Ghost Box*.

7. From Carnesky's 'Case for Support' submitted as part of her (successful) application to the AHRC Fellowship in the Creative and Performing Arts Scheme (2007).

8. Hosted by Miss Amy Lamé, the performance elements on the streets of East London featured Chris Green and Ursula Martinez; the production culminated with a monologue written by Neil Bartlett and performed by Bette Bourne in Toynbee Hall.

9. Trueman reviewed a slightly different show than the one I attended at the Roundhouse, entitled *The Quickening of the Wax* and performed at the Chelsea Theatre as part of its Sacred Festival about six months later.

10. Later restaged at the Latitude Festival, UK (2013) and Cirque Jules Verne in Amiens, France (2014).

11. Attendees at a work-in-progress showing of *Dr Carnesky's Incredible Bleeding Woman* on 16 October 2015 at National Theatre Studios in London received small souvenir bottles filled with a red viscous fluid, labelled 'Dr Carnesky's Snake Oil'.

Earth as Genderqueer Showwoman

Annie Sprinkle, Beth Stevens, and Marisa Carnesky

Marisa Carnesky: It is lovely to see you both and I cannot believe that on a Saturday morning, Annie, you are in full make-up and headdress.

Annie Sprinkle: Of course. I am a Showwoman! That's what we do. Well, Marisa, *your* hair is just so glamorous. I was reminding Beth that I photographed you in a blue satin bikini with white Jewish stars for my deck of *Post-Modern Pin-Ups; Pleasure Activist Playing Cards*.

MC: I am very proud of that. It appears in my Ph.D. You have been so influential to me. I think you gave us all permission to be sexual and excited, in a way that other feminist texts we were reading were not going to.

AS: You showed me that you could be Jewish and sexy. That was a breakthrough for me, because back in the day, I was one of the few Jewish women in porn movies and sexy Jewish was not a thing, and not visible anywhere.

MC: There are more sexy Jewish women now, I think. But certainly, it was not very sexy to be Jewish in England and it still isn't [laughing].

I will start with the term 'Showwomen'. This is an exciting time when gender binaries are starting to melt away. In my last show, which was reinventing menstrual rituals, I brought together a group of women: some of us had wombs, some of us did not. It was a queer exploration of menstruation and ritual. But, in using the term 'Showwomen', I have brought back the word woman in the title. I love lots of different words, and I love trans words and non-binary words, but I also love women words, and I think they can all co-exist beautifully. I wanted to ask you about the act of showing, what it is to want to show and to make shows. I wondered if you could reflect on the relationship between the show, activism, and ritual.

Beth Stephens: For us, I think that it partly has to do with demarcating a ritual space. For one thing, when we dress up in big costumes and invite other people to do the same, that can create exciting expectations for ritual space that blossoms into a great show. There is no business like show business when it is in ritual space. Theatre started with religious ceremonies. And so, we have our priestly, and priestess, wedding outfits, which are always a bit over the top, and sometimes even ridiculous, but they mark that space. Fabulous costumes help create a magic circle that takes us out of our everyday reality. Our costumes say pagan without the Birkenstocks. A showgirl paganism [laughing]. Or a Showwoman paganism. I mean, we are not girls anymore, that's for sure.

It just feels like the world is in such a dire state right now and everyone is so gloomy. This kind of depressive mood spreads like a virus. It does not really hold that many possibilities for imagining change without violence, militancy, or mass extinction. And I think we are in a moment when it is really important to also be able to lift peoples' spirits. Our costumes, props, and activities tend to bring fun and celebration to the work of addressing and performing with and in serious situations. Whether doing that is helpful for environmental causes or not, I mean, maybe we are just fools, but –

AS: The big eco-weddings we performed certainly connected me, a big city girl – I mean city woman – to nature. My connection and love for other-than-human nature, is now so much bigger and deeper. More enjoyable. Big costumes can change your life! Mix that with activism for a good cause and some co-created group ritual, it can't be beaten. And sometimes people that were in our audiences tell us their lives changed too. So, God damnit, we will spend money on our costumes! And for our collaborators' costumes too when we can.

BS: We have money for costumes because I write grants day and night. Plus, I work as a professor. We are not just sitting on a golden egg that produces money for our costumes, although that would be nice!

AS: So true, Beth works really hard to get grant money. But, even if we did not have any money, we would still make fabulous costumes, somehow. Glamour and drag are queer strategies, but also sex worker strategies. When I was eighteen years old and started working in a massage parlour, aka a brothel, I learned that a lot of men go to sex workers because we understood the drama and excitement of lingerie, lighting, props, mirrors, silk sheets, or whatever. We were Showwomen in the theatre of the boudoir.

A couple of weeks ago, Beth and I married Fire up in the Santa Cruz Mountains with about forty artists and activist friends. It was all at once a serious ritual, an attempt to better our relationships with actual fire, since we live in a forest fire zone, and a big, day-long, hot performance art happening exploring fire as metaphor. Also, the whole day was a film shoot for our new documentary film, *Playing with Fire*. All the people who came were our nearest, dearest, beloved community members. Everyone dressed to the nines in fire-themed costumes. Artists Monica Canilao, and Azul Rosa Water Witch made our costumes, accessories, and they decorated everything to the max. Everywhere we looked, they had created magical, ritual space. Costumes, props, bling, and colour are magic. We all felt the love and were forever changed. We all completely bonded with fire and our friendships grew stronger.

MC: I read in your book, *Assuming the Ecosexual Position: The Earth as Lover*, about your *Silver Wedding to the Rocks*, and the performance of Diana Pornoterrorista, richly pouring her menstrual blood on the stage, which made me think of the image of Kali possessing hidden menstrual symbolism, looking at the violent end of one cycle and the bloody beginning of another. I imagined looking at the afflicted Earth and how you would mingle rocks and clay and menstrual blood and hair and leaves. It made me think about the fact that when we see the landscape of Ukraine and of war-torn landscapes, we see the Earth grieving. And I know you explored that in your film *Goodbye Gauley Mountain*, about mountaintop removal coal mining. If we could take an ecosexual action to Ukraine or to a war-torn landscape somewhere in the world, right now; how would you perform or imagine an ecosexual ritual?

AS: That is a great question. I wish I knew *the* answer. I wish I had the ability to stop war. However, I can only offer small gestures towards peace and give some creative gifts and pleasures to people suffering from the war. There are similarities to war and mountaintop removal coal mining. They both use explosives and produce toxic waste, and they both kill people, animals, plants, and worms, pollute the air, and poison the soil and its gazillions of creatures in their wake. War is the worst because there is so damned much of it.

Thankfully I have not lived in a war zone, or been a prisoner of war, or a victim of physical violence, so I cannot even imagine the amount of pain, suffering, and grief of those situations. But I do know that for some humans, ecosexuality offers potential for pleasure and emotional nourishment. Ecosex can uplift the spirits and create some joy. Maybe we could launch Ecosexuals Without Borders and bring ecosexual healing strategies to those in need. We could bring a team of artists to do *Ecosex Walking Tours*, so people can get their ecosexual gaze on, present Ecosex Workshops, distribute printed ecosex educational materials that inspire enjoying sensual pleasure. We could facilitate groups lying outside on the ground together, doing Ecosexual Breathing for healing and climax with big, cosmic energy orgasms. We could do *Free Sidewalk Ecosex Clinics* where our ecosexperts write psychomagic prescriptions for people to find healing through nature. We could produce rituals, create opportunities for sharing ideas and information with some (anti)symposiums. These are all things we do now. But doing them in a war zone would be something else. We would have to find out what people there need and want, beyond meeting their survival needs for food, water, shelter, and heat. As for how to help the ecosystem heal, that is harder. I would do whatever I could; plant trees, clean shit up, maybe learn to defuse land mines, so animals and people do not get blown apart. War is the opposite of ecosex. War is a total turn-off. Ecosex is making love with the Earth and that includes humans. Make love not war.

BS: The Earth somehow survives being continually war-torn. It would be nice to have world peace for a change. A friend of ours told us that last year a wildfire outside of Berlin was detonating formerly undetonated armaments and starting even bigger fires. It is like the ghost of the Second World War coming back to haunt everyone. But now it is climate change that we are describing, the bloody beginning of one cycle and the bloody ending of another. Now, the United States and parts of Europe too are reactivating fossil fuel extraction because Putin is withholding energy resources that Russia had provided to Europe before the Ukraine invasion. The Earth has been so mined and exploited already. I think that is why ecofeminists gender the Earth as female because women and Showwoman Earth share feelings of exploitation and objectification. But even given that exploitation, the Earth always wants to turn towards life. Even the burn scars here in California are bursting with life, where there were horrific fires that torched the land and produced some very toxic reactions. Somehow, new growth is greening the trunks and branches of the redwood trees that were assumed to be dead. They look like little green sweaters, right? I do not want to be Pollyanna or anything, but I think that the Earth has this will to live that is really phenomenal and inspirational.

AS: I just got an idea. We could do a performance ritual where we divorce wars. One by one.

MC: Oh, that is brilliant.

BS: Oh the things we do for art!

AS: As a sex worker, I learned how war and sexuality were connected. I heard stories from vets who had been in wars. They would describe to me how during combat the adrenaline in their body would give them raging hard-ons. Men penetrate men with bayonets and bullets ... and they bleed. War is definitely extremely unsafe sex! Or is it menstrual envy? Defending your homeland when under attack is another thing.

MC: We are all dealing with such difficult times and difficult subjects, such as ecological emergencies and humanitarian crises. But your activism is very embodied and sexual; you are the ecosexuals! But it is easy to connect with your approach because it is about pleasure and joy and it is giving a different outlook on activism.

AS: Rather than saying what we do not want, we try to put our energy into creating what we do want, which is lots of healthy food, clean water, fresh air, joy, and pleasure – for everyone, all in a gorgeous garden of sensual delights. So how can we create that as a kind of antidote to, you know, the world news [laughing]. If we have the luxury and privilege of going for a nice walk in the park or to the beach, we should do it. Let there be pleasure on Earth and let it begin with me. I want to take everyone humpback whale watching. It is the greatest show on Earth!

MC: Reading your book led me to imagine a world exactly as you describe, where ecosexuality and the rituals that you are creating overtake Christianity, Islam, Judaism, and Buddhism, in which we can marry the Earth, Sky, and Sea. What we were really interested in, in the menstrual project was the idea that cyclicity is overlooked and that our bodies are cyclical, men and women and gender non-conforming people. We are all cyclical and the rites of major religions are cyclical and follow the seasons. I was recently performing a Jodorowsky-inspired tarot at the Glastonbury Festival with ten students; we tried to queer and decolonize the tarot and do very positive readings with people. But of course, a lot of these summer festivals, which were founded on things like the Campaign for Nuclear Disarmament, have become these very commercial events, the organizers grappling with how to deal with seas of rubbish thrown onto the land and generated waste.

AS: We have not used the word 'festival' yet. But we like to use the word 'symposium'.

Or better yet, '(anti)symposium happening'. We have done eight Ecosex Symposium Happenings in various countries, with panels, performances, food art, an altar for the ancestors, tabling, costumes, and lots of love and great scholarship. We are going to do a big one in the lower east side of Manhattan in June 2023 at Performance Space New York, the same place where you did your fabulous Duckie Cabaret, when it was called PS122. It is called *Exploring the Earth as Lover*. We would love you to come do something. Maybe you can do something about the menstruating Earth as Showwoman.

MC: Ah, I have not been to New York for so many years. It was such an important time for me. Beth, when I first turned up in New York, I was a stripper and a performance artist in London. And I knew this amazing woman, Tuppy Owens, who is a sex educator. I said to her, I want to go to New York and be a performance artist and how am I going to do it? This was pre-social media, where somebody like Tuppy Owens would give me somebody like Annie Sprinkle's phone number [laughing]. I just turned up in New York and called you and you invited me to your home. I was trying to find work as a dancer, or as a dominatrix and you found somewhere for me to work. Do

Figure 14: Annie Sprinkle Polaroid at *Post Porn Modernist* performance, with Marisa Carnesky and Katia Tirado, 1993. San Francisco

96

you remember this? You did a shoot with me for *ADAM* magazine. You completely connected with me. Tuppy also put me in touch with Jennifer Blowdryer, the wonderful punk writer and spoken word performer and founder of the Smut Fest. She also took me under her wing, and I ended up getting Jennifer to come to the United Kingdom to create a London version of the Smut Fest which was a huge hit here. Then I remember coming back to New York and performing at the Smut Fest with you also for that HBO TV special in the old synagogue.

AS: Yeah, gosh, I forgot about that. Jennifer Blowdryer, by the way, just got married!

BS: But if we were going to do a festival, as opposed to a symposium – which seems more heady – I would love to do one at Chernobyl or in war torn Ukraine or on a mountaintop removal site. I feel like it is easy to do a gathering in a lush, green, fecund spot, but I think these damaged places need love and energy too. Last fall (2022), we produced a symposium about fire at UCSC, the University where I am a professor. One of the first things we did, this sounds a little silly, was contact our Sustainability Office to make sure that we had all the right recycling containers lined up. Californians are pretty well trained to recycle. We try to pay attention to those kinds of details when we are doing an event. However, as I was looking at our bills, I noticed that we ordered a bunch of stuff from Amazon for our wedding performances and symposium. Annie and I are not innocent, we are part of the system too, and as such we are eco-sinners. It is hard not to be in our consumer-oriented system. But we keep trying to buy less and recycle and repair things more.

MC: I know that the organizers of the festivals have a good heart and are often trying to get good information out there and have people like Greta Thunberg speak, for instance. But there is still a bit of an imprint that is left on the land, and I love the idea that you are doing the opposite. You are not going to go and damage a green field; you are going to go and put the green back onto a destroyed landscape. It is almost the reverse of what we would call an outdoor festival. It is restoring the site in a way that is regenerative.

BS: We are not literally restoring spaces, but at least we try to put the energy into damaged places to attract that kind of restoration. We make gestures that we hope can initiate the energetic process of restoring the places that we marry or make films with and about. There is a tree-planting non-profit in San Francisco called Climate Action

Now that we are planning to team up with and actually go around planting trees or doing performances that bring attention to the importance of having trees in the city.

AS: We love Joseph Beuys' *7000 Oaks* piece a lot. He planted 7000 oak trees as art. And beside each tree, he placed a basalt stone marker to bring attention to different kinds of time and growth. He died before the piece was finished. His son planted the last oak. Beuys planted the first oak in Kassel at documenta, and then the last one was planted in Kassel, beside it five years later. Beth and I were invited to be in documenta 14, and our performances began at that site of *7000 Oaks*. It was such an honour to be there and perform with the 7000 oaks. I can die now.

MC: You are very iconic as artists. You have a lot of personality, you wear fabulous costumes, but you are also very collaborative. You create communities. I always felt that you had moved beyond the ego into using your work to build communities. You speak to queer women, trans people, queer people, and interesting arty people, who are a bit unconventional or into green politics. Do you win people over? I wonder if you could meditate a bit on how you use performance art to create communities or change communities.

BS: [laughing] That is a hard question. Ours is a community formed by attraction. We are not trying to win people over or change people in any kind of culty way. We just invite people to join us. And if they want to, they will. Our events often have a majority of women collaborators. Although we always try to have a more diverse mix, we will take who we can. We have plenty of critics, Marisa, believe me. There are people who just think we are full of shit, and of course in some ways we are! Everyone is [laughing]. So, we do not really deny that. Some people critique us by saying that we are dealing with these very serious problems in ways that are not serious enough to deal with these problems and we are like, wow, you may be right. We do use humour. We also engage silliness to make the medicine go down. We engage 'strategies of joy', a term that the Argentinean artist Roberto Jacoby coined when he threw queer dance parties in the streets during the Argentinian military dictatorship, at a time when many people disappeared, were tortured, and killed. Joy was, and still is, an act of resistance and protest because it provides people with the will and the energy to continue to fight for freedom.

People in BIPOC and LGBTQI+ communities are also adopting terms like 'black joy' or 'queer joy'. These ideas and embodied practices help us, marginalized folks, navigate politics, education, or other oppressive institutions that are pillars of our white supremacist society. So, while we do have serious critics, we have strong allies in our professional and friendship networks too. Building these kinds of networks is what we do and we try to nurture our friendships. We prefer to do this in embodied physical space, because we spend so much time working online, which makes us want to physically get together with our friends. In fact, we most often see our friends when we are producing or performing in an event. We do not want to let Facebook and other social media corporations own the word 'friend'. It is important for us to see our friends without the mediation of a screen or some sort of data-mining social media platform. And while real friendship does exist between people online, when one needs a friend to actually show up and be present in the flesh, a million heart emojis are a paltry substitute for physical embodied presence.

AS: We host a lot of dinner parties! Whatever we are doing, we try our best to get a wide mix of people together from all ages, races, walks of life, sexualities, and styles. That is our secret sauce that makes for great happenings.

BS: Much of our work involves going to other places. We only go where we are invited and once there, we invite lots of different groups, local artists, and performers. We are just lucky to have friends who are from different communities. We did our *Wedding to Fire* in two parts because we did not want the wedding to be a huge Covid super spreader. One of the reasons why we do not destroy the land, like maybe people do at Glastonbury, is because we do not do huge events. We appreciate smallness. There is something really appealing about working at more intimate scales and within friendship networks. Our amazing performance director, Joy Brooke Fairfield, came all the way from Tennessee to direct the fire wedding performances. She was a little concerned when we invited a friend who is also a Washoe elder to do the land acknowledgement at our wedding. She was concerned that we might be perceived as tokenizing our friend, and thereby causing harm. And I said, you know, he is a friend. When we work with friends, things can go wrong, and sometimes they do, but friends are usually willing to discuss what happened and forgive us if we were stupid. Whereas, on the internet, it seems that there is very little room for making mistakes. You say one thing wrong, and you get ghosted, or doxed; this is not sustainable friendship because everyone is imperfect, and at some point, we all stick our foot in our mouth, or in our cleavage, or wherever. We are continuously learning to be better allies, and because we grew up with and within white supremacy, we will be in this learning process until the end of our days.

We have made mistakes and some people are uncomfortable with us because of that but we are always open to criticism. We try to be politically astute, culturally sensitive, and careful to ask for consent. Words are very powerful, and we recognize that, but there are worlds beyond words that we try to express and embody. We also try to avoid hierarchy and aim to create a more equally distributed rhizomic network.

AS: Since we do not fit neatly into really straight environmental activist groups, or we have to hide who we are; hide our queerness, my sex work background, we can't wear our big costumes and false eyelashes, so we have had to create our own affinity group. We want to gather with people who care about the environment that are also sex positive, freaks, punks, outsiders, fringe ...

BS: ... queers, and showgirls ...

AS: People in the side-stream. When Beth produced and directed *Goodbye Gauley Mountain*, which was really her first feature film, apparently there were no other feature length queer environmental documentaries. No one has been able to name a single one. That was 2013. It is like, wow, don't queers care about the water, air quality, critters ...?

BS: A lot of queers do – but it did not seem that that was where they wanted to or could put their activist energies.

AS: Yes, they do, but there were very few places for us to connect with back then. Although we loved and learned a lot from those hardcore straight environmental activist groups.

BS: Our work really, in connecting with the Earth and in celebrating sexuality together, is sort of paganistic as opposed to Christianity which creates hierarchies that contribute to the killing of the Earth, discouraging human-nonhuman relationships by demonizing, objectifying, and killing the Earth's non-human beings. In the Christian bible, the book of Genesis says, 'God gave man dominion over fish, the birds, the cattle, wild animals and insects that crawl', which just sets up a really dangerous paradigm. Christians have taken 'God's word' as permission to dominate the Earth's nonhuman creatures, and as we know, Christian domination can be very violent in its quest for worldwide supremacy.

AS: To be fair, there are some decent environmentally conscious Christian groups. Thankfully. We need it all.

BS: But the kinds of beliefs that Christianity has practiced and taught for centuries are essentially spiritually based pro-patriarchal humans, and anti-earth-based nonhumans (including Showwomen). We call this approach, 'Earth as an enemy force'. That is partly why so-called 'religious people' tortured and killed millions of so-called 'witches' because they were very connected with the Earth. Not to mention the death and destruction Christian colonialism has wreaked through the ages.

AS: We like a community that is an ecosystem. In our Ecosex Manifesto 2.0, we say,

> We are aquaphiles, teraphiles, pyrophiles and aerophiles. We are skinny dippers, sun worshippers and stargazers. We are artists, sex workers, sexologists, academics, environmental and peace activists, feminists, eco-immigrants, putos y putas, trans/humanistas, nature fetishists, gender bending gardeners, therapists, scientists and educators, revolutionaries, dandies, pollen/amorous cultural monsters with dogs and other entities from radical ecologies ... Whether GLBTQI, hetero, asexual or Other, our primary drive and identity is being Ecosexual!

We love to pollinate friends with friends. At our last event, we introduced our brilliant grant writer friend, Jeff Jones to environmentalist extraordinaire, Amanda Starbuck, who has been a director for Greenpeace in four countries in South America. He was enthralled by her work and we were happy to have made that connection because we are pollinators. We introduce scholars to artists and sex workers because they can influence each other to collaborate and grow. In other words, we like to bring the Showwomen and queers with flaming fire tassels, glitz, glamour, and fun, which the scholars need, then they can support the showpeople with more resources and write theory about them.

BS: Well, environmental activists really need some fun too, because their work is incredibly difficult with little immediate gratification.

AS: Yes. We cannot assume the ecosexual position alone. We need a variety of communities so we can help each other to thrive. Diverse people but also peacocks, bacteria, mycelia, rocks, bees ... We could facilitate groups laying outside doing Ecosexual Breathing together.

BS: Yes, we are not a singular community. You know, ecosexuals are diverse, not a monocultural community at all. We are a network.

MC: Absolutely. I was always interested in paganism and witchcraft as a teenager and joined a coven. Pagan circles can sometimes be a bit too dominantly white in the United Kingdom, and certainly not always queer spaces. But there are lots of women involved in the Wiccan tradition here and I have a good friend who is involved in a very old Coven. Though when you see old pictures of covens in the 1970s, they seem to be fulfilling quite a lot of male sexual fantasies of the idea of the forbidden or the witch. And in a way queering paganism in the United Kingdom feels quite new.

The way that you connect with Donna Haraway's work, exploring multispecies, paganism, performance art and sex work is rare in the United Kingdom. Or maybe it is happening, I don't know. I am involved in these communities, but even in queer performance art circles, people are not talking enough about the environment, as you say. Those two dialects have not yet come together fully.

To bring it back to the book, my proposition is that the Showwoman has grown up from the showgirl; the Showwoman is a collaborator, she is a part of a collective. She is part of a collective of witches if you like. And obviously moving beyond gender, she is a showperson and we have showpeople who have always been slightly outside and connected to, say, Romani communities or communities that are outside of the mainstream. I see you two as show personages who are connecting these very disparate, different worlds that very much belong together.

AS: Beth and I like to imagine the Earth as our lover. It works well for us. However, the Earth can be imagined as any archetype really; mother, friend, MILF, priestess, God, Goddess, Joker … And it can morph. We imagine the Earth is transgender, beyond gender, all genders. You could imagine the Earth as the ultimate Showwoman as well. Showwoman is an archetype. What more beautiful, adorned, charismatic, and powerful Showwoman than the Earth? Showwoman could be any gender, of course.

BS: The Earth is always performing for us if we take the time to notice. The Earth is the ultimate showgirl/woman. Yet sometimes, showgirls have to defend themselves against exploitative managers and/or producers and sometimes showgirls have to protect and help each other to not get harassed or in order to get good gigs. Once a showgirl always a showgirl, even while aging into a Showwoman who will eventually grow old, die, and become the material of mythology.

AS: Dying is the ultimate show! A great immersive performance art piece.

BS: There is something powerful about the process of dying, returning to Earth and becoming Earth that new life and new ideas can sprout from. We are born from the Earth and to the Earth we will return. Recently, several good friends of ours died. We were lucky to get to visit them during their dying process, which was quite an honour. It is very humbling to see friends who were such powerful, cutting-edge artists and culture makers slow down in the dying process.

A showgirl extraordinaire who just left her big, beautiful body is Carol Leigh, also known as Scarlett Harlot. She was such a super star; a super nova whore artivist with a heart of gold. She famously coined the game-changing term, 'sex work'. We, and scores of others' lives she touched were changed through her glamor, her velvet-gloved power to challenge and change legislation, and her sexy smile. So many people around the world are going to miss her terribly. She had a good peaceful death at home, which was a beautiful blessing and it was completely natural and exactly like she wanted it. Over her lifetime, she had gathered a fantastic archive documenting the international sex worker movement and was having trouble getting it organized and placed. So, Annie and I stepped in to help her. We have placed our archives and six other Showwomen's archives now. We knew what needed to be done. Some of Carol Leigh's sex work community friends volunteered to help, and within two weeks we had a list of everything that was in the archive and we sold it to Harvard's Schlesinger Library. She was very sick, so we helped her negotiate the contract, took it over for her to sign on a Sunday. She left her mortal coil on Wednesday, knowing her archive was safe and sound. A Showwoman's archive is very important for future generations, and it makes her immortal.

The other good news is that after Carol Leigh's death, she became a philanthropist! She had grown up poor, lived frugally and saved, then her mother died and left her some money. So now, she is leaving money to sex workers of colour and sex worker rights organizations she loved. She is a glowing example of love and generosity. An essential part of the cycle of life, which allows the Earth to regenerate and rejuvenate.

AS: What a gal! A legend. Her fabulous costumes have been donated to the San Francisco GLBT Historical Society. Some were made by the person that invented the rainbow flag, Gilbert Baker. They were bosom buddies.

We can think of the whole cosmos as Showwoman. Oh, those glittering shooting stars and those big black holes! We think we know stuff about the cosmos but she/he/they are mysterious. Some of the photographs coming back from space and from the new high-powered telescopes are dazzling. The cosmos drips with sequins and rhinestones. I mean, talk about a costume. The Earth is doing a seductive striptease and a nude dance for us every day. All the world is a live ecosex show stage. It has been fun to think about the Earth as Showwoman. Nature is certainly endlessly entertaining. Better than Netflix!

BS: Yes, thank you Marisa. Now the show(women) must go on! Let's get gussied up and go watch the sunset.

Conquering the World with Hoops

Marawa

In 2007, I left Australia with a hideous backpack and 60 hoops wrapped in a velvet case; except, instead of lonely planet guides and hiking shoes, mine held roller skates, a three-meter static trapeze, various skipping ropes, costumes, three pairs of high heels, and ten sets of good eyelashes. I set off with that ugly backpack on a 'round the world' ticket that never made it past London. I left Australia to see if I could make it as an international showgirl, without really knowing what that was. Ten years later, I returned to Australia with a full set of baby blue Globe-Trotter hardcase suitcases, three leopard print velvet hoop cases holding over 150 hoops, and all the Frequent Flyer cards. This marked ten years of touring as an international showgirl around the world and finally I had the luggage to prove it. First class lounges? Of course! Letters from the pilot? Yes. This was not the caravan touring life of a traditional circus artist (which don't get me wrong, I still love), this was the twenty-first-century skilled circus performer's dream.

Marisa and I met at the Blackpool Winter Gardens in 2007. I was instantly drawn to her, not just because of our matching hair; we also shared a mutual interest in mysterious performers of the past. When I met her, she held herself with confidence and strength and showed me that it was possible to be a performer and a businesswoman. Beautiful, strong, and capable, all at the same time. She took me under her wing. When we left Blackpool and went back to London, I moved in with her and over endless bowls of pasta combed her extensive collection of magic and circus books, studying photos, and reading about performers of the past.

Marisa and I share a common interest in ground-breaking, taboo-shattering, glamorous women, who lived on their own terms. This interest has perhaps something to do with searching for a role model; both of us share different, but similar upbringings: I come from an academic Catholic/Muslim background and Marisa from a strict Jewish household. I was interested in researching the stories of women labelled exotic performers, furthering their stories, making them part of the conversation, and keeping them relevant. This also meant reclaiming ownership of the idea of the exotic woman for ourselves.

Through Marisa, I was introduced to many of the performers and friends that I still work with to this day. Notably, The Insect Circus was the first to point out my likeness to Koringa, known as the first female fakir in the world, who wrestled alligators and walked up a sword ladder. There was not a lot of information available about old circus and variety acts, but with the help of Mark and Sarah from The Insect Circus and Vanessa Toulmin, Research Director of the National Fairground and Circus Archive in Sheffield, I was able to gather as much information as I could about Koringa. The first time I saw a poster of her, it became clear why people felt I looked like her: big hair and dramatic facial expressions.

In 2008, I played Josephine Baker in a show in New York for six months. When I was initially asked to audition, I was offended, thinking that it was just another 'You are a mixed-race showgirl, you could be Josephine Baker!' I did not really know much about her; I knew she wore a banana skirt and that's about it. But after I was offered the role, I dived into research and was amazed at what I found. I discovered more and more about her life off stage: she was a spy and the first person asked to take over the civil rights movement after Martin Luther King Junior was killed. She had twelve adopted children from twelve different nationalities. I had discovered not just a fabulous performer, but also an incredible role model. During my stay in New York, I visited Chez Josephine on 42nd Street, a restaurant that was owned and run by one of her sons, an honorary member of the rainbow tribe, Jean-Claude Baker, who was originally from Germany and was adopted by Josephine when he was fourteen. Sheepishly, I went there for dinner with another performer in the show, Marco Noury. Marco struck up a conversation with Jean-Claude Baker, who was known for always being at the restaurant. Flamboyant, fabulous, and dressed up in Josephine's headdresses, I was terrified when I met him. I was afraid that he might be upset, somehow, that I was playing her in the show. When Jean-Claude found out about the show, he turned to me, took my face in his hands and said, 'but you, you should be playing Josephine!' Relief washed over me, and we struck up a friendship that lasted until his death.

Figure 15: Marawa live shot at Bal De La Rose for Louboutin,
Salle des Etoiles of Sporting Monte-Carlo, 2022. Monaco. © Francois Gautret

For the next twelve months, every Friday, I had dinner at Chez Josephine, often straight after the show, still in my show make-up. He announced me when I arrived: 'Josephine is here!' and then ushered me to a table. I ate her favourite spaghetti and meatballs, while he theatrically retold fabulous stories about his maman. I do not have many regrets in life, but I do regret not having seen the collection of costumes and outfits that Jean-Claude had at his home in the Hamptons. He often invited me, but it seemed like an impossible place to get to at the time. Unfortunately, I never did, and he died in 2015. I often wonder what happened to all the amazing outfits, posters, and photos he had.

This was the first but not the last interaction I had with people who had worked with or known Josephine throughout the years. I performed at Theatre Bobino Paris, which is where her last performance was held. She died after the opening night of her show there, suffering a stroke whilst having breakfast in bed, surrounded by newspapers, which held five-star reviews about her show, or so the story goes. A picture of her state funeral, where one million people lined the streets of Paris, is still hanging backstage. She was embraced in Paris in a way that was never replicated in her home country of America. She tried in vain for years to be a hometown star, but it never worked; and she always returned to Europe, where she was considered showbiz royalty.

Just last week I was in Monaco performing at the sportif venue, where Josephine made her come-back show in 1974. I was performing at Bal De La Rose. It coincided with a Christian Louboutin exhibition, in which there was a headdress that Josephine wore during her iconic show. In a snippet of that performance, she appears in this incredible headdress, with huge blue and turquoise feathers tipped in yellow, pink, and orange, with a turban and earrings attached to the outside. When I looked at this piece in the exhibition, I suddenly realized that as performers, what we do extends far beyond the show. The costumes are extensions of our bodies: real living art! And these pieces will continue to live on after we die.

The show in Monaco also featured Dita Von Teese, whom I have worked with over the years and whom I respect and adore as a performer and businesswoman. I feel I now understand what she has tried to explain to me so many times about the importance of outfits and costumes, which I have always fallen short on. Historically, I have felt that these elements are not as important as the actual performance. But seeing Josephine Baker's glorious headdress, nearly fifty years old, and still vibrant and full of life, I felt like I finally understood more about my legacy for generations of performers to come.

Unlike Dita and Josephine, I do not perform topless; when I played Josephine, this was something that I was very clear with the producers about, even in the audition. I brought it up a few times, but I was not surprised when at the fitting I was presented with a banana skirt and nothing else. It was 2008. I was not young and impressionable; I was unfazed and did not care if I got fired. I have no issue with nude performers (live your life!). It is just not my thing. And no one was going to talk me into it. Thinking back, Josephine is often quoted saying she had no issue performing naked. But I still wondered whether at the time, this was a decision made on her behalf. One of my favourite Fran Lebowitz quotes regarding the #MeToo movement is: 'you choose to be an actress; you don't choose to be a cleaner'. I think about this, when I think about Josephine Baker's opportunity to leave a life of poverty and become a dancer in Paris. She did not get to choose her routines and costumes the way I have. She had to perform in blackface, at times nude, but this gave her a way out. She was a chorus girl who over time worked her way up to being the star of the show; and in doing so she paved the way for performers like me.

My own show *Quality Novelty* focuses on the two things that are most important to me in life: novelty acts and people that specialize in strange skills. This is also connected to my obsession with the Guinness World Records: I have spent many years training and breaking records to the point where I was inducted into the Guinness World Record Hall of Fame 2022. I have broken over twelve records, including spinning the most hula hoops simultaneously (200!), one of my favourite achievements. Marisa's book: *Obsessions of a Showwoman* is exactly the place where stories like mine can live on, inspire the next generation of performers, entertain in their way and on their own terms.

The Making of a Future Showwoman

Empress Stah

I am Empress Stah or Intaglamactic Empress Stah Power Girl.

I lived in London for 22 years and moved back to my hometown in Australia with my husband in 2020, during the pandemic. The thing I did on the last day before I left London was to meet with Marisa Carnesky, the creator of this book, and do an interview for it! Marisa has been a dear friend and professional mentor, guiding me on the road to Arts Council funding, since we met in the early noughties. As a cast member, I delighted in haunting her fairground performance ride *Carnesky's Ghost Train*, where I flew on wires down the platform, as the apparition of a train guard, and later as a Pepper's Ghost illusion after a real life near death experience involving me on a bike and a big red London bus. *Dystopian Wonders* was a research and development project that Marisa presented at The Roundhouse, London, for which I created an act on a bleeding ladder of swords and received a warning about creating a biohazard during a part of the act where I took the blood from my arm with a syringe.

The seeds of my career were planted when I entered a drag queen competition with a lip-synching act, which I won the second year, and a friend asked me to walk in her fashion show, where I came on naked and got dressed on stage. I grew up in the rural town of Mittagong, the eldest of five girls. I am an artist, aerialist, cabaret performer, show producer, director, rigger, teacher, website designer, bookkeeper, fundraiser, company director, all the things that make a Showwoman. I grew up in a completely white town full of very normal people; my dad had a car smash repairs business, and my mum ran an informal childcare centre from the house. I did various forms of dance, until the age of 16, when my interest in boys and booze took over. When I finished high school, I started clubbing in Sydney on Oxford Street and hanging out in gay bars and saw 1980s-style drag queens, who I thought were fabulous.

Growing up in Mittagong, I did not have any influences, anyone to introduce me to cool music. I did have my mum's record collection, so I was always making mix tapes of 1960s and 1970s music and choreographing group dance numbers with kids in the lounge room, when family friends came over for a barbeque. I had a very academic education and have never studied art; an art career was not even on the list in the career advisor's office. Mine was not an obvious progression.

I dropped out of my economics degree, lived in Sydney, and continued with a life of vice for a few years before finding circus, which set me on a new path. I saw some queer performances in Sydney around that time in the early 1990s and was quite inspired by it. In Perth, I became known as Stah, because I had a pink star shaved on my head. I started doing trapeze lessons by chance. I was always the queen of the monkey bars in the playground as a child, so when I was invited to a kids' aerial class, I jumped at the idea, and my feet have never really come back to earth since. In the 1990s, I had a lot of piercings; at one point I had 50 permanent piercings, it was just a lifestyle, aesthetic thing, but also became part of the act. When I dropped out of university, I started nude modelling for life drawing classes. I danced in a peep show in Perth for a while. I started developing cabaret shows, with elements of aerial and fire twirling, some superficial body piercing, lip-synching, and sex toys. I did not go to art school, I had no influences, no mentors, and no references. I was just driven to create these shows for the stage. This is how it all began and then I got a one-way ticket to London.

I find that the traditional aerialist is probably the epitome of a showgirl, tits and teeth. I had a shaved head for many years until I was 40, piercings and muscles. I do not look good in lingerie. The whole burlesque revival came while I was performing what was then referred to as 'twisted cabaret'. I have never looked or behaved like the archetypal femme. I found a natural home for my unique style of performance at Torture Garden. In the early 1990s, when I was running around Sydney with my shaved head, I used to strap my boobs down, which were pretty non-existent anyway, to look more like the gay boys that I fancied. I am not transgender, but there is definitely a very strong masculine side to me. I have often quipped that I am a gay man trapped in a woman's body. I feel I could be cis-male and still be a version of Empress Stah and it would make sense. I am non-binary in a lot of ways; however my pronouns are very much she/her, and I am comfortable with that. I married the queerest heterosexual man I could find. I call us heteroqueer.

In the 1990s, myself as Intaglamactic Empress Stah Power Girl (which was one legal version of my name) and my wondertwin Supreme Commander Stah Power, now Starlady, were on a mission to go to space. I discovered you could actually experience zero gravity aboard a parabolic flight, when I came across the pioneering work of Kitsou Dubois, Morag Whitman, and the Arts Catalyst, who had flown with the Russian Space Agency in the 1990s. Through my research, I discovered that the Zero Gravity Corporation offered such commercial flights. I did a crowdfunding campaign in 2011 and raised half the money to do the flight. It was $5000 and I came up with the rest. I travelled to America and experienced Zero Gravity for a total of seven minutes. This is part of my ongoing project to make a performance in space and was a pitch to Robert Pacitti in 2010, which resulted in a commission for the SPILL Festival of Performance and the show *Empress Stah in Space*.

I had the idea of hiring the Russian Space Agency plane and make a film in it. I asked Peaches if she would write a song for it; she hates rollercoasters and gets motion sickness, so she said, jokingly, that she would write a song called 'Sick Bag' for this space flight, which is notoriously also known as the *Vomit Comet*. I did not get that part of the funding to hire the parabolic plane from the Russian Space Agency, so, I decided that to go to space I had to be like Astro Boy; I needed jets coming out of my feet or my ass, or laser beams coming outta my ass like jet propulsion. I already had butt plug acts, including a diamond butt plug and an eyeball butt plug. In one act, I pull a balloon full of gold glitter out of my arse, blow it up and pop it over my head in a shimmering golden cloud, like alchemy turning shit into gold.

As part of the devising of *Empress Stah in Space*, Ron Athey and I went to Bentwaters, a disused American air force base in Norfolk. This is the site of the biggest purported UFO sighting in the United Kingdom. In the book *Left at East Gate: A First-Hand Account of the Bentwaters-Woodbridge Ufo Incident, Its Cover-Up, and Investigation*, a military eyewitness discusses how these spaceships crashed, and there were aliens taken to an underground bunker at the site. We had permission to go to this site for the day. Concrete had been poured into all the underground facilities when the Americans left the airbase, and there was not much to explore, so Ron and I spent the day doing automatic writing. We were high and writing down whatever came to us.

There were two words that stayed with me from the process of automatic writing: 'iconoclasm / stargasm'. The word stargasm came from Ron quoting his friend Vaginal

Davis. Peaches had agreed to write a song for the laser butt plug act, so I chose to give these words to her for the song. She came back with the song 'Light in Places' that became part of the show with the first iteration of the laser butt plug, which is the one in the music video. The laser butt plug was 17 cm in diameter and the casing, just on the cusp of 3D printing, but not quite there, had gradated laser cut sections of thick hard plastic, glued together and covered in hot glue to try and soften the edges. I had been training my sphincter with various butt plugs from a male gay sex shop, so that I could stretch myself enough to be able to accommodate the device.

I have always been forward thinking. I strive to create something new and original with my work. I was the recipient of a Jerwood Circus Award in 2003 for my solo show *Swinging from the Chandelier*, which played three sold-out nights at the then Circus Space, London. In 2007, I produced a self-funded circus, neo-burlesque, live art mash-up cabaret show called *The Very Best of Empress Stah* at the infamous Raymond Revue Bar in Soho. The aim of this show was to bring my cabaret acts out of the late-night fetish and gay clubs and make them accessible to mainstream audiences. I went on to tour this show around the United Kingdom and to the Adelaide Fringe Festival, Australia, shocking people as I did, which was never my intention. The Arts Council of England and the National Centre for Circus Arts funded me in 2014 to research and develop a show called *Infinite Space*, which included the use of wearable sensors to create real-time motion graphics, which are projections that react to body movements and positions in space. In this project, I started working with drones and this led to the creation of an act called *Starflight*, which features an aerial duet with a piloted drone.

So here we are in Mittagong, creating a new life in Australia, with my London punk husband, Graham. I have established a mobile aerial school and am currently teaching a new generation of young circus artists, empowering these young people to be the best version of themselves. Running the circus school allows me to spend my days going to the gym and training aerial, as I have always done. Gigs are starting to come back, post-pandemic, and in the last three months I have been to Los Angeles and Zurich for performances, which is a long way to travel, but I am happy to be back on the international stage. I have even made a new cabaret act where I am dressed in a yellow rubber catsuit and hood, playing Ernie's Rubber Duckie from *Sesame Street*. Blending both my current worlds, it is rated PG.

Figure 16: Marisa Carnesky, publicity shot for Smut Fest, 1994. London. Photographer unknown

Figure 17 (left): Marisa Carnesky, *Observer Magazine*, 1997. Photographer unknown
Figure 18: David Hoyle and Marisa Carnesky, Queer Up North, 1994. Manchester. © Ruth Bayer

Figures 19 and 20: Marisa Carnesky, *Lady Muck and Her Burlesque Revue*, with Jo Jo and Katia Tirado, Nottingham Now, 1995. © Mark Bushnell

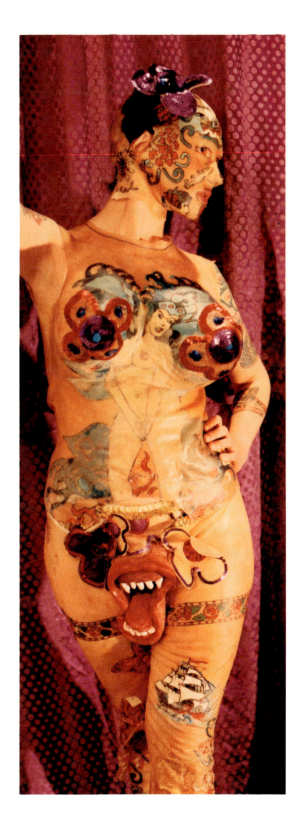

Figure 21: Marisa Carnesky, *Dolly Blue*, tattooed costume by Amanda Moss, Dragon Ladies Studios King's Cross, 1997. London. © Amanda Moss

Figure 22: Marisa Carnesky, *Jewess Tattooess*, Battersea Arts Centre, 1999. London. © Ruth Bayer

Figures 23 & 24: Marisa Carnesky, *Carnesky's Ghost Box*, illusion by Paul Kieve, 2000. London. © Paul Kieve

Figures 25 & 26: Marisa Carnesky, *Jewess Tattooess*, studio shot, 2000. London. © Manuel Vason
Figure 27 (overleaf): Marisa Carnesky, *Jewess Tattooess*, studio shot, 2000. London. © Manuel Vason

126

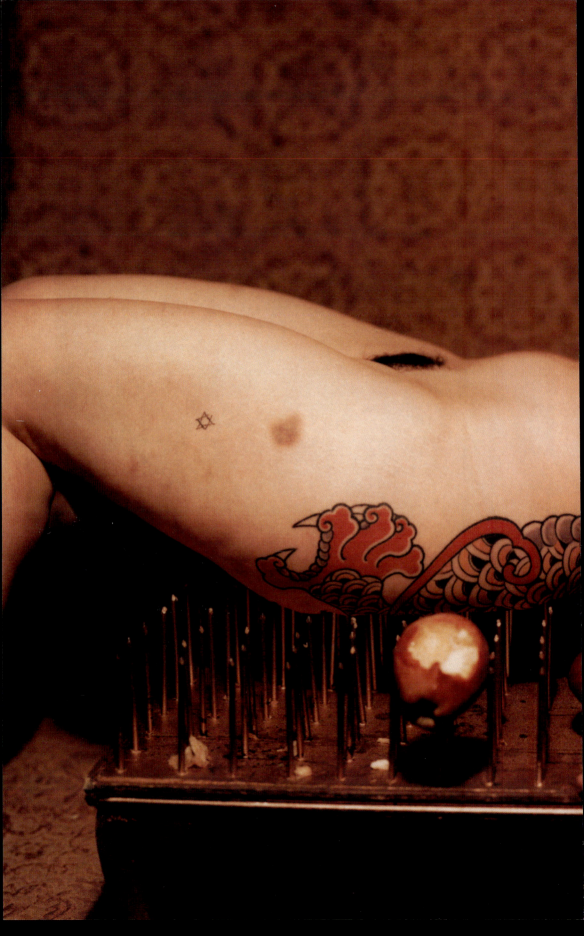

Figures 28 & 29: Marisa Carnesky, *Jewess Tattooess*, studio shot, 2000. London. © Manuel Vason
Figure 30 (overleaf): Façade of *Carnesky's Ghost Train*, Dagenham Docks, 2004. London. © Jonathan Allen

Figure 31: Paloma Faith, *Carnesky's Ghost Train*, Truman's Brewery, 2005. London. © Alastair Muir
Figure 32 (right): Marisa Carnesky, *Carnesky's Ghost Train*, Truman's Brewery, 2005. London. © Alastair Muir

Figure 33 (left): Geneva Foster Gluck, *Carnesky's Ghost Train*, Truman's Brewery, 2005. London. © Alastair Muir
Figure 34: Tai Shani, *Carnesky's Ghost Train*, Truman's Brewery, 2005. London. © Alastair Muir

Figure 35: Marisa Carnesky, *Magic War*, studio shot, 2007. © Manuel Vason
Figure 36: Marisa Carnesky, *Magic War*, Soho Theatre, 2007. London. © Ruth Bayer
Figure 37 (right): Marisa Carnesky, *Magic War*, 2006. © Manuel Vason
Figure 38 (overleaf): *Carnesky's Live Archive*, www.carnesky.com/live-archive. 2020. © Rosie Powell

r stressed puppies, irritable cats, hangover, constipation, flatulence, bilous headache,
h ulcer, anxiety, nausea, morning sickness, good ideas and bad expressions

Fri 16th Feb.
doors open 8.30pm - starts 9.30pm sharp
open until 2am

TIGER LILLIES
your worst nightmare about Love, Piss and Vomit

MARISA CARR
grotesque Music hall stripper extraordinaire

PRESENTS

Phantasmagorical

A BURLESQUE SPECTACULAR OF FRIGHTENING PROPORTIC
TO CELEBRATE
CARNESKY'S GHOST TRAIN

AFTER THE LAST RIDE OF THE TRAIN...
SUNDAY, 19TH SEPTEMBER, 2004
8PM - LATE SHOW STARTS 9PM!
AT: CAFÉ DE PARIS, COVENTRY STREET W1

Conjuring the Weird

Weird Women

Eirini Kartsaki

An open mouth, a devilish grin, two horns located near the eyebrows; enlarged, protruding breasts, signs of leaves, of blood, of scalp, bleeding petals enveloping the body, tendrils threatening to take the self in; an image that takes over, swallowing itself, a monster perhaps, an insistent dance, close to the floor, an opening of the legs, the arms, the mouth; two mouths, one on the head, one on the groin, grinning concurrently, a body whose skin is tattooed, illustrated with signs of leaves, of blood, of scalp, bleeding petals. Violet Rose or Violent Rose, or someone who does not yet have a name, not for all of it, anyway. Not for the weird spectacle that this creature conjures, the unfamiliar territory that it ventures from. The weird spectacle does more than one thing; it distracts, inhabits, and intervenes. It opens up a hole, an egress and asks us to look through it. The monster demonstrates, demarcates the border, and transcends it; it exposes our blind spots, the things we do not know about the self or the things we won't admit. Its hybrid self is a placeholder for what is uncertain and unknowable. It proposes a new configuration of things to come.

The weird, Mark Fisher proposes, is a 'particular kind of perturbation. It involves a sensation of *wrongness*', something that exceeds what we already know, or we are able to represent (2016: 15). It is a fascination with a thing that overwhelms and cannot be contained, '*that which does not belong*', a thing that causes a rupture into the familiar (2016: 10, emphasis in the original). The weird can be thought of as something uncanny or absurd, or an experience that involves a sense of alterity, 'a feeling that the enigma might involve forms of knowledge, subjectivity and sensation that lie beyond common experience' (2016: 62). But also, the weird 'opens up an *egress*, between this world and others' (2016: 19). This irruption turns the familiar into something strange, allows one to look again, to wonder. It is an exercise in learning a new language, in looking at ourselves as if we belong to a foreign land. What we may encounter in this new land through this egress has to do with the inscrutability or unintelligibility of the weird, which points to the inscrutability or unintelligibility of the self (2016: 63). Ursula Le Guin writes about visiting new places: 'I will go to Abbenay, and unbuild walls' (1974: 11). Unbuilding walls, rupturing the familiar or learning to speak a foreign language, are all functions of the weird. The hole, or egress, that Fisher discusses, is also an attempt 'to radically leave the system altogether', rather than simply go against it (Colquhoun 2020: 46). There is some breakage going on here, a rupture into the skin of normality. Weirdness is a tool for rupturing dominant categories, a visual or aesthetic tool, but also a conceptual one (Colquhoun 2020: 47). The dominant categories we use to understand our identity, desire and sexuality are too limited at times and falter in the face of the weird, which, 'in its probing of the innate instability of subjectivity, as well as the world around us, has a tendency to uncover our blind spots and our unknowns' (Colquhoun 2020: 9). The weird entity, Fisher suggests, 'is so strange that it makes us feel that it should not exist' (2016: 15). But

> if the entity or object *is* here, then the categories which we have up until now used to make sense of the world cannot be valid. The weird thing is not wrong, after all: it is our conceptions that must be inadequate (15).

Encountering the weird is slippery, there is nowhere precisely we may locate it, as it does not consist of a singular thing. Describing the weird or its affect always feels inadequate. Weird women, I propose, are artists who challenge boundaries and are uneasy within neat, already existing categories of art, sex, identity, and desire. Their existence is emphatic; yet the categories we already have cannot account for the complexity of who they are. Weird women seem to suggest that a new language is necessary, one that will point towards our unnamed desires, blind spots, and unknowns. The weird not only points to something we do not yet have the language for but also demands a reconsideration of its articulation. The weird could be thought of as another category, but more accurately as a fascination with the uncategorized. This chapter is an attempt to navigate what Fisher identifies as an urgent need to rethink the names and categories available to us and their inadequacy. The weird women I discuss here make a mark on the fabric of experience, stretch out the ways we think about ourselves, our bodies, desires, identities, and propose a new space, place or territory for that which does not belong. Timothy Morton suggests that the weird can be thought of as 'a place for potentially radical disarticulations and reformulations of traditional binaries, starting with self and other' (Morton in Luckhurst 2017: 1041), a space where ideas around the unusual or the odd are unpacked. The weird appears as a placeholder for articulating what does not quite fit into the names, categories, and labels we have access to, what seems wrong in our perception of it or does not belong. The weird points towards what is spilling out of these categories or cannot be pinned down. The spillage, or disarticulation, starts to formulate a different territory, space for, or fascination with the weird. I locate Carnesky's work within this territory. My claim is that Carnesky, amongst other women artists, inhabits a space that refuses to be defined clearly. The work is more concerned with identity and desire that remains fluid and incomplete. Weird women, in my conceptualization, embody a plurality that borrows from different languages, disciplines and creative modes to celebrate hybridity, or what Halberstam calls 'a slippage between language and experience' (2014: 147). Who we are or what we want is always in process and the ways we inhabit the space of weirdness is not necessarily based on a language of names but develops in the process of living and imagining. Weird women continuously evolve and refuse categories, embracing mutation and hybridization as ways of being. Their weirdness creates a rupture into the familiar through which a new understanding of who we are and how we perceive ourselves emerges. This new, weird understanding or conceptualization embraces the unfamiliar, the uncategorized, the inscrutable or unintelligible as tools for unbuilding walls and building forms of belonging. In what follows, I discuss Carnesky's work as well as other women artists that, like Carnesky, have been preoccupied with the task of disarticulating identity. I primarily focus on how artists such as Rocio Boliver, Cosey Fanni Tutti, Narcissister, Lydia Lunch, and Kathy Acker have chosen to offer an account of themselves through interviews or writing, and how these, rather than specific examples of creative practice, might lead to a collective, weird 'I'. These artists' collective illegibility and refusal to fit in forms part of the space of the weird.

The opening image of this chapter describes an instance from the 1997 'The Ballad of Violet Rose' from Carnesky's show *The Grotesque Burlesque Revue* (as part of The Dragon Ladies) at the Raymond Revue Bar in Soho (Figure 39). In this, Carnesky uses specific female stereotypes, such as Dolly Blue, a Victorian showgirl, who transforms into a Tattooed Woman that has taken the skins of sailors to create her own skin, resembling Kali, the Goddess of Death. Carnesky uses these stereotypes in order to inhabit them and, to an extent, reclaim and undo them. She occupies them as examples of the

Figure 39: Marisa Carnesky, *The Grotesque Burlesque Revue*, 1996. London. Costume and photo by Amanda Moss. © Amanda Moss

ways in which social or cultural narratives can inhibit women and create limitations as to how we account for ourselves. Focusing on these limitations and disregarding all other complexity eliminates our plurality and places restrictions on who we are. Justifying one's existence or role through a singular name eliminates the imagining of who we can be. Carnesky knows this; she knows that we are not one thing, a singular identity. In her one-woman show *Jewess Tattooess* (1999–2002), Carnesky inhabits all of her characters: the Rabbi, the macabre fairy-tale aunt, the sexualized, disgraced Jew, the Tattooed Woman. Her characters are sexual, grotesque, monstrous, human, and animal. Her emphasis is on embodying women that have been oppressed by culture, society, and religion. Carnesky, herself, is not afraid to shift focus, experiment with different modes and media. She starts as a stripper in the West End, where she devises weird acts that merge genres and mess up with categories. She is not singular, as a maker, and this shape-shifting process, from her earlier work with The Dragon Ladies, to *Carnesky's Ghost Train, Dr Carnesky's Incredible Bleeding Woman* to *Showwomen* embodies a political indecision that embraces multiplicity, and plurality. Carnesky's political indecision is deliberate and shows a commitment to renewal and metamorphosis. Carnesky also changes her identity by changing her name:

Figure 40: Marisa Carnesky, *Portraits of Anarchists*, 1994. © Casey Orr

> I've changed my name. I've changed it to the name of my grandmother: Carnesky [...] It's kind of a political thing in that all the Jews tended to Westernize their names. I'm now de-Westernizing it, going back to my Eastern European name that is my real name.
> (Carnesky in Bayley 2000: 348)

This transformation is clearly depicted early on in her work. It becomes evident not only within individual shows, as her characters transform from one shape to the next, but also in her body of work as a whole. Most characteristic of this process of metamorphosis is her character Dolly Blue, devised with her then company The Dragon Ladies. In this work, we encounter Dolly Blue, who after being married to Bluebeard, has her legs chopped off and becomes his ship's mast. Her tears fall into the ocean, become oysters and she herself transforms into a diabolical creature of the sea, when the ship crashes; Dolly Blue takes the tattooed sailors' skins and creates her own skin, an elaborate latex skin with fake tattoos, designed in collaboration with and painted by the late visual artist Amanda Moss; Dolly Blue now appears as Kali, Mother of Death and all living beings. She is also now a murdering, avenging woman, Violet Rose, a 'street-walking-carnivalesque whore', who embodies all of the other characters, Kali, Mother of Universe and Dolly Blue (Carnesky in Bayley 2000: 245). The grotesque, transgressive sexuality of these characters seems to spill over and take up space in Carnesky's earlier work. The grotesque element connects to something cavernous, earthy, or hidden. It embodies sexual deviance, but also a sense of liberation, which always exceeds the norm (Russo 1994: 3). The grotesque to do with the monstrous, the strange, the remarkable, but also the hilarious and comic. This is where the grotesque connects with the carnivalesque, 'the suspension and mockery of everyday law and order', a term coined by Mikhail Bakhtin (in Prior 2000: n.pag.). Carnesky's grotesque body is multiple and ever-changing. It 'makes strange the categories of beauty, humanity and identity' and offers a reconsideration of these categories that are based on transcending what we already know (Halberstam 1995: 6). Carnesky's performance seeks ambiguity in her satirical and experimental approach. She is not interested in making finalized statements with her practice, but rather allowing the work to pose 'a series of interrelated questions' (Carnesky in Mock 2020: 46). Her practice encompasses elements of popular entertainment, live art, and sex activism. Bringing together all these distinct genres develops a form of hybridization. The monster, or the outsider, exists in this hybridized space and unsettles the norm, as it destroys and transcends the boundary that separates the here from the elsewhere (Cohen 1996: ix).

Carnesky locates this weird, monstrous, hybrid woman in certain female figures in her production *Dr Carnesky's Incredible Bleeding Woman*:

> One of these witches is Medusa, secluded in darkness, red-eyed and snake-haired, her moonlit gaze so powerful that it must be deflected by a mirror. [...] The Whore of Babylon is another, riding her hydra headed serpent, stealing sperm by night in her decorative attire. [...] Kali is here too, the archetypal goddess destroyer, scythe in one hand, severed head in the other, snakes entwined around her limbs, with multiple arms she presides over a sea of blood harkening the violent end of one cycle and the bloody beginning of another.
> (*DCIBW* Script 2018)

All weird women have something in common: they are unfamiliar, hybrid creatures, desiring bodies who transcend the familiar, demanding a new language and threatening the social order:

> There seems to be a need to bind and contain her polluting, risqué, sexual, seeping, uncontrollable and provocative body. The witch is enslaved in what was once her own domain, the magic world. How then can we use magic to reverse the curse?
> (*DCIBW* Script 2018)

Female figures that won't conform or obey within mainstream culture have been persecuted and demonized. Women with no children, families, or support systems, women who are able to escape the control of the patriarchy and deviate from the norm, will always be seen suspiciously and be perceived as dangerous or risky. These women have been 'othered' by patriarchal systems and their bodies have been thought of as 'foreign bodies' that need to be expelled from the land. The shamanic or magic powers that some of these women possessed as healers, folk doctors, herbalists, and midwives were a threat to capitalist society that promoted a new kind of individually centred work (Federici 2018: 27–28). These weird women's sexuality was also seen as uncontrollable or unacceptable and needed to be domesticated or muzzled. In her 2001 performance *Blowzabellas, Drabs, Mawksa and Trogmoldies*, a contribution to Duckie's East London promenade performance, Carnesky converts the Museum of Immigration

Figure 41: Rocio Boliver, *Needle Striptease*, curator Benjamin Sebastian,]performance space[, 2012. London. © Marco Berandi

and Diversity, once a synagogue, into the Museum of Strange Women: 'here audiences discovered women whose bodies had fused with their trades: a street-seller covered with bagels, a tailor festooned with metal instruments, and a weaver who is enveloped by her long hair that merges into a loom' (Mock 2020: 55). All of Carnesky's work is a museum of strange women: women who are shape-shifting into comedic phantoms or strange apparitions, women who swallow swords that correspond in length to the day of their menstrual cycle, women who become serpents, snake women, part-human, and part-animal; women who refuse to have their sexual, seeping, uncontrollable bodies contained. These women carry within them the weight of others, who have been captured, stifled, tortured, and destroyed. Women who have been oppressed by the multitude of bodily taboos, phobic messages, misogyny, coercion, racism, and narratives of shame. What unites them is a sense of transgression in wanting to be who they are, envisioning new terms of living. These strange women, like Dolly Blue or Lady Muck, or the Incredible Bleeding Woman, radically reclaim their space, identity, and sexuality. They are called different names, which are new and appropriate to the occasion: menstruants, strange women, and Showwomen. The earlier suffocating terms shuffle about, stretch out, and make space for the kinds of things they want to be, allowing for oxygen to burst flooding in.

The specific preoccupations that Carnesky has engaged with around rupturing the familiar, existing as a deviation to the system, or blurring the boundaries between art, sex, identity, and desire are not singular to her project. Disarticulating one's identity and disidentifying with the norm has been the lifelong project of other weird women, amongst which Rocio Boliver, Cosey Fanni Tutti, Kathy Acker, Lydia Lunch, and Narcissister. These women are not only aware of the ways in which they may deviate from the system or appear as 'outsiders', but also make that a key point of identification. Grappling with how they are perceived in relation to the norm becomes part of their work: 'I don't catch normality', Mexican artist Rocio Boliver exclaims in our conversation about categories. Normality or normativity seems to come up a lot in the conversation around weirdness. Boliver tells me that she spent her early years bedbound with kidney disease and used incessant masturbation to amuse herself, while construction workers were perving on her through the window: 'I was in bed for years and when I came out to reality, I felt I was weird to the world' (2021). For Boliver, normality is a disease one is prone to catch, the symptoms of which have to do with

Figure 42: Rocio Boliver, *My Tail of Hairs with Bells* at Embodiment #3 series, curated by Boris Nieslony and Nadia Ismail, Kunsthalle, Unterer Hardthof, Giessen, 2022. Germany. © Constantin Leonhard & BLACK KIT

fitting too comfortably within mainstream discourse. The reversal of this paradigm is significant, as weirdness is not presented here as the parasitic and threatening other side of normality, subordinated to it, but rather as a state in its own right. Boliver struggles with categories when it comes to her own performance practice (Figures 41 & 42); having started as a model and TV presenter, she could not quite fit into the categories of cabaret or performance art: 'It was difficult for me to know what it was that I was doing. I didn't have space in any categories' (2021). Resisting classification or fitting too neatly into specific genres, styles, or schools of thought becomes part of the work. Performance artist and musician Cosey Fanni Tutti proposes that 'normativity is only useful when kicking against it' and that names and categories are to do away with (2022). Eleanor Roberts argues that Tutti's *Magazine Actions*, consisting of naked or semi-naked images often taken in pornographic contexts, resists being classified neatly into one category and that is seen as a strength, rather than a weakness; it prompts continued debate around sexuality and art experimentation and appears as an intervention into the mainstream (2020: 173). Tutti also reverses the normality/weirdness paradigm: 'I don't like acceptance, I distrust it completely, I think I've done something wrong' (Tutti in Petridis 2017: n.pag.). In my personal correspondence with her, Tutti proposes that critics calling COUM's infamous 1976 show *Prostitution* at the ICA 'weird', 'indicates a loss of words and a lack of ability to engage with [it]' (2022). Tutti with Genesis P-Orridge and COUM Transmissions in the 1970s and 1980s reveal a tendency to mess up existing categories and place themselves at the edge of culture. The work intentionally spills out from specific styles and defies convention. It resists not only classification and resolution but also acceptance from the public. COUM's art practice develops a language by drawing on a rejection of limitations and rules, while at the same time it refuses 'to see art as a category distinct from, or superior to, the broader horizon of a *life strangely lived*' (Johnson 2018: 123). In his book *Unlimited Action: The Performance of Extremity in the 1970s*, Dominic Johnson writes:

> What if performance art stages the limits of what can be known, such that knowledge, rationality and the concept of conceptuality itself, are so tortured in the event and thus reconstituted by the baffling, bizarre, deranged actions that often characterise its practice, that the common knowledge of what we thought we knew – the categories of art, life, sex, crime – might seem as new unto itself?
> (122–23)

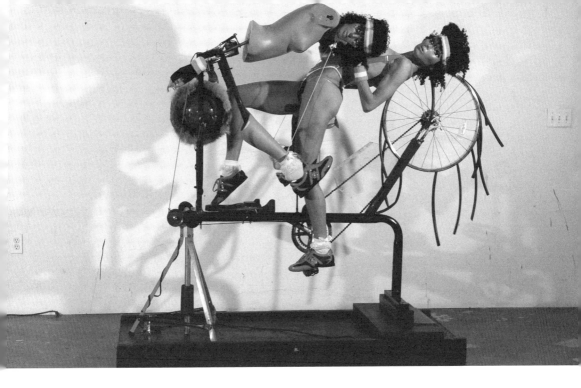

Johnsons' argument connects to Fisher's assertion that weirdness produces new forms of knowledge, subjectivity, and sensation, beyond common experience. Johnson proposes that actions of extremity in performance mess up with the categories we are familiar with. This results in a reconfiguration of the familiar, a rethinking of the recognized and accepted, and a re-imagining perhaps of how we connect to the world. Extremity is one of the strategies that weird women use, but not the only one. Tutti and Carnesky's commitment to invent a new vocabulary, alongside Fisher's contention of the inadequacy of language, re-emphasizes the need to 're-learn how to name things for ourselves' (Preciado 2020: 52). This commitment to a language that does not yet exist highlights the need to suspend our ways of thinking in order to allow for weird forms of knowledge and subjectivity, through the egress that the weird opens up. Through that egress, weird instability and the unknown may enter. These are the ingredients for a new way of connecting to that which is wrong, unfamiliar, or does not belong.

Using instability, weird subjectivities and the unknown as political strategies forms part of the weird's function. Performance artist Narcissister never shows her real face to the world and always wears a mask to perform her fascination with the uncategorized: 'I am definitely interested in resisting categorisation, and that is just part of who I am.

Figure 43: Narcissister, *Self-Gratifier*, photographed in her studio, 2008. Brooklyn, New York.
© Kristy Leibowitz

I am multiracial, my parents come from different backgrounds and different countries [...]. I understand how complicated and messy and unpredictable identity can be' (2022: n.pag.). Narcissister explores gender, racial identity, and sexuality. Her background cannot be easily captured by a singular identity. She works with subverting racial and gender stereotypes while using explicit sexual imagery:

> When I am making work, I have a sort of internal meter; when something feels too hetero or too vanilla or too predictable or too close to something that I have seen before, my internal meter wants to direct ideas towards territory that feels more courageous, more daring, more unknown and sort of stranger. I aim for that; I aim to make work that will satisfy my ideas around strangeness and weirdness or abjectness.
> (2022)

Moving away from the normative and engaging with weirdness or abjectness seems to position the two on the opposite side of the spectrum. However, Narcissister finds that even the categories of conformity and nonconformity do not work in a predictable way and spill into one another. She extends her argument to sexuality and race:

Figure 44: Narcissister, *Winter/Spring Collection*, 2012. Los Angeles. © A.L. Steiner

> People that are gay or queer, thank god, don't behave in any predictable manner, or people that are black, thank god, don't behave in any predictable manner; we are all so complex and we have, each of us, so much depth and richness and so many contradictions in us; I feel the same applies to me, to my racial identity, how I embody womanhood, and my ideas around sexuality.
> (2022)

Similarly to Carnesky, Narcissister embodies her identity, sexuality, and desires in ways that are complex and nuanced; her bizarre imagery or her choice to never show her face and to always perform in her Narcissister masked persona reveals a commitment to re-invent how we appear to the world (Figures 43 & 44). When considering the binary weirdness/normality, Narcissister goes a step further to argue that there is nothing weird about being unconventional or nonconforming; that at times there is much more weirdness in the conventional or traditional options, and that there is nothing weird about the life we are choosing to lead, even when our choices are perceived as weird by some (2022). At times, naming something 'weird' shifts its sensibility, the gesture of naming renders it part of language and therefore something that can be consumed within the context of mainstream culture. Kathy Acker finds a solution to this problem by committing to a desire to remain in the space of the 'fabulous not knowing' (2015: 97). Like the other women artists in this chapter, Acker also refuses to identify with given categories:

> I ask them to whip me and they call me Satan. [...] Me, straight queer gay whatever and where do nut cakes like me fit in who like getting fist fucked, whacked and told what to do? – the only thing that appals me is babies.
> (2015: 32)

When writing to McKenzie Wark drunk one night, she admits that she suffers from some 'weird disease' (46). In contrast to Boliver, who sees normality as a disease, Acker seems to pathologize weirdness; yet, in her work, she strives for it. There is a tension here between, on the one hand, wanting to fit in, being understood, becoming part of a lineage of artists or writers of a certain type, and on the other, allowing oneself to exceed the ordinary parameters of creative existence. Being recognized as an artist requires to an extent being part of a canon, having the ability to be read alongside others. Exceeding that canon sometimes is also recognizable as a key part of it; placing oneself on the edge of culture is only perceived as such *in relationship* to that culture.

Weirdness does not function in a vacuum; something is weird *in relation* to something else; convention, normality, a canonical sense of self (though such thing often only exists as a construct). Pushing against existing categories is only possible because these categories already exist. The paradigm can only be reversed once it exists as a paradigm.

Lydia Lunch names this problem clearly. With her band Teenage Jesus and the Jerks in the 1970s, she calls herself 'No Wave': 'We were angry, ugly, snotty and goddamn vile. [...] We were howling with fucking delight, laughing like lunatics at the brink of the apocalypse in a mad house the size of all of New York City', she suggests in an interview with Dominic Johnson (2016: 29). She identifies not as an artist, but rather as a confrontationalist, an apocalyptician, a refusenik, a hysteric, and an experiential journalist. Like Carnesky who names her collaborators different names, including menstruants and Showwomen, Lunch invents her own language to address herself: 'I document my own hysteria, or political hysteria, or the sexual hysteria of the times. "Artist" seems so fragile. The concept feels so frail' (Lunch in Johnson 2016: 40). Johnson argues that performance art may stage the limits of what can be known. In a similar gesture, Lunch finds the categories of 'artist' and 'post punk' constricting, overwhelming and suffocating. But how can we then allow these categories to open up, stretch out, and become new unto themselves? It is through the rupture that the weird creates; through that rupture we come in contact with weird knowledge and weird subjectivities; through it, we may encounter our blind spots: the unknown, the unknowable, the unnameable, what might remain fluid in the fabulous not knowing. Within the premise of the weird, what we already know is shown in a different light, through the illuminated egress that the weird creates. Weird women make possible this discovery, but also a looking anew at the things we know, the categories we use to denote who we are in this world. Even the category of being a woman seems problematic for some (and indeed there is a question around the restrictions of the word 'Showwoman' that Carnesky herself raises in various points throughout this book or the use of 'women' in the title of this chapter). On the restrictions of this category, Lunch exclaims: '[D]on't let the tits fool you baby, I am a faggot truck driver and you know it. [...] These look like my tits, but they're my balls' (2016: 47, 41). And later on: 'Some of us feel. Those of us that haven't been sexually segregated into being nice fucking girls that smile a lot and act pretty' (Lunch in Johnson 2016: 41). Lunch, Acker, or Boliver use their bodies, identities, and sexualities to explore weirdness. Carnesky does so both within the logic of theatre and through body art. Like Tutti, Lunch, Acker, and Narcissister, Carnesky questions how her sexuality is perceived. Her work can be positioned closer to the work of Narcissister, in that regard, who also uses excess, spectacle, and performance personae to embody weirdness. Whether through fictional characters, performance personae, art experimentation, art writing, or music, these weird women experiment with self-definition and thus transcend oppression, radically positioning themselves against the expected or the norm. The category of 'woman' can indeed be constricting, especially in a time when gender fluidity and nonconformity have become part of the vernacular, at least in some (western, liberal, artistic) contexts. This problem has been discussed by many artists in this book. Tai Shani explains her struggles with the term 'woman'; she interrogates gender categories and differentiates womanhood from femininity and considers feminized subjects as part of a patriarchal order and its libidinous economy. Shani reflects on how certain women-only spaces have been used to exclude trans women and therefore her goal is to think beyond gendered language. I am interested in considering whether terms like 'Showwomen' or 'weird women' become exclusionary of certain experiences that extend beyond the binary. The trans activist and artist Rhyannon Styles describes her approach to those terms in this book; she discusses how even the problematic term 'showgirl' appeals to her, as she came into womanhood in her 30s and therefore missed out on girlhood. In her interview with Carnesky, Styles discusses her experience as follows:

> being a 40-year-old trans person who has a different perspective on womanhood, than maybe as a cis identifying woman, I wish to, in some ways, hang on to the term showgirl, because I never was a showgirl, and I always wanted to be.
> (Styles, in this volume)

The nuance of individual experience cannot be captured by a singular term, as I have shown in this chapter. However, making sure that addressing the complexity of such experiences and making space for everyone to inhabit the space of showwomanry or weirdness is important. My conceptualization of weird women does not only include cis-gendered artists. In fact, it does not only include female-identifying subjects either. Anyone who wants to be part of weirdness is welcome. I focus on specific artists in this chapter because they seem to belong to a space that challenges categories. Women, myself included, that don't necessarily identify with certain categories, such as heterosexual or queer, seem to have no other place to exist. I open weirdness then as a space, rather than a category, for those individuals that find such categories of sexuality, identity, or creativity constricting and suffocating. Like Acker, 'I don't dig het shit for myself'. Like Boliver, 'I don't catch normality'. I do not have to translate my specific experience into one that fits neatly into a single category and therefore I

push against categorization. Queerness could be such a space of transgression, which challenges the expected or the norm, but its particular histories of oppression and marginality do not quite work for subjects that have not occupied these experiences. Weirdness is proposed here more broadly as an alternative space, place, territory with no specific remit or membership. I recognize weirdness as a place of refuge, of openness, and fluidity, where we do not have to make any kind of finite decisions or label ourselves. This writing advocates for weird, unfixed, uncertain ways to relate to ourselves and others, strange terms we can use to discuss and examine our strange desires. Weirdness finds inspiration in opening up categories, stretching them out, widening them, and whacking the shit out of them. Weirdness finds inspiration in inventing new ways of thinking about sex and writing and creative practice, in being utterly outrageous and drunk, like Acker, in masturbating on lit candles, like Tutti, in escaping the kids, the dog, the car and the mortgage, like Lunch, in becoming a hybrid, tattooed, bleeding Medusa or Kali, like Carnesky, in being a refusenik and a self-fashioning apocapyltician, like Lunch, in eating raw eggs and puking, like Tutti, in remaining with that fabulous not knowing, like Acker.

So far, I have identified how Carnesky amongst other women artists has struggled with definition and categorization. Fisher and Johnson have clearly shown how the problem of language is key when thinking about the limit of what can be known. Whether working within the logic of theatre, body art, music, or writing, the artists I have discussed in this chapter refuse to be defined neatly; their weirdness introduces new forms of knowledge and subjectivity; these artists use weirdness in order to undo fixity and reclaim the space of unknowing, find belonging through unbelonging. In her most recent show, Carnesky articulates the discomfort of being named by turning to the problematic term 'showgirl' and undoing its power. She refuses to adopt the names available to her, names that often objectify or diminish women in the entertainment industry. She rejects the term 'showgirl' and invites us to re-think who the showgirl would be, should she be allowed to graduate into adulthood. This is how 'Showwoman' is born to denote all artists who are in charge and do not depend on others, least of all, the showman. Carnesky's proposition is a coven or collective of Showwomen, who use their extraordinary skill to go against the system, transcend dominant categories, and invent new ways of life formation. From their hybridization, or mutation, which is the only way to arrive to oneself, according to Preciado, emerges a new vocabulary and thus

Figure 45: Cosey Fanni Tutti, *Marcel Duchamp's Next Work*, COUM Transmissions, 1974. London.
© Courtesy COUM Transmissions and Cabinet

space to inhabit. As a response to the inadequacy of existing language and the scarcity of terms to denote more than one thing, Carnesky arrives at the term 'Showwoman'. The term encompasses a number of things: a departure from the reductive 'showgirl', a desire to radically differentiate oneself from the showman, as well as an emphatic gesture towards acknowledging that we are not one thing. Carnesky, the Showwoman, performs the imperative of transcending normative language and dominant categories and invents 'a new grammar that allows us to imagine another social organisation of forms of life' (Preciado 2020: 51). The Showwoman's job is that of disidentifying with traditional models of thinking and existing in the world and unearthing weird knowledge and subjectivities. The Showwoman proposes that 'we need to re-learn how to name things for ourselves' (Preciado 2020: 52). The women discussed in this chapter are Showwomen, in that sense. They have refused to be defined by others and have pushed against the inadequacy of language. In this place, this new language or landscape, the Showwoman prevails:

> The whore of Babylon is sick today, she won't be coming to work. The whore of Babylon will not be entertaining you tonight. The whore of Babylon is tired of taking all the blame. She is tired of being a demon.
> (*Jewess Tattooess* 2002)

Showwomanry is an attempt to find space, to find air, to breathe, to resist categories, to imagine a world with a multiplicity of stories and places from which to contemplate living.

There is a tension, however, that emerges from this writing. On the one hand, there is a clear and urgent refusal to fit into categories readily available: the showgirl, the good girl, the bad girl, the slut, the devil, and the deviant. On the other hand, giving a name to ourselves, though it appears as a necessity, it perpetuates the problem of fixity. All artists discussed in this chapter address the issue of language, self-definition, and fixity. They respond to the imperative of not wanting to be named by others that Audre Lorde warns against: 'If we do not define ourselves for ourselves, we will be defined by others – for their use and to our detriment' (Lorde in Goddard: 1984: 45). The space of weirdness urges towards the imperative of keeping identity and difference fluid, allowing ourselves to keep changing, rather than creating more fixed categories. A solution to the problem of fixity could emerge through committing to a perpetual space of transition or mutation, moving 'from one language to another, from one theme to another, from one city to another, from one gender to another – transitions are your home' (Despentes in Preciado 2020: 25). The artists in this chapter re-imagine a landscape, where women can co-exist, work with and support one another: categories, in this case, 'are the map imposed by authority, not the territory of life', Preciado contests (37). His transition is not only one of gender, but also one of place, and language. He finds inspiration in a dream-like world, where we can move from place to place and even conceptualize our own planet, space, or language: 'It's not a matter of thinking that life is a dream, but rather realising that dreams are also a form of life' (37). He dreams of renting an apartment on each planet and moving between them frequently. 'But I'd get rid of the Uranus apartment, it's much too far away' (30–32). His desire is to move from category to category, and never quite settle anywhere. Because living in transition, or at crossroads, allows for a 'radical multiplicity of life and the desire to change the names of all things' (39). Because 'intersection is the only place that exists. There are no opposite shores. We are always at the crossing of paths' (49). From this crossing, it is that Preciado speaks. From this crossing, between the *Incredible Bleeding Woman*, the *Showwomen*, Lilith the Demon, the Tattooed Woman, Dolly Blue, or the Whore of Babylon, it is that Carnesky speaks too. From the intersection of a life's work that never ceases. From this crossing, which is 'a place of uncertainty, of the unobvious, of strangeness' (42), it is that Carnesky speaks, a place not of weakness, but of power. And from this crossing, the artists in this chapter show us a new landscape, where subjectivity 'cannot be reduced to a single identity, a single language, a single culture or a single name' (49). Subjectivity, instead, is plural, fluid, ever-changing, and weird.

Carnesky's creative experimentation has led to this place, this world, this crossing, where the exploitative figure of the showman, who takes advantage and capitalizes on difference, does not have a place. His power is exhausted amidst the multiplicity of new practices of being and imagining that emerge from the crossroads. Because the crossroads emphatically acknowledge the shape-shifting nature of who we are, the desire to oscillate between identities, imagine other ways of living, and exist beyond fixity. In this world, women do not have to give into a singular role, or way of being. They escape from oppressive regimes of sameness; in this world, not having the answer and oscillating between places, human-animal, artist-non-artist, creates a different kind of belonging. Carnesky embodies Preciado's strive against categories in the multitude of communities she invents: 'They say man–woman, Black–White, human–animal, homosexual–heterosexual, Israel–Palestine. We say you know very well that your truth-production apparatus has stopped working. How many Galilees will we need this time to re-learn how to name things ourselves?' (52). Carnesky does just that; while embracing some of these categories, she transcends beyond them.

As the weird refers to something with indistinct borders that remain undefinable, it is hard to locate it in certain attributes, qualities, or contexts. In other words, what may *seem* weird for some may not be for others. Certain practices, behaviours, or modes of being and performing seem strange or weird within the specific context of the neoliberal patriarchy. Because that context requires stability and fixity in order to continue to exist. Carnesky's practice transcends binaries and oscillates between categories, inhabiting a space of slippage, ambiguity, and plurality. This plurality is evident in the multiple stories narrated by Carnesky's theatre practice. The collective 'I' is narrated through stories around menstruation and reproductive struggle in *Dr Carnesky's Incredible Bleeding Woman* or stories of disappeared women between East and West and the haunted borders they had to transcend in *Carnesky's Ghost Train* (2004–14). The artists Carnesky brings together do not shy away from their individuality. Their weirdness has to do with an inability to define neatly who they are but also is read as such within the white, neoliberal patriarchal context. In this light, these artists can be seen as 'partially illegible in relation to the normative affects performed by normative citizen subjects', according to José Esteban Muñoz, embodying not an 'individualised affective particularity', but rather 'a collective mapping of self and other' (2006: 6). In entering the space of the weird, Carnesky is also entering a dialogue with other women artists: she experiments with her sexuality, like Tutti, invents new terms to define herself, like Lunch, transcends boundaries of genres and fuses them together, like Narcisister, and refuses to fit into patriarchal standards, like Acker. Weird women challenge fixed categories and open up the space to discuss art, sex, desire and identity. They mess up categories and inhabit a space that is imaginative, unfixed, and fluid. They propose strategies such as estrangement, disidentification, and disarticulation, which inherently require 'the loss of familiar habits of thought and representation' (Braidotti 2009: 527). No identity is permanent or fixed in the realms of weirdness. There are no statements to be uttered, only conversations to be had. Weirdness holds space for the conflict of always being in between, in the crossroads. It creates a feedback loop between identity, sexuality, and creative practice that is cultivated in a symbiotic way. It does not propose a hierarchical, finite epistemology, but a way of thinking that is messy, disruptive, found outside of dominant categories. A perpetual renewal, self-addressing, and self-fashioning is necessary here, a permission to shape-shift, transform, and be part of a plurality of being that may be perceived as wrong, a perturbation to the system, or that which does not belong. Belonging here takes place through unbelonging and our perceived wrongness becomes community. Through the premise of 'weird women', I envision another way to account for myself and others, inventing new structures to accommodate desire, nuanced identity, and subjectivity. Weirdness as a term is an expansive place that welcomes unease and discomfort, accommodates contradiction, and does not try to resolve it. Weirdness remains undefined, to an extent, and allows for adventure, discovery, and uncertainty; within this space, we can be weirdos who won't fit in, who won't give into the pushing and shoving and squeezing and knocking and ramming and bumming and elbowing. Weirdness distances itself from all these things; it proposes loosened, untethered, untightened, unadjusted, and untailored. Things for which we do not have to crook and bend and adjust but be in any shape or size, even when we mould, out of choice, and take the shape of an artichoke.

Bibliography

Acker, K. and Wark, M. (2015), *I'm Very into You: Correspondence, 1995–1996* (ed. and with an introduction by M. Viegener), South Pasadena, CA: Semiotext(e).

Bayley, B. H. (2000), 'The queer carnival: Gender transgressive images in contemporary queer performance and their relationship to carnival and the grotesque', Ph.D. thesis, Exeter: University of Exeter.

Boliver, R. (2021), Zoom Interview with Rocio Boliver, Interviewed by E. Kartsaki, 22 December.

Braidotti, R. (2009), 'Animals, anomalies, and inorganic others: De-oedipalizing the animal other', *PMLA*, 24:2, pp. 526–32.

Carnesky, M. (2002), *Jewess Tattooess*, Video documentation, Private Link.

Goddard, L. (1984), *Staging Black Feminisms Identity, Politics, Performance*, Basingstoke: Palgrave Macmillan.

Halberstam, J. (1995), *Skin Shows: Gothic Horror and the Technology of Monsters*, Durham, London: Duke University Press.

Halberstam, J. (2014), 'Wildness, death, loss', *Social Text*, 121, pp. 137–48.

Johnson, D. (2016), '"Personality crisis? Honey, I was born with one": Lydia Lunch interviewed', in G. Butt, K. Eshun, and M. Fisher, (eds), *Post Punk: Then and Now*, London: Repeater Books.

Johnson, D. (2018), *Unlimited Action: The Performance of Extremity in the 1970s*, Manchester: Manchester University Press.

Luckhurst, R. (2017), 'The Weird: A dis/orienta-tion', *Textual Practice*, 31:6, pp. 1041–61.

Max Prior. D. (2000), 'Le Freak – C'est Chic', *Total Theatre*, 12:2, available at http://totaltheatre.org.uk/archive/features/le-freak-c'est-chic. Accessed 31 January 2023.

Mock, R. (2020), 'Marisa Carnesky, showwoman', in M. Chatzichristodoulou, (ed.), *Live Art in the UK: Contemporary Performances of Precarity*, London: Methuen Drama, pp. 45–67.

Muñoz, J. E. (2006), 'Feeling brown, feeling down: Latina affect, the performativity of race, and the Depressive Position', *Signs*, 31:3, pp. 675–88.

Narcissister (2022), Phone Interview with Narcissister, interviewed by E. Kartsaki, 21 January.

Petridis, A. (2017), 'Cosey Fanni Tutti: "I don't like acceptance. It makes me think I've done something wrong"', *The Guardian*, available at https://www.theguardian.com/music/2017/mar/14/cosey-fanni-tutti-throbbing-gristle-coum-art-sex-music-hull-2017. Accessed 31 January 2023.

Preciado, P. (2020), *An Apartment on Uranus*, London: Fitzcarraldo Editions.

Roberts, E. (2020), 'Performance and Prostitution: *The Magazine Actions* of Cosey Fanni Tutti', in M. Chatzichristodoulou (ed.), *Live Art in the UK: Contemporary Performances of Precarity*, London: Methuen Drama, pp. 172–91.

Russo, M. (1994), *The Female Grotesque: Risk, Excess and Modernity*, New York and London: Routledge.

Styles, R. (2023), 'Incredible bleeding women I: Rhyannon Styles, Veronica Thompson, Livia Kojo Alour, Marisa Carnesky' in this volume.

Tutti, C. F. (2022), Email Correspondence with Eirini Kartsaki, 7 February.

Their Phantasmagorical Appearances

Tai Shani, Geneva Foster Gluck, and Marisa Carnesky

Marisa Carnesky: We could start by you both saying a bit about how we all know each other and what you do now.

Geneva Foster Gluck: I was in London doing my Master's at Central Saint Martins after doing street performance and circus work in the States. Tai and Paloma [Faith] brought me to a show of yours, Marisa. It was the first time I saw a solo circus-esque performance by a woman in a theatre! A few years ago, I returned to the States to do a Ph.D. in Theatre and Performance of the Americas. My work looks at the legacy of colonialism to consider performances of place and our climate crisis. I still work with circus and spectacle aesthetics, but now, more in context of Western tropes and colonial technologies. I also run a Creation Space in Tucson, Arizona.

Tai Shani: I met Marisa in an elevator on the way to a party. I already knew about *Jewess Tattooess*. I remember you saying, 'Oh, I am working on this project. It is going to tour the world and we are going to go everywhere, and I'd love you to be in it' [laughing]. The first time I performed was in at Home Gallery with you, Marisa, doing the Passover rites. I came from a different discipline, and I felt quite back footed. It was my first encounter being in a purely feminine space, and I really enjoyed that. It has really changed the way I think about what feels safe, what does not. I think some of my naivety made me conservative. I had certain preconceptions around sex work, which I have very different feelings towards now.

MC: You both made such a strong impression on me! I want to ask you both about your creative processes. I remember when I was coming up with *Dr Carnesky's Incredible Bleeding Woman* show, I was in Montana with my ex-husband in a natural hot spring. I had in my mind this image of the dress that would not stop bleeding, inspired by an image from the film *Possession* with Isabelle Adjani. The idea was a blue conservative-looking stage illusion dress that revealed bloody panels. I thought 'that is the show'; I had to do a version of that. You both work with extraordinarily strong images. Does an image lead to a period of research or does it emerge from it?

TS: For me, there is often a fragment of an image. It can be an egg falling out of a window, or something quite abstract. There is a process of transformation that happens through the research, during which the image becomes, somehow, metabolized into an atmosphere. If I am reading about things like ergot and dancing plagues, these become the starting points to think about a somatic imagining of what it would be like to be in a dancing plague and what the medieval imagination would be under psychedelics in a world that is governed by supernatural forces. It is a building of atmosphere.

GFG: I think there is something very sensorial about my process. I begin a project by being preoccupied by a topic, event, or a sense of tension between what I experience and the way that experience is framed by discourse, politics, social norms, and power systems. Images and objects are often core to the way I tell a story. In *Geometry of the West*, a Western show I did a few years ago, I began with the image of a horse pulling a translucent copper box through the desert. This image not only touched on elements of Western expansion and extraction, but also it became a way to tour the work, to collect stories from audiences, and to have a nomadic mini theatre hidden inside a box.

TS: I was talking yesterday, weirdly, about this kind of folk revival that took place around 2004, around the time we did the *Ghost Train*. People at the time did have the internet, but there was such a lack of consciousness around the context of singing traditional folk songs or contemporary folk. This was leading to levels of strange appropriation, but also a glorification of the idea of a simple, noble life on the prairie in America, which did not account for the mass genocidal project that was happening alongside it. These songs which were often versions of Scottish or Irish popular songs brought to the States, held a compelling romance for me that was completely devoid of political context and complexity. I did, for example, research songs where women had more agency in them, but was completely blind to the brutal colonial context of singing an English song on violently stolen land. Thinking back on that time, it was a weird moment of peak whiteness.

MC: Absolutely. As part of the research for *Showwomen*, I have been reading Edward Said's *Orientalism*. I have been thinking about the exotic in relation to the showgirl. I asked Fancy Chance and Livia Kojo Alour, who are women of colour, to reflect, in the show, on the reasons why they want to do sideshow skills or fakir skills. The constructed Orientalist idea of woman as other or exotic has been significant. So many of the women I know in the burlesque community, brown, black, or white women have to deal with the idea of being exotic. We were not talking about that in the 1990s or 2000s. We were not talking about the fact that we were all orientalizing, left, right, and centre. The fact that you are exploring that in your work, Geneva is really important. So, the second part of that question is this: does production, materials and technical realities change your vision? Are you able to create what was in your mind's eye accurately?

GFG: I will pick up on that, but I wanted first to say something about the earlier point. I think people *were* thinking about those topics. Re-enactments are a way to address stereotypes, confront racism, sexism, and systems of domination. These performances ask audiences to reconsider their participation in these systems, like, Coco Fusco and Guillermo Gómez-Peña's *The Couple in the Cage* from 1992–93. Circus, for me, was a way to make a living outside of many of the normative systems, and it was also a site to address social inequalities. At the same time, is the circus also a colonial enterprise? I think the answer to this depends on how this lineage of performance/livelihood is framed, and where its origin is preceded to be. In my early work *The Sugar Beast Circus Show*, I was dealing with topics of colonialism, the colonial imagination, and the reality of being a performing female animal, as I understood myself to be at that moment of my life. But I did not have the language to articulate it in the ways that I understand it now.

But going back to your question about resources, doing cabaret shows, getting hired by venues to do one-off nights, the *Ghost Train* on Brick Lane; these were the opportunities to make work. And they provided me with the resources of money and time to develop my practice, test out ideas, and gain practical experience; it was such a vibrant experience! In the States right now, similar structures of support are hard to come by.

TS: I think there is always a gap between what you imagine and what you come out with in the end. I yearn for this contained, serious, exquisite aesthetic, but it always ends up being quite excessive and campy. I have started painting in the last couple of years and I am getting better, but still, there is a huge gap between what I imagine in my head and what I am able to paint. I have been very fortunate to start making my living from selling work, and that changes how you make work. You become more mindful of longevity, details. Before, I would think that something looks fine, but now I know I cannot have a bowl of gaffer tape behind it, holding it in place. Because someone might buy that, and they want a condition report on it.

MC: I agree. I really want to deliver performances that appear visually as I have imagined them. I am less and less prepared to do club performances, because the lighting is usually really wrong. Next, I want to ask you both about rituals. How do you make an art space a ritual, and how do you make a ritual space art?

TS: For me, there are two main things, transformation and affect. Often, ritual is a rite of passage or an opening of a certain space that does not exist. There is an intensity to ritual; this is something shared with any live, collective experience. I have wanted this sense of complete suspension in the work and for something transformative to happen; through this process of being suspended, you are also suspended from your subjectivity and you are part of some collective ineffable consciousness, or some type of elsewhere.

GFG: Rituals change a space. And this is all I am striving for sometimes. For the last few years, I have been making handmade batteries. These are props in performance and talismans for greater energy-as-electricity awareness. Both the performance and the objects are very ritualistic, they draw on mesmerism and spiritualism to re-find a spiritual connection with electricity, which we take for granted as a utilitarian resource. It is almost ritual working backwards. I am trying to make electricity sacred again as an intervention into our climate crisis.

MC: That sounds amazing! I love the idea of sacred electricity! I tried to create a mass activist performance ritual with clown Lucy Hopkins that people could take part in on an Extinction Rebellion protest, but it did not quite work as I had hoped. I think work made for political protest contexts often needs a different approach to performance made for performance audiences.

TS: I do not think that being a visual artist is a very efficient or interesting way of being political. Within the context of the liberal art world, it feels that what you are allowed to say is ineffectual to a certain extent and what you are not allowed to say is so heavily policed that it becomes neutralized. The art world and its liberal institutions have a certain set of rules, while the art market has a different set of limitations and concerns. But art is not separate from society, it is also built on racism, misogyny, xenophobia, capitalism, things that I explicitly reject in my work but cannot be apart from. That inconsistency sometimes feels overwhelming to me. I talk about communism, but I am

Figure 46: Tai Shani, *Carnesky's Ghost Train*, Truman's Brewery, 2005. London. © Alastair Muir

not a political scientist, and I do not have a blueprint of how we can reach horizontal anarcho-communism from where we are now. What has made a difference for me has to do with keeping the work in this sphere: I have tried hard to keep the work as an affective experience and not allow it to be flattened by politics. I recognize the limitations of what it means to be an artist. I try to think about what I mean when I talk about revolutionary politics in a sphere that is so elitist. I have tried to use my visibility to talk about the politics that I am interested in, in a very direct way and not through the work. When I talk about trans inclusiveness or write about Palestine, these politics do not go through the work. I use my position as an artist that has access to the resources of communication to talk about those things. I can offer a coverlet to other people that do not feel that they want to talk about these things, or that put themselves at risk when talking about these things.

MC: I have experienced similar issues. In *Dr Carnesky's Incredible Bleeding Woman*, Rhyannon Styles performs as part of the show. There was a lot of criticism around the reasons why we have a trans woman in a menstrual show. Rhyannon was part of my company at the time and had been in the Blackpool *Ghost Train*, so, for us, it would have been really harsh and odd not to include her in the menstrual show. I was so glad she wanted to be in it and explore the taboo of menstrual identity from a trans perspective, which I think was very brave of her. When I was working on the *Ghost Train*, I was trying to make more of a community project with it, for it to have a social purpose. But I compromised my aesthetic because the social aspect of the work felt more important. When I look back at it, I see I should not have compromised my aesthetic. Then a new council came in and said that it had lost its vision. You cannot please everyone all the time. It still had my name on it, but it had changed so much that in a way it was no longer my show. It had become something else.

I want to turn to a different topic. I know we all have mixed heritage; we all have some Jewish heritage. I wonder if spectacle is connected to class in some way. My parents were Jewish immigrants from the East End who worked in the rag trade and in restaurants. When I was growing up, if we saw something arty or conceptual on TV, my dad would say, 'well, it is not entertainment, is it? It is loads of rubbish'. I wonder if that filtered down for us, even though you were both born into families with parents who were artists. Is there something that Jewish people relate to unconsciously in terms of the spectacle? Is there something working-class about the spectacular that

Figure 47: Geneva Foster Gluck, *The Magnetic Chamber*, video documentation, 2022. © Geneva Foster Gluck

perhaps conceptual middle-class artists of the 80s and 90s forgot and that you embody because of your heritage?

GFG: I relate to this question because my dad is Jewish. My parents were into living off the land, they were hippies, sustainable folks, but it did not work out. The struggle of how to make money is in each of our lives; my relationship with my body and my ability to dance, do a trick on a rope, ride a horse, ride an elephant, was what I had. I was physically confident and strong enough to do these things, which allowed me to travel Europe, tour India, be part of these otherworldly realities. This was not only fulfilling and the fantasy of being a young girl, but it was the thing I had; I had this body that could do things. I did not have a lot of other resources.

TS: In the last few years, I feel that there has been this strong right-wing pull around Jewish identity and Zionism, and an inability to show solidarity with Palestine or be critical of Israel. Being Jewish does not mean being a thug. You can be Jewish and be something else. A lot of historical politics that I am interested in, like anarchism, or non-violent groups in the 60s and 70s that were very much in solidarity with the Black Panthers, consisted of a lot of Jewish people. To me, there is something important about re-narrativizing Jewishness in the face of this right-wing hijacking of Jewish identity. I do not have a choice in the matter. I am Jewish, whether I like it or not. If there was ever a re-persecution of Jewishness, I would be persecuted, regardless of whether I identify with it or not. Ultimately the questions around identity are always most salient when they are about how the world sees you and not about how you see yourself. This is where the politics of identity play out, when you have no control over them or when they come into violent contact with other ideologies that are hostile to those subject positions. I identify with Emma Goldman more than Golda Meir. There are histories that I feel much more aligned with. I know a few, young trans queer Jewish people that are doing radical yeshiva. I do not participate at that level. But there is obviously a desire for the left or more radical contingent of diasporic Jewry to have an identity that is also public; that desire is being subsumed by reactionary awful politics at the moment.

MC: Thank you for saying that. I am going to go into the last question and perhaps we can reflect on what you both just said through this. The showman exploits difference. He is a con man. What I am proposing is that the showgirl graduates to adulthood. I know you called yourself a showgirl, Geneva, and a showgirl traditionally is in a line-up with other people. She relies on them; she is a part of a collective. The term 'Showwoman' does not currently exist in the theatrical language, other than to talk about women that own circuses and fairground rides. This is my urgent attempt to foreground the term in its political context and in contrast to the showman. So, I wanted to ask: what are the politics of the Showwoman? Does she break the chains?

GFG: As a showgirl, I have always considered myself more like a feral animal. If I am to progress to a Showwoman, then the animal's life is still there and becomes part of breaking down the divisions between things, in the way that your work, Marisa, does by generating so much opportunity for many artists. Tai, I see you doing that too, creating opportunity for folks to share their art in a context that has value and that is transformative.

MC: Can you just quickly tell us about why you went to India? Why did you ride elephants in India?

GFG: Because I could not turn it down. It was a social circus movement. The tigers had been regulated and restricted from the show and the folks who were doing circus in India, who were multigenerational traditional circus performers, had lost one of their big attractions. So, we, European girls, came over and did aerial and trained with the younger performers. It was both very sad and very beautiful; a real insight into colonial, class, and cast relationships. I hung out with elephants, and they played with my toes, and they lifted me up onto their heads. And it was truly magical. I would have never ridden elephants in a circus in the United States. But honouring the history of the elephant in India, and the human-animal relationships that have existed for so long, felt possible in that space. The politics of the circus in India was intense. I was not sure I was doing the right thing by being there, but I had genuine connections with folks who I did not speak the same language with; we trained together, and we worked hard together.

MC: Thank you so much. Tai, are you a Showwoman?

TS: I do not know how much I relate to the category of woman anymore. I do not feel like I am anything else, but I do not really feel very connected to women anymore. I am not transitioning and I am not non-binary. I just do not feel that it is a category that I am completely at peace with at the moment. I try to use non-gendered language in my work. I do not feel bad if someone calls me a woman. And I use she/her pronouns. But there is a lot to be said about femininity and I am more interested in the idea of femininity as a mode of being. In terms of Showwomen, I would first say showperson, perhaps. I think aging is interesting. I was very much responsive in my femininity as a younger person and felt simultaneously on the margins of value as well as a feminized subject within a patriarchal order. I feel a certain amount of liberation not being so much part of this libidinous economy anymore. It also makes me question whether there is something to salvage, particularly when a lot of things that I really used to enjoy, like, women-only spaces, are becoming also really exclusionary to transwomen. For example, my project was called 'City of Women' at first and then a lot of anti-trans people were like, 'yeah, City of Women!' And I thought, no, it is not for you. If you are anti-trans then it is not a city that you are allowed in. So, I changed it to a 'post-patriarchal city', because I am not sure how useful these categories are. I think that they are useful in terms of thinking about progression, tracking changes around perception of gender, like, what is the difference between a showman and a Showwoman.

Gender is a really interesting cog to think about. To me, a Showwoman is powerful, she is trustworthy. She is someone that is also about spectacle but has an inherent power that is not predicated on anything that is tricky or dishonest, a kind of authentic power. It is interesting to think about what happens to that role when it travels through that binary. I am not sure about Showwoman for me, but I am a showperson for sure. And I was a showgirl in my own way and then I was a Showwoman. One of the reasons why I try to get away from gendered language is also to allow men in, in a weird way, because I think that ultimately, if we imagine a bearable future, men have to be part of that too. Everyone's participation is essential for a better world to be possible. I think that also includes people that are not social, or sociable, and people that do not want to be in communes. It is about being as open as possible. That openness also allows men back in, as well, men that are obviously ideologically aligned.

MC: And animals.

TS: And everyone, everything. Yes.

MC: Thank you so much for giving me your time, what a pleasure to have this dialogue with you both.

Penny Slot Somnambulist

Rachel Zerihan

Marisa Carnesky's performance *Penny Slot Somnambulist* (2000–03) was selected by Ron Athey and Vaginal Davis for their co-curation of the first UK Visions of Excess festival (2003), a through-the-night collection of Bataille-inspired performances where performance artists, burlesque dancers, porn stars, and internationally famed actors came together to perform various transgressive, surreal, and exquisite acts. The venue was Johnny Diamond's lap dancing club in Birmingham and the event was part of Fierce Festival's annual programme of live art. Besides Carnesky's spellbinding performance, several other works for solo spectators were on offer, including Kira O'Reilly's moving interaction *My Mother*, Jiva Parthipan's provocative *LICK*, and Nicole Blackman's sensual *The Courtesan Tales*; in retrospect, this fulsome collection of constructed encounters for one person at a time feature in what might be termed the 'golden age' of one-to-one performance in the United Kingdom. *Penny Slot Somnambulist* is an intriguing but lesser-known performance in Carnesky's eclectic oeuvre; aligned with Carnesky's familiar fascination for reworking traditional fairground features it showcases her work's carnivalesque *joie de vivre* whilst evoking a dark rigour that plays across erotic and economic tropes. This short piece of writing draws on French conceptual artist ORLAN's 1977 piece *Le Baiser de L'Artiste* (*The Kiss of the Artist*), to reflect on both women's manipulation of their bodies into sites of sensual transaction and feminist transgression.

The richly theatrical scene that greeted participants to Carnesky's *Penny Slot Somnambulist* was vibrant, alluring, and mystifying. A glass screen set at the end of the small booth separated solo spectator from Carnesky's visual feast. As Carnesky gazed into the multiple mirrors to see her onlooker's reflection, we surveyed her exquisitely painted back. The screen between us had a device installed in which we could insert a coin, if we chose, in exchange for our fortune being told.

Figure 48: Marisa Carnesky, *Penny Slot Somnambulist*, Visions of Excess, co-curated by Ron Athey and Vaginal Davis, 2003. Birmingham. © Roger Bamber / topfoto

In her twenty-first-century construction of *Penny Slot Somnambulist*, Carnesky anchors her fascination for the traditions of the fairground by deliciously skewing the nineteenth- and early twentieth-century practice of touring life-size waxworks of beautiful young women. These figures would be adorned in satin, draped on silk couches, and caged in glass cases then displayed at fairground routes across Europe; Pierre Spitzner's *Grand Musée Anatomique et Ethnologique*, which ran for 90 years, is a well-known example. Carnesky's millennial *Penny Slot Somnambulist*, however, is not silent, conventionally beauteous or the passive recipient of the crowd's gaze.

Deriving from the late eighteenth century, a 'somnambulist' was a sleepwalker or person under hypnosis, also a common figure in fairground attractions. Carnesky's pose in *Penny Slot Somnambulist* combines a contemporary reimagining of the waxwork women and personification of the somnambulist role to pose the question of whether we would pay real money for a premonition from someone in their deepest sleep. The carnivalesque framing of Carnesky's playful invitation both exacerbates the financial transaction that precipitates the exchange whilst the penny slot pittance she asks for lacerates its potential for producing serious predictions for contemplation. In appropriating the part of the *Penny Slot Somnambulist*, Carnesky is resurrecting the fairground's sleeping beauties, letting them speak from their slumber to tell the fortunes of their curious voyeurs; Carnesky's trance-like state is a feminist critique and unruly act.

Carnesky's interactive invitation that straddles erotic and economic uncertainties could be said to have an intriguing antecedent in ORLAN's *Le Baiser de L'Artiste* (*The Kiss of the Artist*, 1977). In this seminal performance, ORLAN produced a sculpture consisting of two parts situated on a large pedestal; on one side a life-size black and white photo of the artist, draped with materials signifying some kind of Madonna figure, beside which onlookers could place a candle upon payment of five francs. Set beside this image of Saint ORLAN was another black and white life-size photograph of the artist, this time unclothed torso only, with an arrow pointing to the top of a transparent plastic gullet where participants could insert a coin. When the artist chose to, she would place herself behind this second board, activating the armoured sculpture's liveness, ready to receive payment from those choosing to pay five francs for the artist's French kiss. ORLAN's feminist force was twofold; she was critiquing the founding iconologies of women in art – the saint and the whore, whilst also taking aim at the art market by making a piece of work that was unmediated, a direct exchange between producer and consumer.

ORLAN's distillation of bodied transaction, sharp cultural critique and invitation for solo spectator interaction is sublimely echoed 25 years later in Carnesky's *Penny Slot Somnambulist*. Howard Caygill's note that *Le Baiser de L'Artiste* 'provides a veritable Mardis Gras of carnival inversions' is explicitly embodied in Carnesky's refracted account of a contemporary Showwoman (Caygill 2010: 81). Part crude feminist cyborg, Caygill's reading of ORLAN as 'fairground slot machine' is freakishly brought to life by Carnesky's penny slot. A contemporary incarnation richly informed by Carnesky's fascination for histories of the fairground and imbued with the artist's corporeal vision, *Penny Slot Somnambulist* is emblematic of Carnesky's commitment to showcasing colourful visual language that embraces figurative over literal representation, ambiguity over clear-cut meaning. ORLAN adopts an armoured sculpture, Carnesky a painted body, yet both women use their bodies as vessels for the performer-spectator transaction. Within constructed artifices, both artists offer their personal services, to one person at a time, for real money. Both artists employ play to transgress; unlike the penetration of ORLAN's anti-art market French kisses, Carnesky draws on fairground traditions to refract the interface between performer and spectator and embrace the carnivalesque tradition of skewing clear-sightedness and valorizing voyeurism. *Penny Slot Somnambulist* is an intimate, almost unassuming artwork but one that binds the histories of fairground and performance art into a gloriously oblique invitation to interact with an exquisitely surreal phantom force.

Bibliography

Caygill, H. (2010), 'Carnival in ORLAN' in S. Donger, S. Shepherd, and ORLAN (eds), *ORLAN: A Hybrid Body of Artworks*, London and New York: Routledge, pp. 74–84.

Shape Changing: The Metamorphosis of a Showwoman

Vanessa Toulmin

As a researcher, I specialize in the history of 'illegitimate' entertainment: working-class recreation – of the circus, showground, sideshow, and a myriad of off-the-wall Victorian entertainment genres. At the time I started, illegitimate entertainment was largely marginalized by the majority of academic studies of entertainment history. So, my worthy research aim was to recover and re-evaluate these overlooked forms, as well as celebrate a history that underpins many of contemporary performance genres and practices.

At the start of the millennium, an enticing invitation to an academic conference arrived; its title was 'Carnivalesque', and its topic 'Carnivals, Freaks and the Grotesque' (Max Prior 2000) – and as it was part of the Brighton Fringe – and I would be among academic soulmates, I accepted. I was accompanied on the journey by my colleague Dr Malcolm Jones from the University of Sheffield, known affectionately to us as the flying willy man for his superlative knowledge of medieval pilgrim badges. Not the pious religious ones from today's holy sites but ones from a darker past revealing a different side of Catholic devotion and I urge you to look up more. But I digress. The conference was fascinating, the talks illuminating and then we were taken into the shows and exhibitions from the gallery; and there she was – the beautiful cork-screwed hair-adorned installation – a living, breathing penny slot machine somnambulist, adorned with magnificent tattoos. This was my first meeting with the artist, performer, and producer Marisa Carnesky, and the muse who would shape my academic life through alchemic forces of transmutation. Little did I know that the artist I first encountered at the Hayward Gallery would be as multi-faced as the nine Greek Goddesses and frankly as terrifying and challenging. At the start of the new millennium, I found my guide, a future companion, and a sister, with whom I journeyed through a maelstrom of magnificent ideas and discoveries from that moment onwards.

All roads to enlightenment start somewhere and my journey to the dark tower started on the world of the fairground. My eco-system was that of the travelling showpeople, born into a family of five generations populated by aunties who danced on the Moulin Rouge and rode the Wall of Death, a grandmother and mother who ran fairgrounds and an extended family across the North of England. It was not until my mid-20s that I fully embraced my heritage and returned to university to record and celebrate it. By the year 2000, I was in possession of a doctorate and a job as Head of the National Fairground and Circus Archive. Even though I was from that culture and I believed I was celebrating its wide and diverse impact, it was only through meeting and working with Marisa that its true performative significance and potential was fully realized.

I could share the many KPIs that we have achieved, the thousands of people who came to our events, the litany of projects we worked on together, but that can be easily googled. Instead, I wish to present an epic poem for the warrior muse who personified the living history of my subject. It starts with the *Ghost Train*, Carnesky's impossibly beautiful, haunting exhibition, an illegitimate theatre with aspects of her heritage and mine, which shaped the first five years of our relationship. It continues with a trip to London to see the spectacle, its extravagantly designed showfront based on the Victorian Ghost showfronts, from images in the Archive. At this point, the relationship was clearly defined: Marisa was the artist, I was the academic; I imparted my scholarly expertise, Marisa transformed it into artistic excellence. In Blackpool this changed, the boundaries blurred, when in 2007 I was awarded one of the first AHRC Knowledge Transfer Awards. The project 'Admission all Classes' was my attempt to celebrate Blackpool's working-class history and to make that history part of Blackpool Council's heritage strategy with Marisa as my guide. Marisa challenged me to become a producer for the project which through live performance could tell the tale so much better. My inaugural lecture as a professor went one step further and became 'Professor Vanessa's Performing Wonders', a live show of film, performance, and music which scandalized and educated in turn (2007). A year later Marisa was awarded an AHRC Creative and Performing Arts Fellowship to study, learn, write, and research, including archival research from the National Fairground Archive, exploring ghost trains, tattooed ladies, magic, burlesque and waxworks, culminating in the exhibition *Memoirs of a Showwoman* (2011). For the next decade, we explored the concept of a Showwoman, how she was defined, by birthright or profession, or through her performance, or through all of these things. Lives were uncovered, archives collected, and new theories imagined.

Over the years, our paths have diverged or became less travelled, but we never lost our yellow brick road – for whoever forgets one's first true love. Marisa's artistic and academic journey is her own making and the shows created, produced, and birthed over that period have been, to quote a nineteenth-century reviewer – as graceful as they are disgraceful. I may have imparted the term Showwoman to Marisa, but it is Dr Carnesky who has used her amazing academic expertise and production genius to bring this together. From Marisa, I learnt how to be a producer, shape ideas and concepts into the reality of live theatrical production, use my academic expertise to shape, and challenge society's preconceptions. From Marisa, I learnt that true knowledge exchange is when the partnership is seamless, integrated, and constantly flowing both ways (Toulmin 2014).

Finally, Marisa was and always will be to me the living breathing personification of all my research activities. Transforming across genres – Maria from Metropolis, the Female Fakir from France, the Lady Clown from Brighton, the Circassian Beauty from the streets of New York, and the doll in a music box from Chitty Chitty Bang Bang – Marisa is truly the archetypal Showwoman. Together we unearthed old stories from which new and beautiful shapes emerged and the archetypal female performance muse, the Showwoman, was once again incarnate.

Bibliography

Carnesky, M. (2011), 'From myths to magic: Memoirs of a showwoman', available at https://www.sheffield.ac.uk/news/nr/1840-showwoman-marisa-carnesky-nfa-1.174178. Accessed 31 January 2023.

Max Prior D. (2000), 'Le Freak – C'est Chic', *Total Theatre*, 12:2, available at http://totaltheatre.org.uk/archive/features/le-freak-c'est-chic. Accessed 31 January 2023.

Toulmin, V. (2014), 'Working class entertainment: Economic and cultural impact on Blackpool', Research Excellence Framework Impact Case Study, available at https://impact.ref.ac.uk/casestudies/CaseStudy.aspx?Id=12213. Accessed 31 January 2023.

Jewess Tattooess

Marisa Carnesky Company

Reino Unido

Madrid
Teatro Pradillo
28, 29 y 30 de enero
20

Marisa Carnesky pertenece a una nueva generación de artistas cuyo trabajo de creación se basa en redefinir los límites de la performance. En sus obras crea un universo extravagante, grotesco y decadente, y recupera para la escena el ambiente melodramático de cabarets y clubs.

En **Jewess Tattooess** Marisa Carnesky mezcla el primitivo melodrama del Teatro Judío con un espacio de actuaciones de feria. La autora crea una performance con connotaciones rituales, donde la nostalgia por el viejo mundo se enmaraña con la ruptura de tabúes fuertemente enraizados en la tradición de una cultura,

Ficha artística y técnica
Compañía: Marisa Carnesky
Concepto, creación e interpretación: Marisa Carnesky
Sonido: Dave Knight, Catherine Gifford, James Johnson
Film: Alison Murray
Vestuario: Nicola Bowery
Tatuajes: Alex Binnie
Fotografía: Manuel Vason y Marcus Ahmad

Friday 21 & Saturday 22 July

DOUBLE BILL

Marisa Carr

Tiger Lady is an exuberant depiction of rude B
entertainers who have challenged ideas of sex
whose subversive upfront work has coloured C
Jewish background, culture and performance
Edwardian music halls, the growth of burlesqu
women of the punk era intertwine with the m
provocative, meticulously researched combina
voicework, live music and elaborate costumes

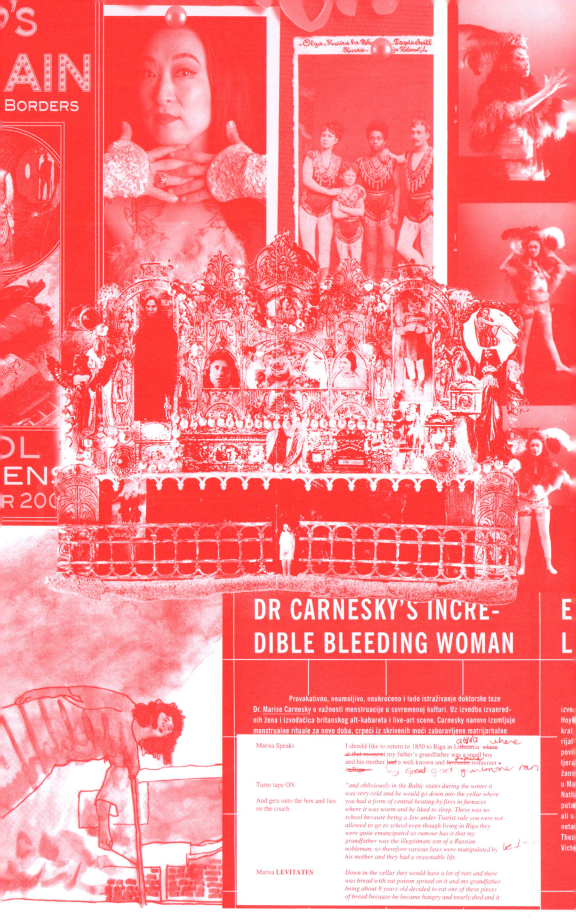

DR CARNESKY'S INCREDIBLE BLEEDING WOMAN

Provokativno, neumoljivo, neukroćeno i ludo istraživanje doktorske teze Dr. Marise Carnesky o važnosti menstruacije u suvremenoj kulturi. Uz izvedbu izvanrednih žena i izvođačica britanskog alt-kabareta i live-art scene, Carnesky nanovo izumljuje menstrualne rituale za novo doba, crpeći iz skrivenih moći zaboravljene matrijarhalne

Marisa Speaks	I should like to return to 1850 to Riga in Lithuania. ~~where at that moment~~ my father's grandfather was a small boy and his mother ~~had~~ a well known and ~~favourite~~ restaurant ~~in Riga~~ — *my great great grandmother ran*
Turns tape ON	"and obliviously in the Baltic states during the winter it was very cold and he would go down into the cellar where you had a form of central heating by fires in furnaces where it was warm and he liked to sleep. There was no school because being a Jew under Tsarist rule you were not allowed to go to school even though living in Riga they were quite emancipated as rumour has it that my grandfather was the illegitimate son of a Russian nobleman, so therefore various laws were manipulated by his mother and they had a reasonable life.
And gets onto the box and lies on the couch	
Marisa LEVITATES	Down in the cellar they would have a lot of rats and there was bread with rat poison spread on it and my grandfather being about 8 years old decided to eat one of these pieces of bread because he became hungry and nearly died and it

Figure 49: Marisa Carnesky, *Carnesky's Tarot Drome* studio shot, 2011. London. © Manuel Vason

Figures 50 & 51: Marisa Carnesky, *Carnesky's Tarot Drome*, Cirque Jules Vernes, English Eccentricity Festival, Amiens, 2012. France. © Sarah Ainslie

Figure 52: Marisa Carnesky as Wheel of Fortune in the set of *Carnesky's Ghost Train*, Spill Tarot, 2009.
© Manuel Vason

Figures 53 & 54: H Plewis (top), Nao Nagai, and Priya Mistry (above), *Dr Carnesky's Incredible Bleeding Woman*, Soho Theatre, 2016. London. © Claire Lawrie

Figure 55 & 56: Rhyannon Styles and Fancy Chance (top) and Marisa Carnesky (above), *Dr Carnesky's Incredible Bleeding Woman*, Soho Theatre, 2016. London. © Claire Lawrie

Figure 57 (overleaf): Marisa Carnesky, *Dr Carnesky's Incredible Bleeding Woman*, Menstruant ritual creation workshop, featuring Amy Ridler, Nao Nagai, Rhyannon Styles, Fancy Chance, Livia Kojo Alour, H Plewis, and Marisa Carnesky, 2016. Southend. © Sarah Ainslie

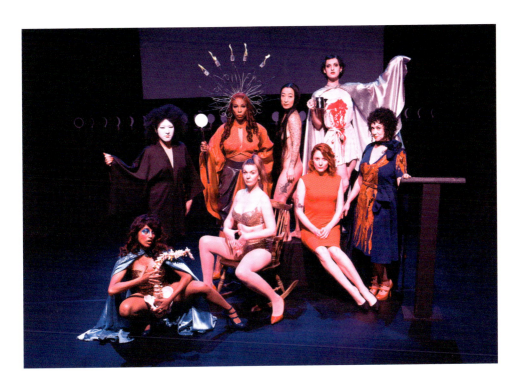

Figure 58 (left): Fancy Chance, *Dr Carnesky's Incredible Bleeding Woman*, hair hanging with the menstruant coven, Soho Theatre, 2016. London. © Claire Lawrie

Figures 59 & 60: Molly Beth Morossa, Rhyannon Styles, Fancy Chance, H Plewis, Priya Mistry, Livia Kojo Alour, Marisa Carnesky, Nao Nagai (top) and H Plewis and Rhyannon Styles (above), *Dr Carnesky's Incredible Bleeding Woman*, Soho Theatre, 2016. London. © Claire Lawrie

Figure 61: Marisa Carnesky, *Dr Carnesky's Incredible Bleeding Woman*, menstrual protest, 2018. Brighton. © Rosie Powell

Figure 62: Marisa Carnesky, *Blood Bath Ritual*, disused morgue, 2016. London. © Claire Lawrie

Figures 63 & 64: Marisa Carnesky and Lucifire (top) and Livia Kojo Alour and Fancy Chance (above), *Showwomen*, Attenborough Centre for the Creative Arts, 2022. Brighton. © Sarah Hickson
Figure 65 (right): Marisa Carnesky, Livia Kojo Alour, Lucifire, and Fancy Chance, *Showwomen*, The Spire, 2021. Brighton. © Manuel Vason

Figure 66: Livia Kojo Alour, *Showwomen*, Attenborough Centre for the Creative Arts. 2022. Brighton. © Sarah Hickson

Figure 67: Fancy Chance, *Showwomen*, Attenborough Centre for the Creative Arts, 2022. Brighton.
© Sarah Hickson

Figure 68 (left): Livia Kojo Alour and Fancy Chance, *Showwomen*,
Attenborough Centre for the Creative Arts, 2022. Brighton. © Sarah Hickson
Figure 69 (top): Livia Kojo Alour, Fancy Chance, Lucifire, and Marisa Carnesky,
Showwomen, Film shoot, 2022. © Rosie Powell
Figure 70 (above): Lucifire, *Showwomen*, Attenborough Centre
for the Creative Arts, 2022. Brighton. © Sarah Hickson

Figure 71: Marawa, Hilton Hotel, Melbourne, 2023. © Jo Duck

Figure 72: Empress Stah, *Stargasm: Light in Places*. © Clive Holland
Figure 73: Eirini Kartsaki, *Protrusions*, 2021. Athens. © Spyros Paloukis

Figure 74: Fancy Chance, *Carnesky's Showwomxn Sideshow Spectacular*, Smithfield Market, 2023. London. © Holly Revell

Figure 75: Claire Heafford and Alex Windsor, *Carnesky's Showwomxn Sideshow Spectacular*, Smithfield Market, 2023. London. © Ruth Bayer

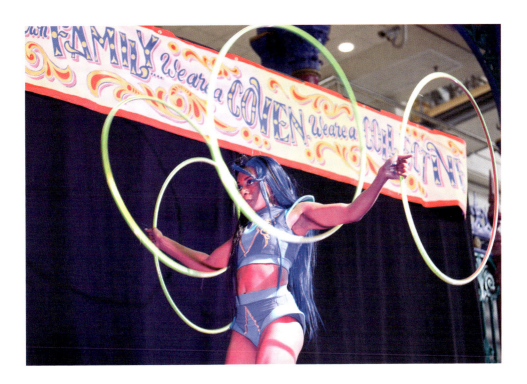

Figure 76: Symoné, *Carnesky's Showwomxn Sideshow Spectacular*, Smithfield Market, 2023. London. © Holly Revell

Figure 77: Missy Macabre and Jackie Le, *Carnesky's Showwomxn Sideshow Spectacular*, Smithfield Market, 2023. London. © Ruth Bayer

Figure 78: Montage by Lee Baxter of *Carnesky's Showwomxn Sideshow Spectacular*, 2023 & 2024. Featuring (from left to right): Tallulah Haddon, Livia Kojo Alour, Katherine Arnold, Claire Heafford, Mysti Vine, Jay Yule, Marisa Carnesky, Meg Hodgson, Lucifire, Fancy Chance, Jackie Le, Molly Beth Morossa, Vicky Butterfly, Kaajel, Livia Kojo Alour. Images © Ruth Bayer and Holly Revell

Figure 79: Montage by Lee Baxter of *Carnesky's Showwomxn Sideshow Spectacular*, 2023 & 2024. Featuring (from left to right): Missy Macabre, Suri Sumatra, Ella The Great, Rachel Acham Seagroatt, Claire Heafford, Rhyanon Styles, H Plewis, Kaajel, Vicky Butterfly, Molly Beth Morossa, Lalla Morte, Chi Chi Revolver, Laura London, Tasha Rushbrooke, Hannah Finn. Images © Ruth Bayer and Holly Revell

Figure 80: Marisa Carnesky, *Dr Carnesky's Incredible Bleeding Woman*, studio shot, 2016. London. © Sarah Ainslie

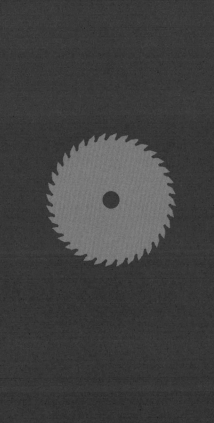

Magic Blood, Mysterious Blades, and Women Who Show

Incredible Bleeding Women I

Rhyannon Styles, Livia Kojo Alour,
Veronica Thompson, and Marisa Carnesky

Marisa Carnesky: Could you all say who you are, what is your practice, and how you got involved in my work and particularly *Dr Carnesky's Incredible Bleeding Woman*?

Rhyannon Styles: I worked with you, Marisa, doing Whoopee shows in the early 1990s in East London. I was then invited to be a part of *Carnesky's Ghost Train* in Blackpool. At that point, I was not yet identifying as a transgender woman, so the fact that you invited me into the *Ghost Train* was a unique experience. Then I worked in *Tarot Drome* and *Bleeding Woman*. I am a writer, performer, and gong practitioner. I offer and facilitate gong meditation in and around Berlin. I have published two books and I am also creating a new performance, which hopefully will premiere next year in Berlin.

Livia Kojo Alour: I used to be known under MisSa and I was a cabaret performer when I started my career in London. In 2014, I walked into one of Marisa's workshops and then I was invited to come and be part of the Carnesky company for the *Bleeding Woman* show; we became great friends, moved in together, and lived happily ever after. We created and toured *Bleeding Woman* together. Now, I am on the *Showwomen* show. I am a vocalist, writer, theatre maker, poet and retired sword swallower, cabaret performer, but circus performer only until the end of this year and then I am out.

Veronica Thompson: I am a performer and creator and perform as Fancy Chance. I sing and do odd dancing when I am asked to. I am a hair hanger and act a bit when the performance needs it. I have been performing cabaret, circus, and neo-burlesque for a long time and I have done a solo show. We met performing in the Whoopee Club in London in the noughties. Then you invited me to be in the *Ghost Train*, and then *Incredible Bleeding Woman* and now *Showwomen*.

MC: Thank you, all. I want, first, to ask Rhyannon, about *Bleeding Woman*, whether the show felt political or controversial for you. And was it different to other shows?

RS: I think the pivotal point for me was when we decided that I should appear from the sawing in half box at the end, completely naked and covered in blood. That was important because it really gave space to a trans woman to talk about menstruation. Had we continued covering my body with the costume, the importance of that would have been missed. That was the changing perspective for me in the show. Obviously, I will never know what it is like to menstruate, but that is not the point. The inclusion of a trans identity in the show was important because we are opening the narrative so that different forms of womanhood and femininity are visible. Also, we are able to look at our differences and similarities in a way that just gives more richness to the topic. I don't think this topic has been explored before in performance with an all-female group.

MC: And it was such a powerful moment in the show. I wondered if you could tell us about the ritual that you made. When you study the cultural representation of menstruation in different cultures across the world, there are lots of themes of renewal and rebirth, and you worked with some of these themes.

RS: At that point, I was going through a challenging period in terms of work outside of performance. I had taken on a different job, and I spontaneously quit. The ritual was a very cathartic experience to rid myself of a lot of that stress that I had been holding on to.

MC: Amazing. Thank you. I am going over to you, Veronica. I want to reflect on the *Bleeding Woman* in particular, in which you had a very iconic performance, both in the ritual in Southend, and then in the show. You created images of rebirth, renewal, and menstruation. Did the process feel political?

VT: This felt like part of a conversation that I was having already, which perhaps had not yet found a space to exist. I do not have a firmly grounded heritage. I was adopted by a white family and raised in a white community as someone perceived as alien. Creating my own ritual felt like creating my own culture and history. *Bleeding Woman* finally gave a language and a vision to something that I already wanted to do. Also, I love being naked in the show, it is so fun. Finally, people are like, yes, let's all get fucking naked. I felt that the show addressed its subject with trans inclusion, Black inclusion, East Asian, and Jewish inclusion and in that way, it was ahead of its time.

MC: Thank you, Veronica. Yes, it was inclusive in a non-contrived way, because we were a company that was working together in the real world and genuinely intersecting before we did this collaboration. Talking to everybody about it and bringing it back to life reminds me of how we all brought a lot of ourselves to that project. I have started dipping my toe into experimental documentary filmmaking, so, we may have to revisit the *Bleeding Woman*. Livia, tell us about your experience in the show.

LKA: When I came out of the *Bleeding Woman* show, I had not yet realized how radical it is to be a woman of colour and to make art and be successful and be seen as a woman of colour, or as a trans woman, speaking up and putting oneself out there in the artistic framework. I was very interested in work that was controversial. There is such a huge stigma around menstruation and everything that belongs to the female body. There is so much censorship around female bodies or female-identifying bodies. I am German and I come from a country, where we actually talk about menstruation and periods more freely than in the United Kingdom. So, it was very interesting for me to find out what a huge taboo the subject is in the United Kingdom. I thought it was provocative, interesting, and important from an activist point of view.

I had an accident sword swallowing and I cut my oesophagus in a couple of places; after recovery, I was interested in finding out why exactly the accident happened. The day it happened, it was the day I came onto my period, the moment I actually walked on stage. I did some research and I found out that, although we always think that it is only the womb that swells up, the truth is that the whole body can swell up too, and especially the oesophagus. With some women this happens less, with some more. Some women swell all over, like me, and internally too. So, I created *The Female Sword Swallower's Moon Calendar*. Since there are so few female sword swallowers in the world, I thought it would be quite helpful to have one. I commissioned a piece of 28 swords that resemble a new moon calendar. The longest sword is safer to swallow on the full moon. During hunter-gatherer times, we were a bit more connected to the moon. We used to ovulate around the full moon and have our periods on the new moon. On the full moon, the men used to go out to get the deer, kill the beef, and throw a big party. And on the new moon, when you went into your coven with all your female and female-identifying friends, you did not swallow a sword. Therefore, on the

Figure 81: Fancy Chance. © Jo Duck

new moon, there was no blade. *The Moon Calendar* has been exhibited in the Museum of Contemporary Art in Bordeaux, and is currently hanging in Dublin, at the Project Art Centre in an exhibition. The artist Ruth Ewan chose the swords, and she keeps touring with them. The swords have got a life of their own now.

MC: Thank you for that. I am going to ask you all a little bit about the word Showwoman. I chose the term in direct opposition to the term showman, which is very much associated with a kind of exploitative side of showbusiness in terms of P. T. Barnum and exhibiting people of difference. Are *we* Showwomen? Tai Shani, for instance, said, she is more of a showperson and is unsure about the word 'woman'. 'Woman' contains the word 'womb', in a sense, too, which can be limiting. Yet, we all have identified at some stage in our lives, as showgirls. I am not a showgirl anymore, I am a Showwoman. Obviously, there are deep issues with the word 'woman'. I am certainly a woman with a womb that did not bring forth any offspring. So, I am not really a womb-an. I am more of a show femme, than I am a Showwoman in a way. But what do you think about the word, if we were to use it as a counterpoint to the word showman?

RS: My journey to becoming a woman is unique in its own way, as I come from a trans history. In a way, I missed out on my girlhood, because I transitioned when I was 30. Coincidentally, my first book was called *The New Girl*. Had that been called *The New Woman*, it would have been an interesting choice of words. I also wanted to write a third book called *Welcome to Womanhood*, because, where I am now, being a 40-year-old trans person, I have a different perspective on womanhood, than maybe a cis-identifying woman; in some ways, I wish to hang on to the term showgirl, because I never was a showgirl. I wanted to be a showgirl in a Vegas show, high-leg kicking with a huge feather headdress. However, I feel that maybe the term 'woman' is more appropriate for me right now. But there is something about the ring of showgirl that I still love and cherish.

MC: In the new show, I say that I was once a showgirl; we were all in love with showbusiness as well as the glamour of the showgirl. But for me, you become a Showwoman when you come into your power and start owning the show; when you become the creator, doing your own steps, not the steps of the choreographer, as it

Figure 82: Rhyannon Styles, *Dr Carnesky's Incredible Bleeding Woman*, Soho Theatre, 2016. London. © Claire Lawrie

were. As a choreographer, but also a gong practitioner, Rhyannon, would you say you are a Showwoman?

RS: I mean, yes. I did not know that definition, because I have not seen your new work, but that very much rings true, in the sense of taking ownership for the whole production and creating the different elements rather than being one participant in a bigger whole. Then yes, I would agree with you, I am doing that and there are various elements in my life that are evidence of that, for sure.

MC: Fabulous. Thank you so much. Veronica, are you a Showwoman?

VT: I am certainly a Showwoman. Even before this show, I was referring to myself as a Showwoman and a showperson. I am going to be two years away from 50. I became a Showwoman a while ago, as I got older. Our lives are constantly filled with shame about being female and aging. I do not know when I started incorporating Showwoman into my language. But it was in reaction to ageism and whatever I had internalized in terms of that. Within our society, we are ageist, sexist, and racist. It is our job to be careful with our words and our conversations about these things. As an entertainer and a performer, claiming Showwoman as my identity is really important. You are writing a book about it, but for me, it is a conversation. I have been thinking about language a lot, and I do not like it when people refer to women as ladies (unless it is ironic) because there is a class element in it that is just fucking ugly. The term 'Showwoman' takes away the overused habit of referring to every entertaining woman on stage as 'Miss', which ensures continuing to keep females as small and as innocuous as possible.

MC: Wonderful, thank you. Livia, are you a Showwoman?

LKA: I used showgirl for a really long time, and I think it was always inappropriate because when I started performing full-time as a show business person, I was already way over 30. So, I do not think this word ever applied to me. However, what Veronica said about misogyny and ageism really rang true to me. This is the reason why I had such a problem calling myself a Showwoman for a long time. It was mainly internalized misogyny. I do not think I experience internalized ageism, as I find the

Figure 83: Livia Kojo Alour, *Dr Carnesky's Incredible Bleeding Woman*, Pleasance Theatre, 2017. Edinburgh. © Roderick Penn

process of aging really fascinating. But I had a problem with the term 'woman'. I am definitely a Showwoman. I will be a Showwoman till I die. I think your work, Marisa, in which we are collaborating with powerful women and female-identifying people has really helped me embrace being a Showwoman.

RS: A few weeks ago, I randomly bumped into Oozing Gloop in a club (I rarely go clubbing). And Oozing Gloop was like, 'oh that fucking Marisa, I have her to thank for everything'.

MC: I do not know if that is true. And I did not know Oozing felt that way, so that is good to hear.

LKA: There are a lot of people out there who feel that way. And I think we are part of that too. The many times you have picked me up when I was like, 'oh, fuck this shit'. If it was not for you telling me that I am a Showwoman, that I can do it ….

MC: I think that you do not always have the life you think you are going to have. But life finds you and you find your path. I have always been a radical and a punk rocker and a showgirl and I have been taking my clothes off since I was 18 years old and a nutcase. Why I thought I was going to end up having kids, I do not know [group laughing]. It turns out that I really love working with and encouraging performers and making shows with really interesting people. Thank you for all your lovely comments. But equally, I think that the shows work, because we have this extraordinary collective power. I want to end on this note: what is the reality of being a Showwoman and how do we cope? What is it really like to go from job to job, from show to show, and navigate the life of a Showwoman?

VT: I will say this. You really have to practice self-care and I think that is across the board for everybody. If you do not practice self-care when you are busy, that opens up the opportunity to do lots of destructive shit to yourself. In the same breath as you need to practice self-care, you also have to practice saying no.

RS: I would say that, if this is your path, it is hard to do anything else and, God, I have tried. But the show always keeps pulling me back, whether that is performing or writing. It is hard to rid yourself of the Showwoman because we are all in the same orbit of consciousness. And that manifests maybe materialistically, in the fact that we are all tattooed ladies or tattooed people. But, at the same time, we come from this similar aesthetic of DIY. We get up, we do it ourselves and we fucking put the show on. And if you are born with that, you cannot let go.

LKA: Both of those things are true. I am learning, I am unlearning. 'The show must go on' is our mantra isn't it. I am currently learning that the show sometimes has to stop. Sometimes the show has to stop because we have to take care of our mental health. I think this is the crucial lesson I have learned in the last two years. This year, I am really trying to enforce it. To make the show always go on, the show sometimes has to stop.

MC: Thank you, all you incredible bleeding women!

Showwomen Who Risk It All

Lucifire, Lalla Morte, Miss Behave, and Marisa Carnesky

Marisa Carnesky: I am going to start by asking you to briefly describe who you are and say something about your practice.

Lucifire: I am Lucifire and I love fire. I enjoy doing dangerous things in front of a lot of people. I like a lot of attention. Sometimes the most difficult things do not look as perilous as they are. You can do a highly dangerous thing that goes unappreciated and then you can do a simple trick that shocks. I trained as a dancer, but I have a very pragmatic, scientific mind. I like to dissect stunts and find out how to perform them relatively safely, and then try and make them look thrilling on stage.

Lalla Morte: I am Thai Knight. I am Lalla Morte on stage. I am a performer who loves doing dangerous things as an idiot person. I say I am an idiot because whatever seems crazy or fun, but mostly dangerous, I will try to do it, even though I have not been trained to. I will find my way, because I am a curious person and, as opposed to Luci, first I will try to find a way to do it, and safety will follow. I started in the night scene as a go-go dancer. I was also a professional make-up artist and worked once on a piece for the Opera Garnier. My now ex-husband used to be a ballet dancer in the company La La La Human Steps in Canada. We met, fell in love, got married, and I was following him on tour. That was around the time I came across your work, Marisa. And I totally fell in love with you and your world.

Miss Behave: I am Amy Saunders or Miss Behave. I never wanted to be a performer. One of the first performers I ever saw in my teens was Luci. She needed me to step in because Dawn [Johnson] got sick. So, I did. I got to be the good baby in a Torture Garden show with Tutu [Tedder] and Luci. I remember seeing you, Marisa, at the Raymond Revuebar doing Dolly Blue. I am an MTV baby, so I am not interested in art or performance at all. I have a complicated relationship with art; I am an entertainer, a salesman. How the room is run, how well things are executed, that is the art for me. I was a flyer and this is where I got my gift of gab. At the time, I was living in Camden and working in the West End. There was a weird bookshop called Compendium Books, where you could find all the Taschen and pin-up books. I found a book called *Memoirs of a Sword Swallower*, and I thought, I love sucking cock, I am very good at it. I reckon, I could do that quite well. I read the book and taught myself sword swallowing.

MC: We all have stories of ourselves as showgirls, but we do so many other things, we run the show, create the troupe, create our own material, manage ourselves and others; we are the businessperson and the artist and the performer. The figure of the showman is associated with controversial ideas around freak shows, ethnographic sideshows, and the idea of the other, the different, or the exotic. As Showwomen, we have a different kind of hierarchy. When we run a team, we work together. So, do we run the show differently than the showman? Are we less exploitative, more collaborative, and more creative?

MB: There is just no fucking way that I would get the treatment I get if I were a man. Whilst someone else is allowed to absolutely freak out because a light is a second late, if I do that, they will say that I have impossibly high standards, which is negative for a woman. Of course, I have impossibly high standards and I will never achieve them. But I have been very lucky to work in what I would call queer spaces or free spaces in Vegas.

L: I do not know if showmen are necessarily always seen as exploitative. There is perhaps a connection with the salesman that Amy was talking about. You can buy a second-hand car from someone who will offer a good deal, but second-hand car salesmen are often seen as exploitative and con men. This is not necessarily true. It is just that men have traditionally been in a position, where they have had the authority and the power to con somebody, while women had different cons traditionally. We have been exploited so often, that most women tend not to want to do that to other people. We can be more collaborative because we are used to having to band together, helping each other out, picking each other up, and bandaging each others' bruises.

LM: My view on this is quite different. In France, where I come from, women in cabaret were seen as goddesses. Today, some women running the show can be more aggressive and exploitative than some men. But this might be coming from decades of not being able to have a voice. As a Showwoman who puts herself and others on stage, I make sure that everyone is treated the way I want to be treated, with respect.

MC: I am very interested in the exotic and the lineage of the showman that exploited otherness and difference. What does it mean to be othered, the weirdo, the outsider, or the exotic? I imagine Lalla, you may have a different experience as a woman of colour within mainstream French society. Why are we drawn to representing ourselves as exotic?

LM: Being of Asian descent, I imagine I may be seen as exotic, but I never tried to push that or use that for my performance art. I actually started as the corpse in my career; that is where my name comes from. I was the dead girl. This is when I met Ane Angel and Paul-Ronney Angel. I invited them to be part of one of my shows. Then they invited me to perform in London when burlesque was starting. This is when I met you, Luci. I thought burlesque was really aesthetic and risqué and sometimes sexy and funny. Being of Asian descent never made me want to use my identity for my art. My body is the journal of all my experiences. My tattoos are really my medicine and serve as a protective layer. I respect my roots, even more today that I am a grown-up and since I have been a mother. I realize how important it is for my spiritual growth and understanding of my family, but I am glad it is not defining me. I have managed to blur the lines in terms of where I come from.

MC: Luci, are you exotic?

L: I have always been drawn to scary women. They were dangerous and exciting, and I wanted to emulate that. Even Diana Rigg, who was a good girl, was kind of tough. I grew up in the countryside, I had motorbikes, and I loved Catwoman. I was always drawn to anatomy and surgery and as a teenager, I worked for a vet. I moved to London after ditching my science career to study dance. I shaved off all my hair. It was the 1990s. I was a riot girl, I loved Tank Girl, I had no hair except for little red tufts, like horns, I wore bike boots, tiny shorts, a big leather trench coat, stomped around, and rode a motorbike. I did not want to be weak. But then it got to the point where I had done so much of the motorbikes, shaved head, stomping around, setting things on fire, angle grinding machinery, and blood that I wanted to push other boundaries. Then I grew to realize that the world is richer and more layered than that.

MC: You all perform thrilling acts, in which you physically take risks on stage. I have always been split between my love of art and entertainment and questioning whether a

Figure 84: Lucifire © Manolo Remiddi

lot of risky live art has a closer relationship to the thrill and fascination of sideshow and circus worlds than it does to fine art. Danger on stage seems to emerge from a working-class entertainment tradition. Luci, could you tell us about the thrill of danger?

L: Nothing is as exciting as the first time you try a dangerous thing, especially if you do not really know whether it is going to work or not. When I started doing dangerous stunts, there was nobody to teach me how to staple myself, or walk on broken glass. We invented our own methods, which is really dangerous, and I am not going to advise anybody to do that. I have a theory that the pain of an act on stage is inversely proportional to the number of people watching. People's attention is a great analgesic.

MB: I taught myself sword swallowing with a see-through shatterproof ruler that I had burned into a point. After I had an accident, my swords became shorter and thinner. I used to do a needle through the neck. I learned later that there is a nerve in your neck, which if you hit, you become paralyzed. I have been just lucky, I guess.

LM: I came to do dangerous or painful things later in my career. My signature act is coming out of the suitcase. For a lot of people, it looks dangerous, because most people are claustrophobic. I had a troupe with my ex-husband and wanted to make shows, in which we would announce no one. All the posters and flyers were drawings and images of us with our birth date and our death date; the latter was the date of the show. We were inviting the audience into one of the first immersive shows in Paris in 2006. All I wanted was to be in a suitcase and be dragged around by my ex-husband until we would end up in the bar.

MC: Is that related to your heritage? Is there a kind of immigrant story behind that?

LM: Perhaps unconsciously, the fact that my parents are immigrants has something to do with it. Or maybe it is because my ex-husband was traveling a lot on tour. He had this big suitcase that at one time me and my daughter were playing with. This is possibly how it started. But then it was also that it was fun to be in a suitcase. I have always been drawn to strange and macabre things, inspired by Grand Guignol theatre. We were calling our shows 'Cabaret Dangereux'. I was the corpse, dragged around in the suitcase. I am very petite, and I have the ability to put my body in the perfect position. It is about finding a way to get inside the suitcase with as many props as

Figure 85: Lalla Morte, *The Wild Rose*, Le Divan Japonais, 2019.
© Monsieur GAC (Gregory Augendre Cambon)

possible and then pop out of it, giving the impression that I am much bigger than I am; it is all about illusion. At the beginning of the specific show, Monsieur Loyal or Monsieur Poudre were giving cards to the audience with the phrase: 'Have you seen this man?' It was a drawing of my ex-husband with a suitcase. My ex-husband then arrived at the venue with said suitcase and me inside; at some point, you could see my arm coming out of the suitcase. It freaked people out and got their attention!

MC: Amy, what are you doing currently?

MB: I am currently living in Vegas. I have been here for five years. I had my gameshow on the strip for three of those years and it was a hustle from start to finish. That said, it was very well received and loved by locals and tourists alike. I am now running a showroom on a classic, iconic, part of downtown Vegas. Vegas is an interesting town and a paradox. On the one hand, I have the absolute dream, and on the other, the entertainment capital of the world is just populated by muggles, and I have never seen anything like it in my life. I have learned that I do not really want to be a boss. I want to be able to work with a small group of people and do damage. Ultimately, I am a maverick punk with little needs apart from self-autonomy and independence. But, in order to have autonomy, you need some power and money.

MC: Don't we all know it. Am I right that you are doing the Cheapshot? And are you also doing the *Miss Behave Gameshow* again?

MB: The bar is called Cheapshot. No, I am doing a variety show called *Miss Behave's Mavericks*, because I have learned (there you go, Showwomen), that however hideous it makes the name of the show, put your name in it; it is part of your security.

MC: Lalla, what are you doing now?

LM: After almost ten years involved in a circus in Paris, my 'contract' was not renewed by my exploitative boss (here we are!). This happened to me, but also to fellow female performers; the boss thought he needed young flesh and brain to mould and manipulate. We had our own identity and were too opinionated and strong minded. It was disappointing because of the way it was done, with no respect. But I learned a lot of tricks during that time. I am now involved in a show called *Les Quatre Femmes de Dieu*. We are four women doing risqué circus and sideshow acts. The four women are the representation of women in society: the whore, the saint, the witch, and the ingénue. It is a circus theatre play. We will be touring in the next couple of years, hopefully. I am lucky to be versatile enough and I can work with bands, theatre companies, and cabaret.

MC: Amazing. Can't wait to see it. Luci, what are you doing now?

L: I tried to leave all the danger behind when I unexpectedly fell pregnant with twins, and I thought, maybe it was not good to continue sticking needles in myself, putting fuel in my mouth, and hanging off things. I thought that it was probably time to lay down the danger and take up the saxophone instead. So, I left it all behind, but then I found myself unable to leave the circus. Except this time around, I have swapped late-night cabarets and nightclubs for theatre crowds. Right now, I am in Marisa Carnesky's *Showwomen*, and I am doing some dangerous things, including putting Marisa in danger. Consensually. I am also in Florentina Holzinger's *Tanz*, which is going to Kyoto next week and is coming to London in November [2022]. I am doing a hook suspension in that. There is a lovely moment in the show, when while I am hanging, there are four female dancers on pointe. They do not like me very much, because I stay up there for a long time and they are just like, oh my God, we get that this is your big moment, can you fucking come down now, please? They are dying on their pointes, and I am having the best time up there.

MC: I have memories with all of you I want to share and maybe you could all give your memories of each other. I remember coming to Paris to perform at the *Cirque Electrique* that you curated, Lalla. I had just split up from my husband and I was very depressed; the show gave me such a boost. I was thrilled to be invited to Paris to perform in the most magical circus. The main thing I remember about that show, and it is the only time this has ever happened to me with the *Bleeding Woman* imagery, is that somebody fainted in the audience from seeing the blood, and an ambulance came. I had a falling ovation! Luci, I remember your Torture Garden show. We all came out in white nighties. In another show, you were dressed as Rosemary from *Rosemary's Baby*. Amy, I remember being with you in the cabaret club called Kabaret. I have memories of you hosting at the Tower Ballroom in Blackpool. The show business had come to life, and you were channelling entertainers. There was that vibe that you always have, where you are very punk, but you embody entertainers of the past. I think you all have that, in a way. You all embody something very contemporary, which is also rooted in nostalgia.

MB: I have a memory of Luci and my first busking gig. We both learned how to do fire. We had needles possibly, and definitely maggots, mealworms, live insects and I could do some swords. We needed to earn money. So, we thought, let's pop on the bus from Crouch End to Leicester Square and do some busking, dressed in sort of Torture Garden garb. After scaring people for about an hour and a half, we had made enough money to pay for our bus fare back to Crouch End. It was a break-even night.

LM: I remember mostly partying together at the Gypsy Hotel in London. I also have this fond memory of when I was following you and the Urban Voodoo Machine on tour with the Pogues! We went to Jay's castle and stayed there overnight. It was so much fun!

L: I remember sitting around Paul-Ronney Angel's table at 7 a.m. the next morning, still chatting.

LM: That is what I remember mostly, us, being ourselves, being silly and laughing and me just watching you guys with admiration. I also have a memory with the three of you. In my research, I had come across the three of you. It was the time I had stopped performing with the troupe. I saw so many inspiring images of you. Then, I came to London and met you in person, Luci and Marisa. Amy, I saw you in a cabaret in Soho and I was so overwhelmed. It was incredible that I was in London and I could see you with my own eyes and work with you. And even become friends with some of you. When you came to Paris to perform at *Hey! La Cie* and *Cirque Electrique*, Marisa, it was magical for me to have you there, the woman I looked up to and who inspired me at the beginning of my career.

L: I have a memory of you, Marisa, coming round to my warehouse space in Bethnal Green; you were doing *Jewess Tattooess* and you needed a bed of nails. We came to see the show at the ICA, and you were there, naked, tattooing yourself on a bed of nails. I remember being blown away by this weird arty space so close to Buckingham Palace and, obviously, your endless charm.

MB: I remember when myself, Luci, and Lisette [Jansen] did *Crafty* for Torture Garden during Halloween. We were three witches, we did some dancing and ended the show with us fucking our broomsticks. I still remember it to this day, because Luci managed it, Lisette did not, and Amy is still trying.

Figure 86: Amy Saunders aka Miss Behave, *The Miss Behave Game Show*, 2018. © Matt Crockett

L: We actually fucked ourselves with these broomsticks. We did not fake it. It was really important that we tried, but nobody saw, it was hidden. This particular part was not for the audience.

MC: I love this memory and the integrity you bring to everything you do, witchy wonderful Showwomen. Thank you, all.

Incredible Bleeding Women II

Nao Nagai, H Plewis, and Marisa Carnesky

Marisa Carnesky: Who are you, what is your practice as artists and how did you get involved in the *Dr Carnesky's Incredible Bleeding Woman*?

Nao Nagai: I predominantly do production and lighting design, and I also, occasionally, perform in a group called Frank Chickens. I saw you at Duckie one evening and that is when you told me about the show and asked me to be a production manager.

H Plewis: My practice has ranged over a few disciplines, but I have come back to settle in my major discipline, dance, and choreography. I currently run a dance company that is based in East London. It is a project that is born out of my many years of work with Marisa and Duckie and my own practice as a solo cabaret, live artist, and performance maker. It is a community dance project called Posh Club Dance Club (P.C * D.C) for older people, drawing specifically on the dance and music cultures of the African diaspora and how that can be studied in an anti-racist and inclusive way to generate collective experiences of joy for an elder cohort of predominantly African Caribbean women, but not exclusively.

MC: It is a happy coincidence that I speak to you two together, because, in a strange way, I think that P.C * D.C and Frank Chickens have some uniquely shared interests.

HP: Intra-actions! They definitely have intersections, yes.

NN: Frank Chickens is an intergenerational pop performance group and my performance community. It has been going for over 40 years.

MC: Am I right in thinking, Nao, that Kazuko Hohki and Kazumi Taguchi founded Frank Chickens in 1982, which was a quirky pop group of Japanese women living in the United Kingdom? They were actually on *Top of the Pops*. The project does not only consist of Japanese women now, but of all sorts of people and it explores Japanese culture and what it is to be Japanese in the United Kingdom. Is that correct?

NN: Yes. The group is still predominantly Japanese women and the songs that we dance with or perform, are mainly written around that era. I remember Kazuko in an interview saying that the criteria to join Chickens is wanting to join Chickens.

MC: And in both of these troupes, there is just so much joy. They are two of the most joyful performance experiences. That brings me to our group! I asked you all to meet twice a month and do the devising project for *Dr Carnesky's Incredible Bleeding Woman*. The idea was that we met in the full of the moon and the dark of the moon over three months. In the full of the moon, we met at my house in Walthamstow to have a party and enjoy ourselves. In the dark of the moon, we stayed at the house in the Metal artists' residency in Southend and we engaged in creating rituals. We were following anthropological theories informed by the Radical Anthropology Group (RAG) about the ways in which menstrual rituals may have been formed in early human culture. How did you feel about creating the performance material at the time? And how do you think it affected you?

HP: The gatherings together outside of this pre-marcated, professional time-space were really key. They allowed us to dig more deeply into ourselves and to extract and access different parts of ourselves.

NN: We had social dinners and talked about menstruation and all sorts of things that were happening in our life and dreams. Each time, Marisa, you shared some of your research. I remember that women in hunter-gatherers' society menstruated together in the new moon, when it was dark, and they had a feast at the full moon, which we were modelling with our gathering. You also mentioned that menstruation resembled women going on a sex strike together. It was really inspiring to think of menstruation as a bodily power. Even if you do not menstruate, you can still menstruate mentally following nature's cycles.

Figure 87: Nao Nagai, *Dr Carnesky's Incredible Bleeding Woman*, Attenborough Centre for the Creative Arts, 2018. Brighton. © Reuben and Jay Photography

MC: I always wanted to be on a retreat, so I organized the devising process of the show as if it consisted of three mini-retreats. You both created extraordinary menstrual rituals. On the stage, we did our acts and talked about our own experiences, but we did not talk about what happened to us in that house.

NN: For my menstrual ritual, I gathered people around outdoors, forming a semi-circle in a field and I sat in the middle and cut my hair. I used my actual umbilical cord that was linked to my mother who died when I was 12. I put the hair in a box with my umbilical cord. Then, I asked women to hold an end of a ribbon each, which was attached to my hair and walk around me like a maypole. Once I was fully wrapped, I unwrapped myself and climbed up a tree and cried on top of it. It was cathartic. It was about cutting that tie.

HP: It was such a powerful image, I will never forget it. The ritual that I performed was not cathartic or transformative in the way that some others were. I was not able to access that part of myself at the time; it was a process of a different gestation, of growing something; of trying to make something flesh or trying to make something inchoate. My ritual was collecting my menstrual blood before becoming pregnant and turning it into a jelly rabbit. By the time the jelly had become a part of the show, I started replicating it as a performance item, as I was pregnant and I was no longer menstruating. Then it turned into a real-life baby, an idea made flesh, which was, I believe, born out of this project and I am forever grateful.

MC: There is something really special about this dialogue. It is very emotional. I have just hit the menopause in the last three months. A lot of those rituals were about release. With H, there was building the baby with magic. With me, there was an attempt to hold a project together and still build a baby. As long as I was able to have my periods, I thought, I would still get pregnant; I will get pregnant at 50 because I am not like other women. I can defy the statistics. Now, I am going through menopause and my periods have stopped for about six months. I feel like I have entered a new phase. I need to do another performance ritual because, I feel, thank God, that is over now. I can stop fixating on it and look into the future. I am glad we did that show because, not having had a child, my periods were at least not wasted. I made a great show out of them. There was magic in everybody that came together. There was a unity.

Figure 88: H Plewis, *Dr Carnesky's Incredible Bleeding Woman*, Attenborough Centre for the Creative Arts, 2018. Brighton. © Reuben and Jay Photography

HP: The reason that became possible was because of the successful way you presented the research, but also because there was that cradle of genius, intelligent research, married with practice.

MC: Thank you, H, for saying that, it means a lot. The show was emotional and you and I were going through a lot in terms of fertility at the time. We supported each other. I know that in the *Bleeding Woman* show, we used the term 'Showwoman' towards the end of the script. We talked about the themes that this book is exploring: women being spectacular, reinventing rituals, and dealing with danger and taboos. Do you relate to the word Showwoman? If the word means people that have extraordinary, strange dance troupes or pop bands or people that perform weird shows about menstruation, do you feel you are Showwomen?

HP: If we are thinking about the expanded concept of Showwoman, I can put myself in there. When I first read it, I felt that I do not fit the bill. Maybe I have vestiges of a Showwoman within me from previous times, but am I allowed to still identify as that? Then, when I think of it in the expanded sense, I think P.C * D.C does deal with taboo to an extent, in terms of older people being sexual and exploring or displaying their wild and carnivorous sexual side. In terms of the spectacular, we do not manage to be spectacular in P.C * D.C in a highly technical sense, but we attempt the spectacular; we attempt the extreme, and the way we reach heights of skill and mastery is defined on our own terms. We are driven and ambitious to get to OUR summit. If we talk about it in more expanded terms, then I would love to think of myself as a Showwoman and I think it is a really important reclamation; but also not just reclaiming territory, but inventing that space as well. This is what I learned from you, and I think it is brilliant and a really important term, and identity.

MC: I think you are a Showwoman because you are the proprietress of an extremely wonderful, brand new, never done before dance troupe. Nao, are you a Showwoman?

NN: I think I am a Showwoman. There is a level of the unknown here trying to identify with a term that does not yet exist. And if this is the case, then, yes, I can be unidentifiable. It would be different if I did not identify as a woman. I do not see 'Showwoman' as a term that holds the sort of social archetype or stereotype of a woman, but is still developing, which is exciting.

MC: It has been so exciting to build this word and world with you! Thank you, both, so much.

Her Spectacular Entrances

Marisa Carnesky

I would like to make a spectacular entrance and announce my work to date; whether engaging with the reinvention of performative rituals, the embodiment of inherited cultural trauma, or the representations of women's sexuality, it always had one crucial, unified goal: highlighting the role of women as subversives, bosses and creators of the spectacular in the arts and entertainment industries and acknowledging their important role. Moreover, I want to elevate performance forms that have been birthed from working-class origins and seen as marginal and illegitimate and explore their deeper cultural resonances.

The work is serious, funny, gritty, sexy, colourful, and psychedelic. I might take you to a future feminist circus or invite you to ride a ghost train across haunted borders. I might ask you to witness the magickal sawing in half and spectacular rebirth of a performer displaying her bold new femininity. We will play with extraordinary props and costumes, me and my collaborators. We will sometimes be naked and covered in blood, sometimes defying gravity, sometimes telling our stories and the stories of others' past. We will challenge the girls we were in ballet class, the teenagers in thick black eye make-up and perpetually transgress, redress, and reinvent as the artist women we have become.

With my 2022 performance, *Showwomen*, I proposed the term 'Showwoman' as opposed to showman, as one that needs to urgently be introduced into the vernacular, defining the Showwoman as using her spectacular vision in acts that are transformative and collaborative, an antidote to the entertainment traditions of the exploitative tropes of the showman. This chapter is going to offer a journey through the trajectory of key influences, people, and ideas, such as the use of blood, Jewish identity, and the important lineage of historical Showwomen, that have led me to this point, as I begin a writing journey to a new solo show about menopause and images of alchemy and transformation. I will discuss *Jewess Tattooess* as well as the research behind *Dr Carnesky's Incredible Bleeding Woman* and *Carnesky's Ghost Train*. Finally, I will offer an overview of some of the findings that led me to create *Showwomen*.

My theatricality embodies a camp sensibility drawn from practices of contemporary burlesque, radical clown, alternative drag, feminist erotica, surrealist painting, horror film, and esoteric ritual. Identifying menstruation as a subject to explore in my practice started in the early 1990s, after attending lectures of the Radical Anthropology Group (RAG). Decoding fairy tale and researching menstrual symbolism in indigenous myths were central enquiries discussed at RAG. This fed into my interest in identifying potential feminist readings and re-readings of the symbolism in fairy tales and myths through the works of Angela Carter in books like *The Passion of New Eve* (1977).

I attended a performance of Annie Sprinkle's *Post Porn Modernist* in San Francisco in 1994, the same year Sprinkle invited me to pose for her *Post-Modern Pin-Up Pleasure Activist Playing Cards* as *The Nice Jewish Girl* (Sprinkle 1994). At this point, I had begun a performance practice looking specifically at my identity as a Jewish-tattooed female performer in pieces like *The Third Traum* (Marlborough Theatre, Brighton 1991). I created a series of radical stripteases/new burlesque short performance pieces that I performed in alternative nightclubs at art spaces including the ICA, the Pullit X Gallery, and sometimes in conventional striptease pubs, as well as events like sex educator and sex positive disability rights campaigner Tuppy Owens' infamous party The Sex Maniacs Ball. I joined Feminists Against Censorship (FAC), a London-based activist pressure group founded in 1989 that met at Conway Hall in London.

Working with FAC, I programmed and produced the New York inspired London version of Smut Fest with its founder Jennifer Blowdryer and Tuppy Owens in Camden in 1994 as part of the Ten Days of Anarchy festival that was going on across London. We programmed a variety of emerging artists exploring different modes of sexual representation through short performance pieces in a cabaret format. Dressed in a 'psychobilly' style crossed with vintage lingerie, I performed a piece where I sung my rewritten version of a Noel Coward song 'Don't Put Your Daughter on The Stage Mrs Worthington', followed by a striptease where I cracked raw eggs over my body. It went down really well with the audience.

Women in entertainment history and particularly women as sexually provocative performers in striptease and burlesque were areas I had researched prior to creating the work *Jewess Tattooess*, both as an emerging performer in arts contexts, nightclubs, and galleries and at the Theatre Museum Archive formerly located in Covent Garden. This research led to the formation of the company Dragon Ladies and the season of work in what was then the infamous sexual entertainment venue the Raymond Revue Bar in Soho (1997). With sculptural body pieces made by the late artist Amanda Moss that featured caricatured enlarged breasts, tattooed skin, and a vagina dentata made of layers of latex, the work we presented there was expertly rendered through Moss' vision to create eerie imagery that looked sexually explicit, yet at once nostalgic and emotive. The work weaved feminist readings of myth and fairy tale into a surreal, sexual cabaret revue landscape. We had the work featured in the *Independent* on Sunday, with the headline 'How do you get a £5000 Arts Council Grant to bring grotesque burlesque to the Raymond Revue Bar?' (Anne Treneman, *Independent*, 7 February 1998).

Jewesses and Tattoos

In *Jewess Tattooess* (1999–2002), my own experience of growing up identifying as Jewish and the conflict of this with my choice to be tattooed became the backdrop of the work that explored the complex relationship and cultural contradictions of identity and belonging. The work examined my dual position of both an emotional attachment with Jewish cultural traditions and yet a desire to break free from Judaeo-Christian religious structures. Ultimately, beyond my own joyful childhood memories of my Jewish upbringing, the work focused on how my identity has been shaped and marked by histories of genocide, immigration and the changing landscapes of Europe. The marks expressed through tattoos performed as a visceral map of my conflicted sense of heritage and cultural dissidence. My tattooed body became a fluent landscape, examining, exposing and proposing how to embody inherited cultural trauma and gendered politics. The tattoos were then a way for me to challenge traditional life choices through my skin.

In the work, the taboo of the tattoo in Judaism is turned on its head and reclaimed as a subversive expression of my complex relationship with my Jewish identity. The archetype of the Whore of Babylon riding her hydra-headed serpent and Lilith's relationship with the serpent of Eden, represented as demonic manifestations of women's sexuality in Judaism, serve in the work to connect me to ancient Jewish representations of women's menstrual blood, sexuality, cyclicity, and synchronicity.

The relationship between taboo blood, menstruation, sexuality, and bodily decoration in Jewish tradition, and my choice to become extensively tattooed informed my autoethnographic journey into the performance project. *Jewess Tattooess* looked at the representation of mythological Jewish figures like Lilith, at representations of women's sexuality as demonic and in particular at blood taboos around marking and drawing blood from the skin. The supposed ban and taboo of tattooing is attributed to the Leviticus quote; 'Ye shall not make any cuttings in your flesh for the dead, nor print any marks on you: I *am* the LORD' (Leviticus 19:28).

I was not alone as a young counter-cultural punk feminist in my decision to challenge my cultural heritage through the ritual of tattooing in the 1990s. This was being echoed across a generation of women transforming the tattoo as 'a reclaiming of their bodies and a form of resistance to normative femininity, or at least an alternative to it' (Thompson 2016: 6). On another level, my draw to tattoos was a response to a cultural heritage of persecution. Learning about the numbers tattooed on the victims of the Nazi Holocaust and seeing images of multiple starved and dehumanized bodies piled up, indiscernible from each other, made me want to have a body that could not become unidentifiable. I wanted to consciously embody my identity through my skin in a form that could not be erased and in doing so become part of an anarchic subculture.

The work focused on my choice to be tattooed as a medium and metaphor through which to question my cultural heritage. While transforming the body permanently through the act of tattooing, I documented myself getting tattooed, and I was photographed during each stage, reflecting and writing about the entire process. The tattoo which covers my entire back took eleven five-hour sessions of tattooing over nine months to complete. I also recorded conversations with the tattooist Alex Binnie during these sessions and the sounds of the tattoo gun entering my skin, as well as collecting all the drafts of the design in process.

This process of collecting material led to a one-hour performance work *Jewess Tattooess*, revealing these findings through creative vignettes that were woven together to create a montage of spoken word, film, and performance actions in a non-linear, visual, and spoken narrative that utilized found images and newly commissioned video work by filmmaker and collaborator Alison Murray, collected stories, new monologues, choreography and stage illusions and an element of live tattooing. The work contrasted the blood drawn by self-inflicted tattoos with the ancient menstrual blood taboos surrounding the Jewish woman's body. The work was devised by drawing on personal memory and family heritage as well as stories from Yiddish folktales. It incorporated material collected from Holocaust survivors of transforming, by choice, concentration camp number tattoos with new decorative tattoos and the taboos against marking the body in Jewish tradition. Through a weaving of this material, I examined the complex relationship of the tattoo to Jewish culture.

The work featured live performative actions where I emerged from a huge paper Star of David through the floor; I was covered in bandages *Mummy* style from which I cut myself out. Then, naked, I put on a 1940s hat and shoes filled with blood and walked across the star dripping the blood onto the paper. I went on to tell short stories through live monologues and filmed characters I played. They included a concerned Rabbi trying to reason against the act of tattooing and a macabre eighteenth-century Eastern European Jewish fairy tale grandmother figure. In the show, a narrative of a Jewish girl that runs away from the *Shtetl* to join the fairground as a tattooed lady emerges. Murray used a camera effect to transform my face and we worked intensively to find unsettling vocal styles for the characters.

The taboo of women's blood in Judaism was touched on with the action of using a tattoo machine to mark a Star of David around my belly button through drawing blood to the surface of the skin. Creating a wound shaped as a Star of David live on stage was an image that sought to consolidate the emotional complexity of the work through a fully embodied performance action. Both operating in the realm of live art and contemporary theatre practice, the work was bold and bodily, equally driven by monologues and performative images.

For the diverse audiences that saw the work, the metaphor of tattoos highlighted the wider theme of radical forms of reinventing and expressing new cultural identities. Creating subcultural expressions that embody inherited stories of loss, torture, genocide, and escape was a regular subject raised by audiences in post-show question-and-answer discussions. The work then evolved through the practice of performing it in different contexts, which ranged from the ICA and the Battersea Arts Centre, the Los Angeles International Festival to an outdoor theatre festival in the medieval Palestinian/Israeli town of Acco for the Acco Festival of Alternative Theatre and contemporary theatres in Madrid, Dublin, and Ljubljana between 1999 and 2004. Touring *Jewess Tattooess* to the Acco Festival in 2003 in Israel/Palestine indicated the significance of autoethnographic practice and lived history. Situated in a predominantly Palestinian Christian medieval port town in Northern Israel, the

Acco Festival is a unique experimental theatre festival that brings together Israeli, Palestinian, and international artists. Performing the piece to a mixed secular and religious audience raised extraordinary responses. A Hasidic woman was very moved by the work, coming over to me to say: 'I understood … I feel the pain of these taboos on my body also, even though it is not tattooed' (Acco Festival, audience feedback 2003). A Palestinian Christian man found the work moving, seeing the clash between cultures 'that was written on the body' (Acco Festival, audience feedback 2003). Yet a secular, non-religious Israeli woman viewed it as unproblematic for a Jewish woman to have tattoos. This was because national identity was more important to her as an Israeli Jew than religious Jewish customs (Acco Festival, audience feedback, 2003). Performing the work at the Acco Festival opened new questions about the placement and context of it affecting the premise of the concept. As a British Jew from a conservative diasporic cultural tradition, a tattoo estranged me from my Jewish identity, yet in Israel, in this context, it did not.

Further themes raised in *Jewess Tattooess* around immigrant identity, cultural displacement, and generational culture clash surfaced in discussions with Eastern European performers I worked with in the London cabaret scene, many of whom had fled the Balkan wars and worked as dancers in the traditional London striptease venues. The possibility that immigrant journeys and refugee experiences from East to West, particularly women's stories of displacement and struggle, had not significantly changed in a century of changing borders, resonated with the stories of women I was meeting.

Hearing their stories of exile and displacement and the way they navigated low spaid and illegal work as a survival strategy brought to mind the familiar stories of struggle and displacement of Jewish refugees over a century earlier. These women, like the Jewish migrants in the nineteenth century, also have a history of migration from East to West.

An idea emerged for a new project, a travelling 'ghost train' ride that explored images of disappeared women between borders. *Carnesky's Ghost Train* evolved from *Jewess Tattooess*, from my interest in lost stories of my Eastern European Jewish cultural heritage, and of the travelling fairground tattooed showwoman in the nineteenth-century popular entertainment that led to a ghost train about women and migration. *Ghost Train* built on a Jewish story of disappearance to explore wider narratives of displacement following a mourning mother looking for her disappeared daughters in an unknown town somewhere in Eastern Europe. In this work, the theme of writing on the body then became a bigger structure, a temporary building that houses performances and images of a series of nomadic bodies: the body of the *Ghost Train* purpose built and inscribed as a living memorial to disappeared identity.

An Emotional and Bloody Rollercoaster

Carnesky's Ghost Train was a large-scale production that involved building from scratch a state-of-the-art operational ghost train touring venue, designed in a collaboration I led with a creative team of designers, engineers, and performers. The original cast included artist Tai Shani, Turner prize winner, musician Paloma Faith, Brit Award Winner, visual and circus artist Geneva Foster Gluck, actor Violetta Misic, performance artist Dagmara Bilon and dancer Agnes Czerna. Inside the ride moving sets, performance stages and bespoke illusions were built to house the cast of performers. This work grew from the earlier one-woman show *Jewess Tattooess* (1999) and then *The Girl From Nowhere* (Riverside Studios 2003), where I rode around the stage in a singular fairground ghost train carriage disembodied from its original ride, whilst telling stories of women's migration from East to West, including those of my own Jewish family. It featured images drawing on magicians' assistants levitating and enclosed within confined magic box spaces. It followed the theatrical traditions of a stage magic show, featuring increasing levels of spectacular illusion. Focusing on themes of disappearance and defying physical and geographic boundaries, the stories increased in dramatic intensity as the performance progressed. In the performance, the magician's assistant is divided and her transforming body becomes a metaphorical site of political conflict and a carrier of multiple identities.

These images and stories fed the creation of *Carnesky's Ghost Train*, bringing the woman's body as a site of magical and cultural change into an ensemble piece where a series of characters and scenarios could be created. The context of a haunted house/ghost train ride provided a holding form that promised a thrilling journey into darkness and the unknown. The work explored images and stories of war-torn refugee and disappeared women crossing haunted borders between Eastern and Western Europe. It toured successfully for five years in the United Kingdom and Europe (2004–09) and then became the resident art project on Blackpool's Golden Mile for five more years, between 2009 and 2014. It received critical acclaim in *The Times* and *The Independent* with a four-star review in *The Guardian* and was ridden by an audience of over 50,000 people over its ten-year life.

The ride followed the story of a mourning protesting mother informed by the *Women in Black* activist movement looking for her daughters who had disappeared from a devastated town. The performers played the ghosts of migrant women who embodied the liminal spaces between loss of culture and identity, geography, and memory. These ethereal characters in tattered dresses were situated in train carriages and fragmented stations that went nowhere, never arriving at their destinations. The characters I created were all on a journey that had no end, a mother looking for her lost daughters, her daughters looking for her and the way out. The language and metaphors were bold and immediate. The desire was to create a work that would resonate emotionally with truly diverse audiences from a multiplicity of ethnicities, age range, racial, social, and economic backgrounds. The intention was to create a travelling nomadic ghost ride that could be presented outside of traditional contexts of both arts and fairground, positioning the work politically as neither and as both. The ride grew from exploring an immigrant heritage and looking for answers on identity from a disappeared culture; locating a lost heritage in order to construct new identities. Geographic borders crossed by ancestral blood families leading to new cultural and sociological borders, crossing between a time of nostalgia and inherited sadness now mingled with the resonances of new feminist futures, unfixed, unmarked, and open to all possibilities.

Carnesky's Ghost Train sought to knowingly use the 'scare attraction' genre in all its tawdry exploitation art of gore to create a sense of the uncanny and placelessness, where old world nostalgia and emotive images of loss and disappearance collided with the schlock abject horror of a fairground ghost train. The original exploration on ghost trains and ride designs was the beginning of my research journey at the National Fairground and Circus Archive at the University of Sheffield, where I went on to become a fellow in 2008 and which now houses my archive. Images of rides and fairground façades, temporary travelling entertainment palaces fascinated me, particularly images of Victorian ghost shows.

Bill Luca posits that ghost trains are thought to be derived from the famous American *Pretzel* brand rides premiered in 1928 and created by Leon Cassidy; these are the first dark rides in which people in carriages were jolted around a sharply turning track (Luca 2015). This was fused with the earlier tradition of the ghost show, magic lantern and phantasmagoria presentations. These were exhibitions of illusory light and smoke effects with ghostly projections popular in the late nineteenth century such as the exhibits of French showman and inventor Etienne-Gaspard Robertson, whose phantasmagoria show Marina Warner describes as: 'Teeming with devils, ghosts, witches, succubae, skeletons, mad women in white, bleeding nuns, and what he termed as "ambulant phantoms"' (Warner 2006: 149).

The shock and fascination of taboo topics including the undead, the odd and curious body feature across the nineteenth-century popular fairground, carnival and sideshow entertainments including waxwork sideshows, freak-shows, and theatrical booths. As part of my initial research when creating *Carnesky's Ghost Train* I rode ghost trains wherever I found them on my travels, including the since burnt down ghost train on Brighton pier. This ride with my collaborator, choreographer Mim King, proved a more bizarre experience than expected. The ride mechanics failed and we were left sitting in the dark, in a stationary carriage by a lonely dusty green monster for over ten minutes. A live actor in a mask and a bin liner appeared and did his best to keep us scared for the duration. It was a performance inside a dark ride that created an abject thrill; the performance of a bizarre improvisation using sound, breath, and proximity to disorientate and disarm. Unknowingly, in its broken state with the impromptu performer, the ride combined aspects of a variety of fairground entertainments creating a new horror narrative affected by real events.

Similarly, *Carnesky's Ghost Train* sought to tell the horrors of real events of migration and disappearance, structured and contextualized through the narrative of the experience of riding a ghost train, creating a multisensory, shock-filled, and otherworldly atmosphere. The costumes and performances did not suggest genderless, abstract ghouls but the unique relationship of women to blood and the abject. The tropes of the traditional horror ghost train then were turned on their head, with the shocks, thrills, and fear rooted in history, cultural identity, and the emotions of intergenerational loss.

The choreography had frenetic movements where some of the performers clutched their skirts as if protecting a pregnancy or in pain. It was always my intention to show images and stories of displacement from a female perspective. I wanted to create images specifically of women's memory and loss between borders and between lives, an art experience that fell not just between genres but between history and location.

The marketing of *Carnesky's Ghost Train* drew on the aesthetics of the fairground and horror cinema in an attempt to attract diverse audiences through popular culture tropes. Posters and flyers used fonts and colours from traditional British fairground sources and typography from 1970s horror films. The intention was to draw on the well-established western leisure activity to visit the seaside and go on a theme park or fairground ride or see a magic variety revue featuring a line-up of circus skilled showgirls, even if the ghosts are immigrants and the showgirls are women who bleed.

Incredible Bleeding Women

In 2015, I first premiered *Dr Carnesky's Incredible Bleeding Woman*, a full-length show touring from 2016 to 2019, that examined existing religious and cultural menstrual rituals with the intention of reinventing new alternative feminist performative ones. The project created these rituals using theories that ranged from anthropological studies of synchronicity in traditional human cultures to the autoethnographic testimonies from the performers involved. A unique group of intersectional cabaret and live artists joined me in this cabaret, bringing a range of skills, cultural interests, and backgrounds, from hair hanging, stage magic, and sword swallowing to live art practice and queer journalism. They were Fancy Chance, alternative cabaret star and circus hair hanger; Livia Kojo Alour, burlesque performer, poet, and sword swallower; Rhyannon Styles, trans rights activist, queer writer, and performance artist; Nao Nagai, lighting designer and musician; and H Plewis, performance artist and choreographer. Aesthetically, the performance work drew on traditional entertainment tropes of bleeding women in popular culture and media, from classic horror film imagery of women possessing paranormal powers when menstruating, to women bleeding in stage magic performance and parodies of sanitary product advertisements. The work revisioned and reinvented rituals associated with menstruation into contemporary feminist performance and activist practices. We devised the show through a process where I asked the cast to meet me once a month, for three months every new moon, staying overnight together and creating performance material. The overarching desire of the work was to raise awareness and expand notions of the cultural identity of menstruation, exposing hidden mythologies, reframing popular representations and exposing ingrained social taboos in mainstream western consciousness.

The show began with a performative lecture, led by me as 'Dr Carnesky', a camp character developed from aspects of my persona and aesthetic interests informed by historical and thematic research. 'Dr Carnesky' presented her 'Menstruants', my collaborating team of performers, as if she were an anthropologist exhibiting her subjects, a flamboyant circus Showwoman, a *magicienne* with sleight of hand tricks, and a carnival sideshow con artist posing as a doctor. This eccentric academic lecturer, using slides and films, both upholds and defiles the institution of instruction about the body, as she plays with the tradition of ethnographic shows in Victorian popular entertainments, the politics of cultural appropriation and perceptions of traditional anthropology, to explore the magic of menstruation. She asks the audience through her evidence to question the very origins of magic: 'What if I told you the origins of all magic, of all ritual, since the beginning of time was menstrual, would you believe me?' The cabaret then offers a unique performance experiment in synchronicity where the 'Menstruant' participants each perform their own individually devised rituals live. The performance swings between the fictional, the factual and the autoethnographic, working with abject images, horror, and variety of stage tropes. Questions are then posed to the audience. The character of 'Dr Carnesky' is a punk-cabaret *détournement* of the archetypal Aunt Flo in menstrual advertising – the popular euphemism for getting your period – and a formal Mistress of Ceremonies, crossing into moments of hysteria and horror. At moments, she is authoritative like a supposed medical instructor, at others, an illegitimate entertainer dealing in shock, taboo and spectacle, or a female parody of the 'showman' in the tradition of variety theatre who linked the acts and spoke directly to the audience. Lastly, she breaks her camp façade to join the collective and deliver intimate personal testimony and an activist call to reclaim our bodily cycles.

The Menstruants brought their own stories and characters to the work. Fancy Chance executed a minimal live art choreography, where she drew a red line down her body after taking a lipstick out of her vagina, culminating in applying lipstick to her lips relentlessly until it becomes a clown-like mouth. She went on in later runs of the show to talk about her experience of taking birth control as a woman who is clear that she does not want to have a child – and the negative side effects it caused for her. Livia Kojo Alour, the spoken word artist, at the time was known as MisSa and had worked as an international burlesque performer and sword swallower for a decade. She created a moon calendar of swords of varying sizes in response to having a sword swallowing accident when she was menstruating, where she grazed her oesophagus that had left her fighting for her life. She discussed her research on the internal changes the body goes through during the menses. H Plewis explored her journey to fertility through creating a performance object made of jelly moulded into the shape of a rabbit that she froze each month and infused with her own menstrual blood collected each time. She created a choreography with the jelly rabbit and explored in her monologue her pursuit of conception. In later versions of the show, she brought her baby daughter Sula onto the stage who was conceived at the end of the process and was actually born on the premiere of the work in 2016 at UCL, on which day Molly Beth Morossa performed as

her understudy whilst she gave birth in a nearby hospital. Rhyannon Styles explored her trans identity as a woman as well as her relationship to the menstrual cycle through the practice as research process of devising the work. She had created a cathartic piece during the process where in an old cheerleader outfit from her years in cabaret she made a performance in the beach in Southend – burying balloons in the sand and responding to the landscape and her emotions of facing her transition, which resulted in a frenzied screaming performance on the shore. She showed this film in the body of the live show and explored the notion of menstruation as a signifier for cyclicity in culture as a queer and eco feminist action against patriarchal norms. In the process, Nao Nagai had explored her feelings around the loss of her mother at a young age to inform a ritual performance in which she took part of her umbilical cord that had been preserved since she was born and climbed a tree and tried to connect with her feelings about her loss. She created a character and an image that drew on the Japanese myth of the Yokai – a mythical character that explores serpent imagery in her response to the project research, exploring the relationship of serpent imagery to menstruation across world cultures. The piece then came together with an extraordinary prop made by Nao using a traditional Kabuki mask of a young girl on an extendable neck, almost like a giant umbilical cord, creating a puppeted second floating head to spectacular and moving effect.

Figure 89: Nao Nagai, Amy Ridler, H Plewis, *Bleeding Women Ritual Workshops*, artists' residency, Metal Culture, 2015. Southend. © Sarah Ainslie

I created a scene that was filmed which I then spoke about it in the show. The film was of me getting into a bath full of blood. The blood was theatrical blood – but before filming I added a little of my real menstrual blood I had collected. It was a stark image with my coloured tattooed body against the white porcelain bath and the blood running over my skin. I literally washed in the blood. We filmed it in an old morgue – in an industrial tiled room where bodies had once been washed. The concept for the film came from the idea of reversing the Jewish Mikvah ritual, where the *niddah* – a woman who is menstruating – washes off any last traces of menstrual blood from your body. The *niddah* is associated with notions of ritual impurity and menstrual uncleanliness and in some Jewish interpretations is actually seen as dirty and contagious: 'And if a woman have an issue, *and* her issue in her flesh be blood, she shall be put apart seven days: and whosoever toucheth her shall be unclean until the evening' (Leviticus 15:19: 140). The *niddah* separates herself from the community, to rejoin only after the ritual of the *mikvah* bath. Feminist debate on the rituals of menstruation practiced in current Judaism as outdated and misogynist are counterbalanced by some as a reclaiming of the Mikvah as ritually empowering as a woman-led space. Rabbi Haviva Ner-David suggests that the tradition of *tumah*, the ritual impurity surrounding the *niddah*, was misinterpreted in a misogynist medieval culture and calls for change in Jewish interpretations of menstruation that could 'create a positive understanding of what it means to be a *niddah* and to replace medieval interpretations of *tumah* that include notions of pollution, danger, and filth' (Ner-David 2005: 197).

In the piece, my idea was to bathe in the menstrual blood, akin to stories of Cleopatra bathing in milk, to luxuriate in this sacred substance as a symbol of power and joy, not of dirtiness and shame, to wash it on. As I showed the film during the show, I talked about my experience of miscarriages rather than the Mikvah. The film was not made to literally represent miscarriage but became a poignant image to associate with the trauma of it.

As the show progressed, we started to perform as a cast on the stage together and performed two spectacular acts. One was a sawing in half illusion where we reversed the trick and brought Rhyannon Styles on in two parts of the separated magic box, as if she had already been sawn in half. H Plewis and I then put the box and her back together and then split it apart again. I wanted to create an image where her naked legs covered in blood were sticking out of the box. Rhyannon also decided she wanted to emerge from the box naked and show her trans body to the audience. We were then joined by Fancy Chance, Livia Kojo Alour, and Nao Nagai for a finale where I performed a 'psychic surgery' on Fancy Chance, lying on the now connected sawing in half box, extracting what looked like flesh from her belly. From here she was connected by her hair to an aerial line and flown upwards to perform a full hair hang simultaneously bursting blood bags hidden in her hair which dripped down her body as she swivelled in the air by only her hair. This was the end of the show.

This cabaret explored abjection, radical anthropological perspectives on witchcraft, the origin of the commune, and the revelation of hidden menstrual mythological figures. It further unpacked and addressed the parallels between trans-activism and menstruation as metaphors for rebirth, proposed feminist reclamations of death-defying nineteenth-century carnival sideshow skills and new theories of understanding misogyny in stage magic. It was a menstrual activist call to arms, combining personal testimonies which were both serious and emotive alongside the researched material, in a manner that was both rigorous and a spoof of research modes themselves. Drawing together aspects of autoethnography, memoir and imagined fictions, the work combined and interspersed aspects of lived experience into a performative landscape that drew from the proposed real and the fictional. The transition from process to performance included dramaturgy from Kira O'Reilly at National Theatre Studios (2015). O'Reilly was the first to see the material gathered through the process and explore with me how to crystallize the work into performance actions and identify a unifying aesthetic. In a production where I join the cast as a performer and direct and facilitate devising, at a certain point I need an outside collaborator to help me facilitate my part. With clarity and precision, O'Reilly worked intensively with me to find the essence of each piece and focus on the heart of the action. Later in the process, with O'Reilly relocating to Finland, I asked Florence Peake to look at the work before we ran it at Soho Theatre during Christmas 2016/17. Peake asked some questions about my original intentions for the work and encouraged me to include my own story of miscarriage into the piece. The show started its touring life and we realized the work often spoke as a cathartic experience for audiences. A number of women in the audience over its four-year touring life were moved to tears and wanted to talk afterwards.

As audience reactions grew, we created a monthly activist meeting inspired by the show in collaboration with Dr Camilla Power and the Radical Anthropology Group – who became known as The Menstronauts. We facilitated a number of meetings and workshops open to the female and menstrual identifying public to create menstrually inspired performance actions on the landscape. Between 2017 and 2018, we created

outdoor rituals across London including a marking of the cyclicity on midsummer eve on the Greenwich meridian line, and 'Red Riding Hood' Halloween march through Soho. We joined Polish feminist groups in support of reproductive and abortion rights and marked the anniversary of the Match Girls strike of 1888 on the site of the Bryant and May Factory in Bow.

A Radical Cabaret School and a New Degree

Alongside my work as a performance maker has always been an interest and practice as a teacher and facilitator. Teaching in various institutions as a visiting lecturer throughout my career, I then established my own part-time 'school' in the late 2000s through a residency at The Roundhouse. This became known as 'Carnesky's Finishing School'.

In the press release for Carnesky's Finishing School (CFS) in 2017 working with creative producer Lara Clifton, we called the classes 'an esoteric St Trinian's for the queer cabaret generation, Carnesky's Finishing School has been helping people discover and hone their creative talent since 2008' (Carnesky and Clifton 2017). Spanning fifteen years of

Figure 90: *Menstruant Action*, Red Riding Hood March, 2017. Soho, London. © Claire Lawrie

independent performer training, performance education, and radical stagecraft in the United Kingdom, CFS helped to launch a whole new generation of bold, transgressive performers onto London's mercurial alternative cabaret/performance art scene. CFS began in 2008 as part of a two-year artist-in-residence experimental project at London's Roundhouse and went on to hold regular courses at the Bethnal Green Working Men's Club from 2010 to 2015. It toured in pop up residences all over the United Kingdom, including tours to venues in Wales, Scotland, Blackpool, and festivals Bestival and Latitude. In 2017, we took over the former iconic Foyles building in Soho in the heart of London before its demolition. Its last incarnation was at The Tramshed in Southeast London providing courses live and online throughout the Covid pandemic. Eschewing more traditional methodologies in favour of classes such as contemporary cabaret, situationist clowning, radical burlesquing, esoteric PE, trans-metamorphosis, performance art, new spoken word, anarchic stand up, alternative circus skills, new magic, future drag, progressive wrestling, immersive horror shows and unpopular expressionism, CFS occupied a unique space in which emerging and novice performers received a level of support, guidance and mentoring that fell between workshop, experiment, direction, and showcase.

In 2019, conversations with Jeremy James, Artistic Director of the Tramshed about the future of CFS initiated the proposal to run a new BA based on the classes that had been established. The Tramshed had begun a dialogue with Rose Bruford College about the venue being used for its courses and with The Tramshed set to be refurbished, James was keen to launch a new course alongside it. Friend and peer performance artist and educator Brian Lobel was at Rose Bruford and had just launched a new course called BA Theatre and Social Change. Over the next two years through the pandemic, Brian worked closely with me to translate my methodologies into a new BA. BA Contemporary and Popular Performance (CPP) started in 2022 with a new cohort of students ready to join a new kind of degree exploring the crossovers between the popular and the radical, new performance forms and traditional variety skills.

CPP grows on a yearly basis establishing a curriculum that combines new performance creation and specialized and popular skills in a theatre school, art school, and circus school marriage, working closely with industry partners like Punchdrunk, Duckie, Certain Blacks, and Glastonbury Festival to provide really exciting placements. The year 2022 also saw additional classes and workshops from wrestling and gymnastics sportswoman and justice campaigner Claire Heafford, aerialist and Shunt theatre collective member Layla Rosa and Phoebe Patey-Ferguson, performance academic and activist. The BA is truly informed by the experience of making and producing performance, to feed the BA students with knowledge, opportunities, touring and festival work that creates a strong sense of collaboration and professional practice. The cohort becomes a performance family and a company, a preparation for what can happen outside the structure of classes. Standing in the theatre of the newly refurbished Tramshed, we dream of shows that we will work on together in this space – finding and defining our odd creativity, our specialist skills, our shifting and mutating identities, our own unique gang.

There's No Women Like Bloody Showwomen

Showwomen as a project in its own right was first conceived in 2008 when I was working on a fellowship with Professor Vanessa Toulmin, the founder and at the time Collections Manager of the National Fairground Archive (NFA) at the University of Sheffield. Toulmin is like a tornado of knowledge on the history of popular performance, circus, variety, fairground and, as she calls it, 'illegitimate entertainment' in all its myriad forms. She came from the fairground community and established the NFA in 1994 born out of her original research and commitment to bring greater representation to working class entertainment history and legitimacy to its under-celebrated workers. It went on to become expanded into the National Fairground and Circus Archive (NFCA).

> The collection embodies the history of popular entertainment in the United Kingdom from the seventeenth century onwards, covering every aspect of the travelling fair, circus and allied entertainments as well as the culture, business and life of travelling showpeople. The NFCA provides a primary source of research and teaching material to a wealth of popular culture and history from the unique viewpoint of the travelling entertainment industry.
> (Toulmin, NFCA website, 2016)

Toulmin introduced me to the term 'Showwomen' which was generally used in the fairground community to describe a woman who is the proprietor of a ride, circus or fairground amusement, or theme park. It was clear that me and others like me were inhabiting a space that straddled the worlds of performance art, the burlesque showgirl, and the woman who ran the show. We now could be re-evaluated, renamed, and promoted in the ranks of showpeople to Showwomen. Contemporary cabaret had changed the popular performance landscape, the making of new performance that explored and evolved old tricks was growing in clubs, festivals, theatre, and broadcast media. And there was a new style of boss emerging. Showwomen bosses.

From women who were stone eaters to fire walkers, women who hypnotized alligators, women who presented crucifixion shows, from wall of death riders to escapologists, the closeness of death as entertainment and the edges of known boundaries are themes that have preoccupied audiences and women entertainers over the last two centuries. These entertainers, regardless of their extraordinary acts, would have been commonly referred to as showgirls, even though they were soloists with rare individual skills, often topping the bill in variety entertainment. The word 'Showwoman' is currently a marginal term associated only with women proprietors of fairground rides or circuses. It does not, as the term 'showman' does, denote a special flair for entertaining, spectacle and bravado, or for breaking of taboos through an exploitation of the extraordinary, exemplified by P.T. Barnum and his exhibition of differently able-bodied performers in the eighteenth century. How could a Showwoman differ and yet have an equal status as a consummate entertainer and provider of spectacle, beyond running the fairground ride or the circus ring? If such a term were to be elaborated on and represented fully in the dictionary, it would potentially identify women who have the power of Showwomanship, a bombastic theatrical flair and an extraordinary skill, most likely within the worlds of 'low brow' variety entertainment. It could also define a woman who manages and produces large-scale spectacular shows with a great talent for creating a buzz and getting publicity in inventive and risqué ways.

Without the Showwoman in the common vernacular, we are exposed to a society of the spectacle drawn by the patriarchal showman, and he can be cruel, exploitative, and brash. I suggest that a Showwoman could expand and be defined beyond the above and have different qualities to the showman. She could not only be a new kind of grown-up showgirl in charge of her own material and career, that harnesses her taboo, abject, forbidden, death defying, or extraordinary body in spectacular feats, but she could possess collaborative as opposed to exploitative revolutionary potential. We need to birth the term Showwoman to offer alternative visions of spectacular matriarchal entertainment utopias. With the term Showwoman, we can have this new identity, this new kind of risqué performer, that does not exploit or control her cast, the women she shows, as perhaps the showman is thought to. Showwomen are a collaborating group, a coven, a collective bound by shared experiences of visceral euphoria, applause, loss, shame, abjection, hustle and struggle, marginalization, and the fight against

Figure 91: Signed publicity photo of Koringa, 1943. Photographer unknown

patriarchal injustices. Because the woman menstruates and shares this taboo with other women, her troupe can inherit the proposed power of the menstrual collective, as a group bound to each other with a body that defies temporary death and taboo. If her women though do not menstruate, if her cast are trans, non-binary, men or animals, they are still part of the menstrual collective. They together are the model of the cyclical group that can perform acts of ritual and separation from the everyday as part of a process of inclusive group identity.

Historical British Showwomen of the nineteenth and twentieth centuries could include Koringa, working in the Bertram Mills Circus in the 1930s who hypnotized crocodiles and put her head in their jaws, the stunt motorcycle rider known as Marjorie Dare who toured a wall of death to English seaside towns in the 1930s and Florence Shufflebottom, a snake handler and a knife thrower touring a western skills circus show in the United Kingdom during the 1950s. Shufflebottom passed away in 2014. In an article by Oliver Wright for the BBC News Leeds and West Yorkshire website, he describes elements of her acts:

> She was used as a target for her father's knife, axe and tomahawk throwing act and, from the age of five, performed as a snake-charmer. Her final trick – named the Kiss of Death – was to place a snake's head inside her mouth. (Wright 2014)

Koringa's work was also preoccupied with the image of a woman's relationship to the serpent. An act somewhere between magic and circus, she was a headline speciality act, rare for a woman, let alone a woman of colour in the United Kingdom in 1937. It is assumed from her publicity materials that she was a brown woman from a French Moroccan background, although there is a possibility she was presenting as a brown woman and was white. It is debateable if her act was a white woman's colonialist fantasy of the exotic and the woman as other or a genuine attempt at a multicultural performance identity. Her performance character came from the western fixation with Orientalism, popular throughout the nineteenth and twentieth centuries (Toulmin 2007). As well as her crocodiles and snakes, she climbed a ladder of swords, walked on broken glass, had a concrete block broken on her stomach, laid on a bed of nails and levitated. She is often seen in pictures with the cross of Lorraine, known as the mark of the French Resistance drawn on her forehead and she claimed she was an active spy that worked for the French Resistance, hypnotizing animals to help soldiers cross enemy lines. Toulmin suggests this may just have been propaganda for the French

Resistance or publicity for her act, and it is not known if she was actually an active spy. Koringa exemplifies that Showwomen not only existed in the heyday of British variety but also had subversive performance personas and were involved in political activism of the time. In the popular history of cabaret and variety as a transgressive form during the Second World War in Europe, the Weimar Republic is cited as a hotbed of sexual transgression and radical cabaret exemplified by performers like Anita Berber who 'consciously broke every social and theatrical convention of her time' (Gordon 2006: 1). Koringa personifies the existence of UK-based pre-war iconic women popular performers. Although UK theatres 'went dark' in 1938 Koringa re-emerged post-war and continued performing into the 1950s making headlines like: 'Crocodile Fell Into Preston Orchestra Pit':

> An eight-foot crocodile, infuriated by a fall into the orchestra pit, its jaws gnashing and its tail lashing about smashing musical instruments and stands, provided an entirely unrehearsed thrill for the second house audience at the Preston Palace Theatre last night. The crocodile, one of six used by Koringa in her female fakir act, is named Goebbels and, like his namesake, appears to be very keen on 'putting himself over'.
> (*Lancashire Daily Post*, 17 February 1942)

Evatima Tardo was a Showwoman that impressed Harry Houdini himself; he described her as a 'woman of exceptional beauty, both of form and feature [...] and a fearless enthusiast in her devotion to her art' (Houdini in Ricky Jay 2003: 26). Tardo performed in America in the late 1890s, her work involving the exhibition of her claimed ability to not feel physical pain. On stage, she would be bitten by poisonous snakes and stop her own heartbeat by stopping the circulation of her blood flow. Tardo also had a popular crucifixion act in which she had herself nailed to a cross and suspended there for over two hours at a time, as reported in the *Chicago Chronicle* in 1898 in which she was quoted: 'Before I gave the nails to the doctor I had them steeped in deadly poison [...], there wouldn't be any fun unless I had prussic acid on the ends' (Tardo in Jay 2003: 27).

The crucified woman with snakes ritually bleeds without dying like Jesus, transforming and perhaps returning the Christian spectacle of rebirth from a patriarchal to a matriarchal image. The crucified woman is in league with her serpents, not the victim of them. She ritually embodies the role of menstruant and transcends the role of showgirl and stage magician into shaman. Showwomen who topped the variety bills and traded in skills of spectacle, shock, and wonder remain obscure in entertainment

Figure 92: Lulu Adams, Bertram Mills Circus, National Circus and Fairground Archive, circa 1937. Photographer unknown

history. Yet, their legacy lives on in the extraordinary women performers who are part of a re-emergence of radical corporeal feminist cabaret, contemporary working Showwomen like Empress Stah, infamous 'Laser Butt Plug' inventor and circus artist, Miss Behave, *La Soiree's* premier female sword swallower, creator of the anti-variety Las Vegas show *Miss Behave's Gameshow*, and Fancy Chance, tattooed performance artist and circus hair hanger. With my reworked illusions, new writing and body art performances, these are women that I have worked alongside for nearly twenty years, as a co-performer in cabaret clubs, theatres, and circus tents in their curated shows and they as performers in my curated shows.

We form a new community of women performers that can be defined by a new application of the word Showwoman. By reinventing the context of the variety show as a platform to expose bodily taboos and misogyny, the work offers new visions of potential feminist variety personas. The new Showwoman then has the potential to rewrite the practice and performance of historical extraordinary entertainments with risqué wit and subversive spectacle.

In 2022, I created the production of *Showwomen*, the untold herstory of British working class entertainment from immigrant, queer, activist, and occult perspectives. 1930s body magic star Koringa, 1930s pioneer clown Lulu Adams (Figure 92) and 1880s teeth hanging aerialist superstar Miss La La inspired an exploration of lesser-known stories of extraordinary women in variety performance from a century ago. The performance of *Showwomen* compares them to the lived experiences of exceptional performers today. I narrated and performed alongside collaborating stars hair hanger/comedienne Fancy Chance, sword swallower and spoken word artist Livia Kojo Alour and physical and fire performer Lucifire, interweaving live action, in-depth interviews, and archival footage to create a dreamlike landscape mixing death-defying stunts, strange and emotive acts, political resistance, and secret backstage rituals. The show asks why and how women perform dangerous and taboo acts and explores the legacy of forgotten and marginalized diverse British entertainers.

In a press release, I describe what audiences have in store from the work: 'Expect witchy collective going-ons in full leopard print, naked crocodile women scaling walls, ladders of swords, live hair hanging, never ending pom poms and ectoplasmic clowns, *Showwomen* channels entertainment heritage to create visons of new matriarchal performance futures' (Carnesky 2022). The work toured the South-East, culminating in a headline spot at the Theatre Tent in Latitude Festival. I also made a short accompanying ten-minute documentary film, which we now look to expand into a full-length film.

My drive to make shows gives me a deep sense of purpose and enables me to be part of a community of performers, makers, and producers. There is never enough time, money, or hours in the day to make all the shows I want to. On average, I work on 40 short-form performances with students every year and I make a new touring work every two years. I have started plotting my next show and its creation. It is a solo where the red blood of the past will turn gold as I explore stories of menopause through transformative acts.

The Showwoman has arrived to re-address the definition and bring the full flesh to the history of showpeople; the untold herstories surfacing in the now. The Showwoman is ceremonial: first, she issues the invite; she tells the community that the show is coming to town. She has authority: she commands the curtain to rise. She always makes a spectacular entrance. She leads the ritual of the show: she casts the perimeters of the space, she proposes the beginning of the show, holds the centre of the ring, and closes the circle at the end. She is witch-like, her work is traditionally the proprietress of working-class popular entertainments, she is the boss. She runs the show. Her showwomanly spectacle is different to the showman's, because as a former showgirl, she really knows how to collaborate. Most importantly, her vision is not about exploiting difference. Because she is different. She is showing herself. Because she wants to.

The transspecies Showwoman's body is transformative. Like the monarch butterfly, her extraordinary feats of flight are always under horrendous threat. So now is the time of the Showwoman with her shedded skin, her old marks, and her brave new connections. She shows us that variety entertainment was diverse even a hundred years ago; her perspective might be the immigrant, the witch, the daredevil, the activist. She has always been here, but sometimes she is obscured. She often appears in wartime; she is subversive; she is spectacular; and she makes covert actions for radical change, using her incredible talents in circus and variety. Like the tarot reader, her plight is a divinatory return to the generative, from the ruins of the war-torn city in the forgotten theatre, she enacts a never-ending rebirth, a shedding of skin; she is the alligator that escapes her oppressors and survives to reinvent herself. Her imagery is earthy, fiery, watery, and fleshy. She makes herstory, she makes new visions of new matriarchal utopias. She conjures her she-desseors, her herstorical counterparts, the ghosts of

Showwomen that she has unknowingly embodied. She uncovers hidden connections and lost stories. This is the Showwoman: she endures, she is part of a collective, she decolonizes the exotic, she transcends oppression, and she never misses a show.

She is the Showwoman, the Showwoman, the Showwoman.

Bibliography

Baskin, J. R. (2002), *Midrashic Women: Formation of the Feminine in Rabbinic Literature*, Hanover and London: Brandeis University Press and University Press of New England.

Carnesky, M. (1994–2019), Full production details and credits for all Marisa Carnesky work, available at http://carnesky.com/productions/. Accessed 19 January 2023.

Carnesky, M. (2022), Press Release for *Showwomen*, available at https://carnesky.com. Accessed 4 January 2024.

Carnesky, M. and Clifton, L. (2017), Press Release for Carnesky's Finishing School, available at https://carnesky.com. Accessed 4 January 2024.

Carnesky, M. and Power, C. (2016), Menstronauts Facebook Group, available at https://www.facebook.com/groups/136504193446334/. Accessed May 2017.

Carter, A. (1977), *The Passion of New Eve*, London: Bloomsbury.

Fanni Tutti, C. (2014), *Cosey Fanni Tutti: My Life is My Art, My Art is My Life*, available at http://www.coseyfannitutti.com. Accessed 30 March 2014.

Fonrobert, C. E. (2000), *Menstrual Purity, Rabbinic and Christian Reconstructions of Biblical Gender*, Stanford, CA: Stanford University Press.

Frankel, E. (1996), *The Five Books of Miriam*, New York: G.P Putnam's.

Gordon, M. (2006), *Voluptuous Panic: The Erotic World of Weimar Berlin*, Los Angeles, CA: Feral House.

Grahn, J. (1993), *Blood, Bread and Roses*, Boston: Beacon Press.

Jay, R. (2003), *Jay's Journal of Anomalies*, New York: Quantuck Lane.

Knight, C. (1985), 'Menstruation as medicine', *Social Science Medicine Journal*, 21:6, pp. 671–83.

Knight, C. (1991), *Blood Relations Menstruation and the Origins of Culture*, London & New Haven: Yale University Press.

Lancashire Daily Post (1942), *Crocodile Fell into Orchestra Pit*, National Fairground and Circus Archive, University of Sheffield.

Luca, B. (2015), *Send 'em out laffing*, available at http://www.laffinthedark.com/. Accessed May 2015.

Machon, J. (2009), *(Syn)aesthetics: Redefining Visceral Performance*, Basingstoke: Palgrave Macmillan.

Machon, J. in Jensen, O. and Munt, S.R. (2013), *The Ashgate Research Companion to Paranormal Cultures*, Farnham: Ashgate Research Companions.

Mock, R. (2008), *Jews and Sex*, Nottingham: Five Leaves Publications.

Ner-David, H, in Shail, A., Howie, G., and Ner-David, H. (2005), *Menstruation A Cultural History*, Basingstoke: Palgrave Macmillan.

Power, C. (2017), *Rule by the Moon*, available at https://lunarchy123.weebly.com/. Accessed November 2017.

Shuttle, P. and Redgrove, P. (1999), *The Wise Wound*, London: Marion Boyars Publishers.

Sprinkle, A. (1991), *Post Porn Modernist*, Amsterdam: Torch Books.

Sprinkle, A. (1995), *Annie Sprinkle's Post-Modern Pin Ups Pleasure Activist Playing Cards*, Vancouver: Gates of Heck.

Sprinkle, A. and Stevens, B. (2017), *Sexecology: Where Art Meets Theory Meets Practice Meets Activism*, available at http://sexecology.org/. Accessed June 2017.

Stephens, B. and Sprinkle A. (2021), *Assuming the Ecosexual Position: The Earth as Lover*, Minneapolis and London: Minnesota University Press.

The Bible (2008), *Authorized Kings James Version with Apocrypha*, Oxford: Oxford University Press.

Thompson, Y. B. (2015), *Covered in Ink*, New York: New York University Press.

Toulmin, V. (2007), 'Koringa: From Biknar to Blackpool: A female fakir's story', *Cabinet Magazine*, Issue 26: Magic, available at https://www.cabinetmagazine.org/issues/26/toulmin.php. Accessed 13 June 2015.

Toulmin, V. (n.d.), *National Fairground and Circus Archive*, available at https://nfa.dept.shef.ac.uk/holdings/collections/shufflebottom.html. Accessed 13 June 2015.

Warner, M. (2006), *Phantasmagoria*, Oxford: Oxford University Press.

Wright, O. (2014), 'Florence Shufflebottom: Staring at life down the barrel of a gun', available at https://www.bbc.co.uk/news/uk-england-south-yorkshire-29893893. Accessed June 2016.

Radical Bodies of Work

From the Finishing School of Marisa Carnesky: Lessons in Doing It Together

Phoebe Patey-Ferguson

Was anything ever finished in the finishing school? The prospectus promised to be *the* 'School for Illegitimate Entertainers of all Persuasions', in which Carnesky created a space where students can finish themselves – and each other – off.[12] Ready to graduate into the big wide world of performance equipped with all the lessons they needed to thrive and flourish. To *finish* school and set out together armed with a scope and grasp of their unique practice as artists. To *finish off* the staid, the traditional, the commercially driven, and the politically and aesthetically conservative. To resurrect the radical, the weird and the adventurous. Carnesky's style of radical cabaret is a practice of continued curiosity, driven by indeterminacy, open-ended investigation, and chance encounters. But! Things can still be *finished*, maybe even polished, to impeccably high standards, to standards that defy what might generally be perceived as *finished*.

Carnesky's Finishing School has shaped over a decade of performance makers of all ages and in the early stages of their careers.[13] Since starting at the Roundhouse in 2010, pupils have been admitted into what has been described as an 'esoteric St Trinian's for the queer cabaret generation'.[14] Held across various venues such as Bethnal Green Working Men's Club, online, and for a short time in 2016 occupying its very own basement property in Soho, the Finishing School has been a rite of passage for many self-respecting troublemakers working in experimental performance to 'discover and hone their creative talent' (McLaren 2016). The school has had a significant role in transmitting and defining the distinct set of practices that comprise contemporary alternative cabaret in the United Kingdom today.

You would be hard-pressed to find many working performers tearing up the cabaret stages in London who have not had some contact with the teachings of Carnesky. Her school, and its (very friendly) rival run by Duckie (the Duckie Homosexualist

Summer School or DHSS), has fixed up and made sharp a whole generation with an uncompromising generosity, wholehearted advocacy, and a light sprinkle of aesthetic whipping (for more on DHSS see Walters 2020: 179–231). These extra-institutional educational programmes of professional training and development often go largely unnoticed while being of extraordinary value to the overall health and continued success of nightlife which revels in risk and experimentation – particularly in the capital, but with ripples across the globe.

Entering the Finishing School is also to enter a Carnesky performance, where the *mise-en-scéne* is an imagined academy for unruly miscreants to learn some manners and how to do things properly. There is already a tongue-in-cheek set-up in which everyone is role-playing to some extent. Heike Roms identifies that 'acknowledging training, not just in the formation of a performance artist but as a part of their continuing practice, also means valuing experience, expertise and professional standing as an essential part of performance art and live art work' (Roms 2020: 118). In an interview with Ben Walters, Carnesky explains her vision:

> I've been obsessed with the idea of stage schools since attending them as a child – I loved the movie *Fame* and I've always had a vision of wearing lots of beads and leading strange, esoteric and politically motivated theatre and movement classes. I feel it's in my blood. In fact, it seems a lot of renowned London stage schools were led by Jewish grandes dames: Sylvia Young, Anna Scher … I aspire to be the tattooed avant-garde queer version!
> (Walters 2016b: n.pag.)

Along with the acquisition of techniques, imaginative skills and practical instruction in working the cabaret circuit, education is also held as the practice of pretending together, of believing in the show you are living in which is urging you towards breaking open your potentialities. So – we all have something to learn from Dr Marisa Carnesky. Here are five lessons to study to ensure you get top grades:

Lesson One: DO IT TOGETHER

Being a pupil of Carnesky's Finishing School means you are no longer alone. You are now part of a ragtag bunch of art weirdos who all want to make something happen. Upon entering the classroom, everyone agrees to the expectations to support each other, collaborate, and foster camaraderie.

DIY (Do It Yourself) arts education has a rich history in radical cultures, subcultures, and countercultures. Outside of sanctified institutions who lead with their own agenda, it places the 'learner at the centre of the experience' in order to 'follow their own interests and explore the world in whatever way they chose' (Heddon 2020: 151; Gauntlett 2018: 11). DIY citizens have been defined as individuals who are 'making themselves up as they go along' (Hartley 1999: 159). It is easy to see why queer subjects are drawn to DIY practices and the Finishing School has been predominantly attended by queers with myriad genders, sexual identities, and relationships with post-human, cyborg, goblin, and other experimental notions of self. In general, the self-creation of DIY approaches can be considered positive for queer and feminist people, particularly as we are resisting the regulation of identity that characterizes the lived experience under a right-wing totalitarian government (Ratto and Boler 2014: 5).

Part of a DIY sensibility is an action-oriented ethos, things should really happen, projects fully accomplished and acts should be finished. It is about getting things done conjointly regardless of difference. In her study of live art training, Dee Heddon highlights the standing criticism of DIY as a term, in that its 'concept of self-reliance continues to privilege the individual over the collective' (2020: 152). Many scholars and collectives have proposed that *Do It Together* (DIT) more accurately describes the kinds of queer feminist spaces which are 'united by a shared investment in the affective, emotional, empowering and transformative potentials of independent, deprofessionalised cultural productivity' (Armstrong 2009: 95). Therefore, as Red Chidgey identifies, '*individual action held within a collectivity* is really the basis of cultural resistance' for any community resisting an authoritarian identity regulation (Chidgey 2014: 103, original emphasis).

In Carnesky's Finishing School, the learning, realization, and actualization of performance are all shared. No-one is at the centre of the experience, as co-creation is at the heart of the public-facing graduating show and the sum of the cabaret is always greater than its parts. However, students are also under the close eye of a mentor of high artistic standing and are required to pay attention to the expertise that delivers the next instruction. This could appear to put the school at odds with the usual suggestion that DIY and DIT approaches are horizontal, peer-to-peer pedagogies that privilege relational modes of knowledge production, discovery, and exchange among equals (Chidgey 2014). Instead, these relational modes are enhanced by a camaraderie that is enforced by the performance of authority carried out by Carnesky as the 'teacher'. This performance might be of a strict school mistress, but in practice

Carnesky takes an approach that is 'relaxed and creative', leading by the 'carrot, not the stick' (Walters 2016b: n.pag.). Submitting, together, to this performance as pupils empowers a togetherness through a camp playing along – an idea further explored in Lesson Four.

In this way, the Doing It Together characterization of the Finishing School is more akin to the prominent modes of drag training in the twentieth century, where there are clear inheritances of skills, a passing on of information, with a shared sense of striving towards equality, empowerment, and excellence. The designation of drag 'mother' in order to join a 'family' is a queering of the typical nuclear ideology. This structure is present in many local drag contexts across the globe but was popularized – and exemplified – by the queer Black and Latinx house mothers in Harlem documented in the film *Paris Is Burning*, released in 1990. In his work on drag training, Stephen Farrier has observed that 'alongside advice on a "look" and the "structure of performance", a mentor [...] will also pass on an understanding of investing in a community' (177). He further explains that

> This kind of exchange of performance training and skill which has an appearance of a family structure [...] might form a feral pedagogy, whilst also mirroring family exchanges in other popular forms of performance, particularly circus entertainment families, who reproduce their skills within a family set-up.
> (2017, 118)

Carnesky takes the parodying of these familial structures into a more formal arrangement with the 'camping' of the notion of school, and not just any school, but the Finishing School which is supposed to transmit the absolute correct behaviour from teacher to student.

Queerly approximating the 'school' as another (potentially oppressive) social institution like the family which transmits values, oppressions, and limitations and transforming it into a space of community learning not only creates a space for learning how to be an accomplished and exciting performer but also ensures the continued survival of pupils as working artists in the fierce London arts scene. In practice, Carnesky's approach facilitates the circulation of shared knowledge between pupils as well as from instructors to students – however, as Farrier emphasizes, 'these flows of skills are specifically located' (177). Therefore, the students' work at school is inevitably imbued

Figure 93: Carnesky's Finishing School at the former Foyles Building, 2016. Soho, London. Featuring Claud Palazzo, Oberon White, Scarlett Lassoff, Gwen Delune, Tracey Smith, Tallulah Haddon, Tom Cassani, Marisa Carnesky, Jasmine Shigemura Lee, Fauve Alice, Rene Eyre, Felix Huxtable. © Sarah Ainslie

with Carnesky's particular approach to performance, shaping to varying extents the work and practices of those who enter and graduate.

Doing It Together means being a solo performer who enters the school to be held collectively. This is an antidote to the isolating experience of a landscape of dominant individuating pressures; one in which many queer performance contexts echo the dog-eat-dog ethos of reality TV drag espoused on *RuPaul's Drag Race* that prioritizes the singular 'winner' and 'beating' the competition. The Finishing School offers a chance for cooperation, mutuality, and compromise – the idea that someone else being better also makes you better. This approach does not end when Carnesky's school bell rings but permeates out into the gloomy, glittery streets of the city and has created material transformations for the togetherness of all those working in nightlife contexts.

Lesson Two: DO EVERYTHING

> It's not like we're actors who just turn up to do our own part, it was very much the circus in that we all put the tent up and we all take it down together.
> (Tom Cassani, Finishing School Alumni)

Upon graduation, pupils of the Finishing School should be consummate in knowing every aspect of the industry. They should know everything from how to pitch programmers their show to how to pitch a tent at a festival, from how to communicate their cues to a sound tech to how to manage a queue for the show, from how to create their props from the pound shop to how to run a public workshop. A sense of self(less)-reliance is fostered that (from Lesson One) values and cherishes all aspects of communal labour that are required for the show to get on. As this is school (and so not the real world), you can try everything out. You might not be good at all the tasks all of the time and that is accepted as part of the learning process – after all there is a structure of mentorship there to catch you. You Are Doing it Together!

There is a pragmatic understanding that to be a contemporary cabaret, drag, and/or live art performer is to be a freelance worker, with all the egoistic entrepreneurial hustle that requires. This position intensifies the force of neoliberalism which already 'requires individuals to become entrepreneurs in their own lives, making choices within a highly volatile world and taking individual responsibility for their failures' (Bockman 2013: 15). In his study of solo performance, Stephen Greer states that 'if entrepreneurialism grants autonomy, it might also serve to isolate' and identifies the self-driven requirement for artists to be 'responsible, productive and self-actualising individuals, and to do so through the orderly stage-management of their life stories' (Greer 2018: 10). Learning a set of expanded skills that might fall under the broad umbrella of 'stage-management' is necessary for continued survival while producing and selling the extremely valuable commodity of performance in this current flaming late-capitalist nightmare (Blackwell-Pall et al. 2021: 42–43).

It is impossible for stage management to be a solo activity. Furthermore, following artist and queer icon Peggy Shaw's declaration that 'I am a solo artist and, by virtue of that, a collaborator' (2011: 39), we understand that no-one is ever truly alone on the stage. Particularly in nightlife contexts, collaboration and cooperative support are necessary – partly due to the community nature of these spaces and partly due to economic precarity. It is the reality of these situations that you might have to be someone's stooge, make-up artist, costumer, sound tech, prop operator, or any myriad of roles before or after your own set. And this offer is always returned. Recognizing mutuality becomes an act of political resistance, operating in the cracks of the dominant system. Building your own skills becomes about something you can offer someone else – a focus on what you can give and not what you want to take.

This recognition of the *real* social, political, and economic conditions of the spaces of cultural production for the kinds of performance Carnesky fosters means that, first, her pupils are trained in operating successfully as workers in order to survive in an arts scene shaped since 2010 by policies and ideologies of austerity. Second, graduates are encouraged through political education to be engaged in changing and challenging those circumstances through increased shared support. Third, artists are trained in imagining different and better futures for the industry and the wider world which centres agency, multiplicity, and mutual support. One such possible future that pulls on these threads is theorized by Finishing School alumni Oozing Gloop in their growing body of work on Commucracy which desires 'to ensure *individual* autonomy within collectivised living'. With confidence, Gloop proposes 'The Commucratic Question: What are the commons of this situation? And how can we democratise them?' (2020: 9).

Lesson Three: CREATE A MOMENT OF WONDER

Now the tent is erect what will happen inside it!? The first two lessons are methodologies of backstage pedagogical practice, ethos and effect, but none of that can make an appearance unless there is something to put on stage in front of the anticipating audience. In terms of class time, stagecraft is the primary activity at the centre of Carnesky's lessons. Each pupil is required to make a distinct 'act' in their time at the school, to be performed to a paying audience at the end of term and usually toured as part of a Finishing School showcase to festivals such as Bestival or Latitude. Most alumni continue to perform the acts they develop at school for years on various circuits.

As with most occult practices, it is not appropriate to go into detail about the exact teaching arsenal Carnesky uses to approach her workshop pedagogy. This repertoire holds significant power and any attempt to reproduce them here risks dilution. Therefore, the below ABC (and so on) is offered in broad strokes as required to enable insight without cheap replication:

A is for ... Active!

Doing practical exercises designed to get everyone moving, loose and in their bodies.

B is for ... Book!

Tasks such as free writing open up each pupil to explore what they have entered the space carrying and get it down on paper as material to be played with.

C is for ... Construct!

Every performer needs structure. Cabaret slots are short and you have very limited time to set your scene, introduce what/who/where you are, to make everyone pay attention to you, create your desired affect, and be unforgettable. Alumni Jo Marius Hauge shared the structure Carnesky created for their act:

1. *Entrance*
2. *Two Levels/A Level Change*
3. *Directional Change (Blocking)*
4. *Reveal (Physical?)*
5. *MOMENT OF WONDER*
6. *4 Images*
7. *Exit*

Hauge reflected that 'these were suggestions of elements you might have, broken down for you. Not at all in a prescriptive way. More like, here are some building blocks for you' (2021). Absolutely anything could happen between or during these steps and everyone's scaffold will necessarily be a different shape between entrance and exit – but having a pace and knowing the steps helps focus the act.

D is for ... Discover a MoW!

A Moment of Wonder (or MoW!) has, in Hauge's own words:

> ten million ways of happening [...] either through a reveal or after what you've set up comes together. To me it felt really expansive, anything that makes people go 'Oh! I didn't expect that!' It can tie something together, or bring something back, or completely change what's happened before, or destroy something you've set up. It doesn't have to make sense, it doesn't have to make the audience cry or shock them or any unifying reaction. It's just like this open idea of wonder! So, if I pull something out of somewhere, or I'm now glowing, or slime is pouring out my nose – that doesn't have to make sense or tie everything up it just has to try to be wondrous.
> (2021)

E is for ... Explore stuff!

Bringing in big boxes of tricks with wigs, capes, fabric, masks, and other assorted 'stuff' can spark inspiration and encourage the work to be differently ambitious. The sculptural, the visual, and the textual are all held in dialogue with the movement of the body and voice.

F is for ... Find your archetype!

However outlandish an act is, it still must be legible for an audience to really pay attention – are you the witch, the hero, or the jester? Considering which archetype a persona might be, or working out what it currently is, gives a framework to anticipate projection. This draws on Jungian notions of the collective unconscious as projections that embody societal struggles and recognizable figures. It gives a point from which to connect to and then subvert expectations.

G is for… Guest teachers!

Outside eyes are always important. At The Finishing School, Lisa Lee, co-founder of The LipSinkers, joined and offered essential feedback on each pupil's work in progress. Carnesky called Lee her 'co-tutor', but descriptions of Lee's presence by pupils cast her in the role more akin to an Ofsted inspector or cheerleading coach (Walters 2016b: n.pag.).

H is for … Heart!

It is important to be true to yourself at all times. As Hauge acknowledges above, there are a 'million ways' to put these lessons into practice. Carnesky ensures that the work of one pupil never looks or feels like anyone else's. Each pupil is unique in the artistic collision of the moment. Furthermore, radical political cabaret starts by focusing on the body as the main site where the state exerts control and therefore anything that is fully embodied has to be idiosyncratic.

I is for … Intensity and Integrity!

Cassani spoke of how Carnesky would make pupils consider how to 'push this further'. Asking,

> How do you make it more of the thing that it is? If it's sexual, how do you make it more sexual? How do you make it more grotesque? How do you make it *more*?! Not for the sake of it, but how to make it cabaret? Make it more of a show? How do you make it bigger, louder and punchier in three minutes? (2021)

In their tutorage, Carnesky and Lee encourage pupils to do anything they want, however whacky, but to be really good at it. The magic trick has to be exactly right to be magical. The lip sync has to be on point. If there's dancing, you have to nail your routine.

Many pupils reflected on how Carnesky encourages everyone to expand their comfort zone. A student might arrive knowing they want to do something traditionally recognizable on the nightclub stage such as be a beautiful drag queen and do a lip sync. They would be asked 'why?' Carnesky would then take the identified motivation behind this desire and embolden them to pick apart their drag, dismantle their concept, and create a new monster out of it. The aim is to create something unlike anything seen before; to create something weird, personal, subversive, and unexpected.

J is for ... Joyful submission!

Signing up for the school is agreeing to the terms set out by Carnesky. There is no option to be a wallflower or to avoid the group numbers. As Cassani recalled,

> It's like ... whether you like it or not, you're doing it! Because that's what we're doing and that's what the whole show is. It's this entourage. The story is we're her pupils and she's been teaching us this mad stuff. We have to set the scene together and get everyone going for what we've got to show and tell.
> (2021)

... and Z is for ... Zeal!

Whatever you have planned to do, when you get on stage you have to bring all your energy, enthusiasm, and passion to it. An audience will always respond to commitment and gusto!

Lesson Four: CABARET IS A (CLASS)ROOM

> The word cabaret means room. It could be a bar with a stage, or a theatre, or indeed a classroom – the point is the gathering of people in a space and the unique encounter that results when they exchange not just energy but also words, actions, feelings. The cabaret space is closer than the proscenium-arch theatre to a more empathetic, progressive learning environment in which the teacher facilitates rather than dominates, leads the conversation rather than remains the only voice heard. The physicality of the space is important too: the lighting set-ups that allow for eye contact between performers and audience, the ability of the acts to walk among and touch the punters, the cultivation of a sense of dialogue, not monologue.
> (Ben Walters, *A Cabaret Classroom*, 2016a: n.pag.)

As Greer has identified, using the term 'school' in the context of radical performance training recognizes its own position as an assumed outsider status. Drawing on the work of Bryant Keith Alexander, he argues that 'the paradigm of performance studies has the capacity to capitalize on the implication of "school" within relations of power and social practice to reveal, interrogate and challenge "legitimated social forms of teaching, learning and knowing"' (Greer 2020: 216). The framing as 'school', along with uniforms, blackboards, and role-play, is a deliberate camp strategy of constructed artifice which only draws attention to how much this is *not* school, or like any school anyone ever actually had to attend. It is a fantasy school that poses as a school in an exaggerated fashion (hence calling to mind comparisons with other fictional schools such as St Trinian's).

Education is serious business. Access to education is one of the defining societal determiners which shape an entire society. In *Notes on Camp*, Susan Sontag identifies camp as 'a sensibility that converts the serious into the frivolous' (1964: 1). Of course, it is not performance that is frivolous but the required performance of being at school with its petty rules and strict hierarchies. But the campness of the Finishing School is never shallow frivolity, following Bruce la Bruce's investigation on camp, it is 'an existential condition as much as a sensibility: an enormously serious and profound frivolity'. He continues, accurately contradicting Sontag identifying that camp is 'by its very nature political, subversive, even revolutionary' (LaBruce 2013: n.pag.). LaBruce declares that camp should be 'a kind of madness, a rip in the fabric of reality that we need to reclaim in order to defeat the truly inauthentic, cynical and deeply reactionary' (2013: n.pag.). The first step is to 'celebrate, elevate and even worship qualities of deviance, difference and eccentricity', and this aesthetic and political aim of camp is fully harnessed in the Finishing School (n.pag.). Camp*ing* school also helps circumvent and reclaim difficult feelings about hierarchy and control in educational contexts, freeing each participant up to the possibility that being instructed by someone highly experienced can be hugely beneficial and pleasurable.

Apart from the fact that most schools reject any notion of fun, for many of the pupils that have attended Carnesky's classes, school was a place that reinforced their 'misfit' status –particularly as queers. bell hooks centres the belief that reinvigorating a learning experience with excitement, fun, and pleasure is at the core of transgressive, revolutionary pedagogy:

> *Excitement* in [...] education was viewed as potentially disruptive of the atmosphere of seriousness assumed to be essential to the learning process. To enter classroom settings [...] with the will to share the desire to encourage excitement, was to transgress. Not only did it require movement beyond

accepted boundaries, but excitement could not be generated without a full recognition of the fact that there could never be an absolute set agenda governing teaching practices.

(hooks 1994: 7, emphasis in the original)

hooks explains that excitement about ideas is only the first step. Real excitement is generated by 'our interest in one another', a shared attentiveness of 'collective effort' which requires everyone to ... Do It Together! (1994: 8)

It has been established that radical performance pedagogy can and does exist through artist-led training as exemplified in Guillermo Gómez Peña and Roberto Sifuentes' book *Exercises for Rebel Artists: Radical Performance Pedagogy* (2011)– a book which documents the activities and methods of the international performance troupe La Pocha Nostra. hook's work brings a consideration of how radical pedagogy has the potential to transform the space inside an institution as well as outside of it. Although the work of the Finishing School and other Radical Cabaret training has been forged independently of official educational establishments, Carnesky now brings this learning into delivering a Bachelors of the Arts degree programme in Contemporary and Popular Performance at Rose Bruford College in partnership with Tramshed in Woolwich.

It remains an open question whether educational and arts institutions are able to nurture truly practice due to their structure, histories, social, and economic dynamics. Both institutions in which the new course is based have their own threads of radical history. Rose Bruford College's legendary Community Theatre Arts course formed some of the most important contemporary figures in British theatre and the wider creative fields including current Principal and Booker Prize winning author Bernadine Evaristo, director Paulette Randall, playwright and project manager Patricia St Hilaire (who together formed Britain's first Black women's theatre company, Theatre of Black Women, in 1982), as well as alt-cabaret's producing stalwart Simon Casson – co-founder of Duckie. Tramshed is the home of the Greenwich and Lewisham Young People's Theatre (GLYPT), who have been working locally for over 50 years to deliver workshops and creative opportunities to as many young people as possible. Since the 1970s, Tramshed has been home to cabaret and comedy nights such as Fundation (with Gareth Hale and Norman Pace), The South of Deptford Comedy Club (with Julian Clary and Harry Enfield), and this progressive history is continued in nights such as Tramtastic, a fully accessible club night centring those with learning disabilities.

Tramshed is already enacting alternative institutional dynamics by leveraging their accrued social, cultural, and economic capital to take a proactive role in the service of their local area by operating daily as a vibrant community hub.

As Stefano Harney and Fred Moten warn in their work on the 'University and the Undercommons', there is always a risk of radical practice, mystery, and togetherness being depoliticized and neutralized through the professionalization at work in the university (2013: 22–43). However, the stability of infrastructure that gives respite from the precarity of freelancing should not be overlooked as it can offer (when it is functioning correctly): adequate, guaranteed, regular payment for labour; increased care and student support services; collegiality and cooperation between teachers and researchers; opportunities for research support, development, and scholarship; accountability and complaint processes; and greater disabled accessibility through increased resources. There is always hope things can be altered from the inside and a fugitive space of transgression to be carved out in any classroom. As hooks writes: 'the academy is not paradise. But learning is a place where paradise can be created. the classroom, with all its limitations, remains a location of possibility' (hooks 1994: 207).

I am now teaching alongside Carnesky and my sincere hope is that, alongside many other colleagues, we will be able to bring the excitement, pleasure, weirdness, experimentation, and subversion of school into transforming the institutional space of higher education. This new course does not replace the importance of independent, artistic-led artist training, but is a new branch that expands possibilities for valuing cabaret and nightlife performance as a vital artistic form: another room in which to stage an encounter.

Lesson Five: CONTINUE TO CELEBRATE

The public-facing performance work is the most evident outcome of the school – the 'profession' which people graduate into. The community-building element is vitally important too, as the art scene is formed from an often informally structured, complex, fluid, and dynamic set of social groupings which allows people who have non-normative selfhoods and (often) even less normative performance practices to be connected on and off-stage and for new forms to be forged and future possibilities to flourish.

After the show: Dance. Chat to as many people as possible. Toast what went well in your work. Loudly praise what went well in other people's work. Don't go home immediately.

Clear up your own shit. Help clear up other people's shit. Get really good at doing your make-up in a festival portaloo. Firm up your star status. Get bookings. Keep in touch with your teacher. Offer to help other people set up their space. If you don't get booked create a new context. Start a night. If you need it, someone else will. Hustle. Don't do it alone. Namedrop that Marisa taught you, so people know where you've come from. Teach others. There is always more to learn – we are never finished.

Bibliography

Armstrong, J. (2009), 'DIY feminism: A dialogical account', Ph.D. thesis, London: University of East London.

Blackwell-Pal, J., Boyle, M. S., Dilks, McGuiness, A., Mader, C., Mckeon, O., Moravec, L., Simari, A., Unger, C., and Young, M. (2021), 'Marxist keywords for performance', *Journal of Dramatic Theory and Criticism*, 36:1, pp. 25–53.

Bockman, J. (2013), 'Neoliberalism', *Contexts*, 12:3, pp. 14–15.

Cassani, T. (2021), Interview with Author [Zoom], 1 November.

Chidgey, R. (2014), 'Developing communities of resistance? Maker pedagogies, do-it-yourself feminism, and DIY citizenship', in M. Ratto and M. Boler (eds), *DIY Citizenship: Critical Making and Social Media*, Cambridge, MA: The MIT Press, pp. 73–85.

Farrier, S. (2017), 'International influences and drag: Just a case of tucking or binding?' *Theatre, Dance and Performance Training*, 8:2, pp. 171–87.

Gauntlett, D. (2018), *Making Is Connecting: The Social Power of Creativity, from Craft and Knitting to Digital Everything*, London: Polity Press.

Gloop, O. (2020), *Commucracy Now! The Revolution is Buffering*, London: Oozing Gloop.

Gloop, O. (2022), Interview with Author [Zoom], 10 January.

Greer, S. (2018), *Queer Exceptions: Solo Performance in Neoliberal Times*, Manchester: Manchester University Press.

Greer, S. (2020), 'Training for live art: Process peadagogies and new moves international winter schools', *Theatre, Dance and Performance Training*, 11:2, pp. 214–228

Harney, S. and Moten, F. (2013), *The Undercommons: Fugitive Planning and Black Study*, Wivenhoe: Minor Compositions.

Hartley, J. (1999), *Uses of Television*, London: Routledge.

Hauge, J. M. (2021), Interview with Author [Zoom], 8 November.

Heddon, D. (2020), 'Professional development for live artists: Doing it yourself', *Theatre, Dance and Performance Training*, 11:2, pp. 145–61.

hooks, b. (1994), *Teaching to Transgress: Education as the Practice of Freedom*, New York and London: Routledge.

LaBruce, B. (2013), 'Notes on camp/anti-camp', *Nat. Brut*, 3, available at http://www.natbrutarchive.com/essay-notes-on-campanti-camp-by-bruce-labruce.html. Accessed January 2023.

McLaren, J. (2016), 'Carnesky's finishing school arrives in Soho', *Run Riot!*, 9 September, available at http://www.run-riot.com/articles/notices/news-carnesky%E2%80%99s-finishing-school-arrives-soho. Accessed January 2023.

Ratto, M. and Boler, M. (eds) (2014), *DIY Citizenship: Critical Making and Social Media*, Cambridge, Massachusetts: The MIT Press.

Roms, H. (2020), 'Training for performance art and live art', *Theatre, Dance and Performance Training*, 11:2, pp. 117–25.

Shaw, P. (2011), 'On being an independent solo artist (no such thing)', in J. Dolan and P. Shaw (eds), *A Menopausal Gentleman: The Solo Performances of Peggy Shaw*, Ann Arbor: University of Michigan Press, pp. 39–46.

Sontag, S. (1964), 'Notes on "camp"', *Partisan Review*, 31:4, pp. 515–30.

Walters, B. (2016a), 'A cabaret classroom', *Exeunt Magazine*, 14 September, available at http://exeuntmagazine.com/features/a-cabaret-classroom/. Accessed January 2023.

Walters, B. (2016b), 'Summon the courage: Marisa Carnesky on fighting with theatre', *Run Rio*, 17 October, available at http://www.run-riot.com/articles/blogs/summon-courage-marisa-carnesky-fighting-theatre. Accessed January 2023.

Walters, B. (2020), 'Dr Duckie homemade mutant hope machines: The Ph.D.', Ph.D. Thesis, Queen Mary University of London.

Finding Power in Pathos

Alex Lyons

Desiring to be a part of Carnesky's Cabaret collective, I joined *Carnesky's Radical Cabaret School* in 2020; it was the peak of lockdown, when the world felt heavy and COVID-19 had dominated our lives. The many approaches of facilitation implemented by Carnesky within her school have left a lasting impression on me, in particular, the phrase 'finding power in pathos', a term she taught within the school (Carnesky 2020). Pathos is defined as a feeling of sorrow or sadness. Pathos for some artists is also employed as a device to establish an emotional connection and to evoke a feeling within the audience. For others, such as Carnesky, employing pathos is a way of revealing and finding power in one's identity, using personal experiences to cultivate a feeling of shared identification and political transformation.

An example of when I experienced the pedagogical efficacy of pathos in Carnesky's work was within her performance *Dr Carnesky's Incredible Bleeding Woman* (2016): on the stage's backcloth, a video is projected. I watch Marisa Carnesky's naked body move towards a bathtub of blood. She slowly steps into the tub and begins to lower herself down, submerging the lower half of her body in the red liquid. With her back in view, Carnesky bends forward and cups the bloody water in her hands; her vertebra protrudes from under her skin before she lets the liquid wash over her. The motion is repeated. She cups the liquid, raises her hands to her body, and releases. As the ritualistic movement continues, Carnesky tells the audience a personal and devastating account of the recurrent miscarriages she has experienced.

In this performance, Carnesky and her assembled group of radical cabaret artists perform a series of menstrual rituals that explore both an ethnographic and personal response to menstruation, tracing menstrual journeys of gender identity, feminism, loss, life, activism, and kinship. What I encountered in the moment of Carnesky's story is an intimate exchange of trust and empathy, a revealing of something personal, and a permittance to look inwards at my own relationship and view of menstrual blood. An often-tabooed topic was transformed into a site of power and reclamation.

This approach to performance that privileges a sense of empathy and connection was echoed in Carnesky's teachings within the school. The online version of *Carnesky's Radical Cabaret School* ran for the duration of eight weeks towards an end goal: to assist in or produce a short performance. Each week the group was set a new creative inquiry through a video module Carnesky had designed for the course. These modules suggested a series of performative prompts to do at home which helped layer our performance work and find connections to the political, to the everyday, to the self, asking us to creatively reflect upon our own experiences within the world in order to inform our artistic development. The structure of Carnesky's course reflected upon the processes and principles that she employs in her own performance work. This was particularly recognizable in the module Carnesky entitled 'Trans-metaformism' which focused on the dialogue of transformation, asking the group to draw from our memories to 'reveal our identities' and find our very own 'power in pathos' (Carnesky 2020). Here, pathos was framed as a creative methodology in exploring what is important and urgent within our work as artists. Within live art practices, the context of pathos can reveal an artist's political and personal ideologies to an audience in hopes to highlight or confront a particular issue drawn from their identity. Performance artist Martin O'Brien provides an apt example, employing body-based practices to challenge representations of cystic fibrosis and sick bodies. Co-founder of the Live Art Development Agency (LADA), Lois Keidan in Maria Chatzichristodoulou's book, *Live Art in the UK: Contemporary Performances of Precarity* (2020) discusses how '[l]ive artists are negotiating complex, loaded issues, such as difference and representations of identity' (Keidan in Chatzichristodoulou 2020: 13). The paradigm of pathos in this instance was to challenge our understanding of what performances of identity politics can be and how our voices can reverberate to audiences.

The exercise invited each person to draw upon either a difficult or happy memory from our childhood and perform it in an opposite emotion. The memory acted as a catalyst for connection and conversation, driven by an urgency to share something about ourselves. I found pathos in the memory of being thirteen years old, feeling ashamed of my vulva and protruding labia. I spoke about my desire to remove parts of my inner labia in my teenage years before understanding that the way I felt towards my body was the product of internalized misogyny. Carnesky had phrased the exercise as a means of 'break[ing] the taboos that are inside of ourselves' (Carnesky 2020). The object was not to disclose any potentially triggering details but rather to reveal an authenticity and stake to our work that could be processed and experienced by an audience.

For me, performing this exercise required a certain degree of vulnerability and risk, a discomfort in sharing something personal to articulate the deeper issues that my work explores. Yet, what I discovered was how the intimate quality of finding power in pathos can be transformative, both personally and creatively. As a neurodivergent woman, I have often found it challenging to verbally communicate my ideas on stage. Pathos encouraged me to uncover validity in my voice by retelling the story without masking behind pre-recorded audios, communicating a more meaningful and responsive message around my memory. In their chapter, 'Dyspraxic approaches to teaching Live Art in a "neurodivergent"/"normodivergent" classroom' (2022), Sumita Majumdar and Daniel Oliver discuss how the 'foregrounding of subjective experience and identity politics, was key to [Oliver] embracing his own divergent modes of being and doing in his performance practice' (Oliver and Majumdar 2022: 218). Similarly, embracing my identity politics and lived experiences through pathos enabled an acceptance of my own neurodivergence when creating work. Through this process, I was able to expose a deeper sense of my identity that enabled an intimate, visceral, and authentic exchange with the audience around the themes of gender, queer identity, and body politics. As the topics of my work are inherently intertwined with taboo in cultural and social contexts, the breaking of taboos within myself felt immensely cathartic. Indeed, Carnesky's approach not only allowed space to break a taboo within myself but also sought to draw out some distinctive reasonings behind the complexities of my work.

Across the group, individual voices and stories emerged inside our collective online space, stories that resonated, stories that established connections with those listening and stories that gave an insight into different lived experiences. I felt a closeness to the artists, a familiarity usually only encountered through kinds of kinship wherein pathos also contributes as a strategy for connection and mutual understanding. As a listener, you are offered an intimate insight into the person in front of you. Whilst the performances produced sought to be transformative in the themes they addressed, transformative action also took place through simply being able to take up space, allowing for otherwise invisible identities to be seen.

Carnesky nurtured a group of artists who wanted to make an impact and led us to understand that there is solidarity in performance. Being a part of this collective made the world feel less isolating in a time of physical isolation. Our collectivism was a production of taking up more space, an invitation to find power in our identities, a provocation for change, an exploration of ideas, and a community. There was an urgency to create and question what is at stake in the work. Carnesky's teachings allowed us to achieve a sharing – an intimate understanding – one that facilitated the audience to truly connect with both the performer and the performance. *Carnesky's Radical Cabaret School* provided comfort in a place of chaos, a community in a time of displacement, and gave space to a group of rebel rousers to unleash their creativity and be heard. What could be more radical than that.

Bibliography

Carnesky, M. (2020), 'Trans-metaformism', *Carnesky's Radical Cabaret School* [Recorded Lecture]. Session 3. Tramshed, 20 October, available at https://vimeo.com/468246310. Accessed 23 September 2022.

Chatzichristodoulou, M. (2020), *Live Art in the UK: Contemporary Performances of Precarity*, London & New York: Bloomsbury Publishing, Kindle e-book.

Oliver, D and Majumdar, S. (2022), 'Dyspraxic approaches to teaching Live Art in a "neurodivergent"/"normodivergent" classroom', in P. Whitfield (ed.), *Inclusivity and Equality in Performance Training: Teaching and Learning for Neuro and Physical Diversity*, New York and Oxon: Taylor & Francis, pp. 217–31.

The Coven

Amy Ridler

I met Marisa Carnesky in 2009 at an after party at the Soho Theatre, when a mutual friend introduced us after a Michelangelo & The Black Sea Gentlemen show. Not long after this first meeting, I found myself sitting on the floor of Marisa's house, in front of a roaring fire, listening to Mae West and having my tarot read. We talked and talked all evening, red wine flowing, and vaguely discussed the possibility of me working on a show (I was doing make-up at the time). The evening ended with us watching *Dances Sacred and Profane* and me crashing out on the sofa. That night, in 2009, I had no idea that I would work with Carnesky Productions, let alone still be collaborating with Marisa thirteen years later.

When asked to write this piece, my first thought was: I am no Showwoman. Then I started thinking about the women behind the scenes, the women who support, the women who promote, and the women who, like Marisa and I, are a sounding board for each other's ideas. Of course, the women who perform are Showwomen, but from the performance springs community. The connections that are born from the show are often lifelong. Carnesky Productions is a middle finger up to every man who has profited from a woman's ideas or skills. It is a team and becomes family. A group of women who are equal, whether you are, like me at the time, a 20-year-old trying to figure out what I wanted to be or an established internationally renowned performer. When you are working in the company that does not matter, and it is a very special and rare dynamic to be a part of. I realize, as I get older, that it is not normal to start a sentence with, 'Oh yeah, here is my friend the – insert: sword swallower/ hair hanger/ fire breather', but it is a great privilege. If you have ever been on a tour with Carnesky Productions – my mind instantly goes back to the entire cast sharing a flat in Edinburgh for a month, or in a show – I am reminded of countless tour bus rides

Figure 94: Fancy Chance and Amy Ridler, Metal Culture, artists' residency, 2015. Southend. © Sarah Ainslie

(sometimes Transit van in the earlier days), all piled in, early hours of the morning singing our hearts out to *Picture This* – you are bonded. It is unspoken.

My role within the Carnesky coven changed as my confidence grew. Marisa had asked me if I wanted to be part of the company the evening that she read my tarot, and I, a young goth struggling to make ends meet as a make-up artist/barmaid, had jumped at the chance. What I learned that night was that if Marisa says something, she follows through. *Dystopian Wonders* was just about to start a UK tour, following its successful run at The Roundhouse. True to her word, Marisa invited me to join the tour, and thus, my involvement in the world of Carnesky Productions began. My first role was as an anatomical body in *Dystopian Wonders* (2010). The brief was simple: lay on a table whilst a contortionist pulls out your entrails. I was no performer, but even I could manage that. *Tarot Drome* (2012) saw me take on the role of make-up artist for the cast at The Old Vic Tunnels and, later, at Bestival. Looking up at the roof of a big top, at the Cirque Jules Verne, I remember consciously stopping my conversation, and walking away from the rest of the cast to take a moment to appreciate that I was really there. In my early 20s, just dropped out of an art foundation degree, no big plans for the future other than wanting to be a writer, there I was, working on a queer, feminist, occult circus show in Amiens.

Dr Carnesky's Incredible Bleeding Woman (*DCIBW*) is another project that has been really important to me. Marisa asked me to join the initial research project and development of the show. The research for *DCIBW* was unlike any other project I have worked on. Marisa, Rhyannon Styles, H Plewis, Livia Kojo Alour, Veronica Thompson, Nao Nagai, Lara Clifton, and I travelled to the seaside to stay at Metal Culture, Southend, the Artist Residence. Every new moon, we ate together, spent time reflecting on our cycles and moods. We engaged in rituals – each led by one of us. We workshopped ideas and spoke openly about personal experiences in our past. As we sat around the table, you could feel that this work really meant something to each of us. The coven – as we dubbed ourselves at some point during the project – was strong. There was a gentleness when dealing with each other, with stories of experiences that were workshopped but never shared outside of the group. That gentleness continues and it has fostered a fierce loyalty to protect and defend each other to this day.

Marisa has been bringing women together for over twenty years. A company made of women, when even the crew and tech are predominantly women, feels like a shift. During the time I have had a role within the company, I have seen so many performers work with Marisa at the beginning of their career and go on to make amazing and important work. The Carnesky alumnae is vast. I have also met a host of influential Showwomen: sharing a late dinner with Annie Sprinkle and Beth Stephens in Bethnal Green after their film premiere, or sipping cocktails at the Barbican Martini Bar with Lois Weaver and Peggy Shaw. The net is cast wide. For me, it began by meeting the cast of *Dystopian Wonders*, but it became an opportunity to meet and work with women who are integral members of the performance and live art world. These women shaped the woman I am today, which is a direct result of a shared thread that runs through so many of our lives.

The Department of Feminist Conversations in Dialogue with Marisa Carnesky's Live Archive

Mary Paterson and Maddy Costa
for the Department of Feminist Conversations

1. Orientations

Q: Where does your history find you?

On impact with the border, the name is amputated. Letters shaved off, syllables chiselled. Appropriately shrunk, the name can be held before the body as a mask: better still, it becomes a tool of assimilation, fashioned and gifted back to the owner by immigration control. (The tool is not guaranteed to be effective.)

The mutilated name stands for the whole, as the colonizer stands for its empire, subsuming identities, eliminating complexity. Any narrative it once held – akin to the clear, concise histories conveyed through names as occupations (smith, baker, cook), as indications of learning (clark, robert), as markers of roots in place (heath, dale, ford), and of course the belonging of patronymics – all comparable story is discarded as inessential.

'Among human beings', writes Simone Weil, 'only the existence of those we love is fully recognised' (2005: 291). Those who are not loved do not require names by which they recognize themselves, only names by which they might be stamped and shunted into order.

And yet.

There is a bit of a complication here, says Marisa Carnesky in *The Girl From Nowhere* (2003). These names, their languages, are strung through the body like veins. Behind the masks are mutable relations of name to place, place to map, map to land, land to story, story to imagination, and imagination to possibility. Animated by desire, bodies keep moving, moving despite borders, moving to (through) the chaos where order does not reach.

Q: When did you first feel yourself disappear?

Bodies keep moving where order does not reach.

'As a consequence of its embodiment', writes Guilia Palladini 'the archive ceases to have a domicile and is forced to embrace nomadism and migration' (2017: 15). She is writing about one archive in particular – the books committed to memory in François Truffaut's film *Fahrenheit 451* (1966) – and she is talking about archives in general: the way that archives survive through transmission from body to body.

Marisa Carnesky's *Live Archive* opens with a rag-doll image of a woman: dark haired, pale skinned, and brightly clothed. Click on one of the words around her body and you will zoom in to see the rag doll is made of the kind of half-magic you find backstage at a theatre: reams of crumpled satin, disjointed mannequin parts, bicycle wheels, high-heeled shoes, old umbrellas, vintage telephones. You can almost smell the old leather and cracked vinyl. You can almost feel your fingers winding through the curly telephone wires. These are props from the past and of the past. Perhaps you recognize them as things you have seen in one of Marisa Carnesky's shows; perhaps you recognize them as the kind of thing you might have seen.

Imagine I am with you while you look. Imagine that I am your archive; I am the hook that catches on to the frayed threads of your library of secrets and pulls them out, limb by limb, for you to remember. Imagine I am your half-anecdotes, half-documents, half-photographs, and half-life. I am naïve and childish in my recollections. I am committed to memory. I am on the move.

Zoom in to the rag doll and here is another body: the real body of Marisa Carnesky. Here, she is rendered twice unreal: unreal because this is not Marisa Carnesky of course, but a digital representation of her; and unreal because this is not the person Marisa Carnesky but the performer, who presents a version of her, curled up temporarily inside one of her rag-doll body parts. This real/unreal Marisa Carnesky – the person, the performer, the magician, the Showwoman – is here to introduce you to the films of her past shows.

The archive (that archive, this archive) 'is entrusted to the chance agency of other bodies', says Palladini, 'who choose to take up its affective potential and become its new archiving impulse' (2017: 15).

Each film shows the real body rendered once again unreal: past versions of Carnesky, recognizable but different, appearing in grainy footage in long-demolished spaces in long-disappeared times. Perhaps some of the films are as real to you as a memory: the smell of a Victorian theatre, the sound of bodies hushed by the dimming of the lights, the sudden apparition of a troupe of people gliding on roller skates onto a stage. Perhaps others are fragrant with strangers' movements; a sideways view of bodies sitting inside a performance venue, the muffled audio of a hidden cameraman, the silhouettes of people's heads.

Your memories reach out to the archive, while the archive reaches out to you.

Imagine we are with them all: we soak their senses into our own skins, render our own ideas real and unreal and entangled with them; part-memory, part-magic, part-document, part-dream. This is how the archive is transmitted from one body to the next. This is how the individual dissolves into the collective. This is how we learn to cross borders.

Q: What have you lost to obsolete technologies?

This is how we learn.

Once upon a time there was (a woman) (a midwife) (a gossip) (a witch).

Each with her own (knowledge) (skill) (perspicacity) (magic).

Magic: 'premised on the belief', writes Sylvia Federici, 'that the world is animated, unpredictable, and that there is a force in all things' (2004: 173). A force that capitalism sought to (contain) (supplant) (suppress) (eliminate).

I pull (she pulls) (we pull) a card from the tarot deck. (Rider-Waite, illustrated by Pamela Colman Smith, first published 1909.) The High Priestess: lodged between strength and establishment, black and white, masculine might and masculine order. Her gown a waterfall, blue as the sky. Moon at her feet, ready to prick her.

Once upon a time, 'the very existence of magical beliefs was a source of social insubordination', writes Federici (2004: 143). Or rather, 'the belief that there are lucky and unlucky days, that is, days on which one can travel and others on which one should not move from home' (2004: 142) made labourers (unreliable) (chaotic) (irregular) (ungovernable).

Pull another card. The Empress, upright on her cushioned throne, stiff with responsibility. Robe stamped in pomegranates, the fruit that consigned Persephone to a life half in hell.

Science, philosophy, religion, all required to destroy 'a universe of practices, beliefs, and social subjects whose existence was incompatible with the capitalist work discipline' (2004: 165).

Another card. The Magician: sword and wand at his command, cup and coin of plenty. In the *Tarot Drome* (2012), a re-imagined, animated, living-breathing tarot deck commandeered by Marisa Carnesky, the Magician pushes swords through the body of a (woman) (midwife) (gossip) (witch). This is a collaborative act, she escapes the blades unscathed.

Once upon a time, writes Federici, there was a fleet of fishermen who, far out at sea, missed the anti-woman propaganda that elsewhere resulted in executions. Back on shore, they were the only men known to intervene against the persecution of witches (2004: 189).

Another. The Hanged Man. Suspended. Caught in time. Caught by fate. Ballet slippers on his feet, head crowned with a glowing halo.

These may not be the canonical interpretations. Interpretation is no simple matter.

Q: What remains hidden when the final layer is removed?

Existence is no simple matter.

Perhaps there was a time when the archive thought her body might contain herself, or her idea of herself, or of who she might become. Perhaps there was a time when she thought she might align with other people's dreams of the future, might grow up to become one of those most imaginary of creatures – let's call them Men – whose words live in fresh print on new pages, copied down for centuries, etched into the school curriculum, inked into the minds of young travellers in time.

Or perhaps she knew, perhaps deep down she had always known, that she would be one of the frequently forgotten, the centuries-silent, the heavy-bodied, the dirty, the mucky, the animal people – let's call them Women – who lunge from border to border, who haunt the edge-lands of their mother tongue.

The archive parades herself in front of you, her skin, her limbs, her hair stretched out like a beautiful poem. She hides in the shadows, her magic, her music, her tricks hidden like a delicious secret.

She says some words in a forgotten language and cuts the delicate blanket of our skin.

2. Bodies, Real and Imagined

Q: Where does your history find you?

Cut the deck to the open-mouthed lion, its jaw and forehead caressed by the hands of Strength.

The reclaimed name is an act of resuscitation: air into the bellows that fan the fire that sets ideas aflame. It is the revelation of always present ghosts, skeletons reassembled, bones injected with marrow.

The reclaimed name is a swelling stomach, the roll of fat through thighs, long fingers with short nails, or short fingers with long nails, dimpled cheeks – face or buttocks – and especially, especially, an unfurled tongue. Touching the teeth of each added letter, spelling out with relish the name so long left behind.

Deep in the roots of Carnesky – akin to carnival – are the word for flesh, the word for cutting. This is a name that refuses order.

The reclaimed name is a spell, an incantation. An act of self-compassion. An expression of potential.

Q: When did you first ~~feel yourself~~ disappear?

An incantation:

Dressed like a doll from the age of zero. Look, look how she cries! In her sun-yellow ballet slippers, you could lick her up like ice cream. Sticky red syrup – no, wait, that's her lips.

Dressed like a doll at ages five, six, seven, face a rose garden of pilfered paint. Wind your fingers through her curly hair. Look how she teeters in her mother's shoes, tiny model feet like Cinderella. Not herself in these shoes but future vamp, future crisis: each girl re-creates the image as though she were the first. Her doing, or your seeing? Unanswered question.

At eight the monster turns. A gnash of teeth, a flash across her eyes, not so much twinkle as a lightning strike. The rage, the dirt, the muck, it's coming – it's coming – it

passes, brief storm.

Still mother's perfect angel, father's poppet. The first sign of blood is a false alarm.

Eleven / twelve / thirteen – annoyance / fourteen – defiance /

Sixteen and here comes trouble. Dressed pure goth, black from head to roller-skated toe. Sticky red syrup pours down her legs, daring – willing – another to drink it. Showgirl showing what mother and father would hide. Nipples slash through puppet strings, the cut that leaves no scar.

Later, much later, slipping off the mask. It has the texture, colour, folds and creases, pocks, and open pores of real decaying skin.

Q: What have you lost ~~to obsolete technologies~~?

The bodies in the *Live Archive* are partial selves, real and decaying, just as the archive (that archive, any archive) is a partial repository of the past. Summoned to the screen in a variety of ages and resolutions, a variety of costumes and personas, Carnesky's bodies perform the differences between them. Here, in *Jewess Tattooess* (1999–2005), is a young

Figure 95: Marisa Carnesky, *Showwomen Ritual Action*, The British Library, 2019. London. © Ruth Bayer

body that declares its Jewishness upfront; here, in *Dr Carnesky's Incredible Bleeding Woman* (2015–19), is an older body that centres her wisdom, her leadership, her womanhood.

'When she is in question', writes Sara Ahmed, 'she begins to question herself' (2017: 170). Ahmed is writing about how it feels to be socialized as a woman, but she could just as well be writing about how it feels to be socialized as any non-rich-non-white-non-male in history. Zoom in, and you will see that her sentence contains another interpretation. When your existence is in question, must you question yourself? Or can you, yourself, ask questions?

'*Jewess Tattooess* was a one-woman show from the late-nineties', says older-Marisa-Carnesky, revealed to be hidden in the rag-doll's upper arm. 'I used techniques and forms of illusion, and film and performative actions', she continues, giving nothing away. The screen cuts to an image of a bandaged woman emerging from a spot-lit stage, like a mythical birth of the Invisible Man.

'Jewess' is a designation – a pejorative in modern English. It means a woman and a Jew – not just a woman, in other words, but also a Jew. (A body rendered twice unreal.) 'Tattooess' echoes the pejorative with its rhyme. At the same time, it asks the question: what kind of person can be both these things at once?

What kind of woman?

What kind of Jew?

What kind of (body) ( ) (witch)?

The questions and omissions in the *Live Archive* – its understanding of its own state of incompleteness – is, of course, what constitutes the 'liveness' in its name: both what makes it alive (mortal and time-bound) and what makes it live (active in the present moment). Carnesky introduces us to her work but tells us none of its secrets. This archive is not a series of explanations but a collection of stories that flicker on-screen like fireside tales.

And the questions and omissions in the *Live Archive* are also what constitutes it as an archive of Carnesky's work – itself a series of partial tales that explore the borders of silence and speech, of inscription and scars, of present and past.

Martha Schoolman says there are two questions that scholars must ask the archive (my archive, our archive), in order to acknowledge its holes, its omissions, its propensity to tell tales: '"what does the archive want from me?", [which should be placed] in active, reflexive tension with the question, "what do I have the right to expect from the archive?"' (2019: 27)

Imagine we can hear the questions the *Live Archive* is asking.

Imagine we invent the questions to ask in return.

Imagine we are a woman rendered invisible, stripping away the masks, costumes, identities imposed on her, naming the layers one by one.

Q: What remains ~~hidden~~ when the final layer is removed?

Let the layers be: one, categories. Two, classifications. Three systems of division, including dogmatic insistence on male and female gender, and resulting hierarchies of priority and subsidiary nature. Four, nature. No, not that. Four, natural selection. Five, differentiation between species, between human animals and non-human animals, between body and soil, between the swirl of a snail shell and the curl of a galaxy, between contour lines of a fingerprint and contour lines of a mountain slope rendered in two dimensions.

Where there is a pattern also lies chaos. Chaos: 'an overabundance of resources', writes Elizabeth Grosz, 'beyond the need for mere survival' (2008: 7). Six, reduction of existence to mere survival.

Art is rooted in this abundance, this 'superfluousness of nature' (Grosz 2008: 10), a dance or song of pattern and chaos. The woman (I) (you) comes (we come) to the archive seeking the 'peculiar relations that art establishes between the living body, the forces of the universe and the creation of the future' (Grosz 2008: 3).

Zoom in to the archive (that archive, this archive), find:

The living body: hormonal, messy, sprouting hair, spilling blood.

The forces of the universe: tidal, gravitational, magnetic.

The creation of the future: *Marisa Carnesky's Incredible Bleeding Woman*, who rejects imposed borders between body and earth, earth and solar system, movements of sea and blood, and turning moon.

Also:

The menstrual cycle: an overabundance of resources that Carnesky reclaims as a metaphor for all ecological cycles, for the natural rhythms of the planet, those undulating features that the border disregards or tramples over or attempts to fix. Those undulating features that capitalism disregards or tramples over or attempts to fix.

Beyond category, beyond classification, within chaos, lies contradiction. For instance: the contradiction between a desire for fluidity and Carnesky's wayward aspiration to synchronize menstruation at a global scale (it would, she suggests, change time and reverse the world order).

Chaos is overabundance is art is sensation and sensation, Grosz offers, heralds 'the evolutionary overcoming of man' (2008: 22).

Seven: man.

3. Silence

Q:

Why histories? Why not herstories? Why not stories liberated from gender? Why not stories (fabrication) instead of stories (fact)? Why not stories without a singular you? Why not stories in fragments that refuse to ( )?

Q:

When did you first feel yourself disappear?

Q:

Do you know how many languages are now extinct? Their final exhalation still present in the air, gathered in the cloud on the edge of the moon.

Q:

-?

4. Hauntings

Q: Where does your history find you?

Pull another tarot card. Justice seated on her throne, sword in right hand, scales in left.

Count the centuries in which men believed that the womb was a living thing (superfluous) inside a living thing, an animate being (overabundant) with independent impulses (chaos) that could affect a woman's mind, appetite, and levels of moisture, all of which measured imperfect against the body of man.

Count the decades of belief, explicit or implicit, that the womb is the origin of all diseases, that the birth of a female is a departure from nature (beyond the need for mere survival), that woman is man deformed.

Count the years of the assertion that a woman must give birth to retain the slightest balance, that the womb not subject to procreation will asphyxiate and in this suffocation begin to wander around the body, that intercourse (penetration) but also sneezing (expulsion) might ensure the womb retains its proper functionality.

Count the men who believed these things in one tally and the women dismissed, mistreated, and violated as hysterics in another.

Count the men who, for centuries, continued to believe these things through misreadings and predetermined interpretations of ancient Greek medical philosophy in one tally and the women murdered as witches (gossips) for midwifery, intuitive medical practice and rejection of male supremacist thinking in another.

Weigh up trauma, torment, suffering on one scale, resistance, refusal, abandon in the other. Add to the second scale the erotic: 'a resource within each of us', writes Audre

Lorde, 'that lies in a deeply female and spiritual plane', offering 'a well of replenishing and provocative force to the woman who does not fear its revelation' (2007: 53–54).

Watch bodies unfurl free of binaries, into the nature seen by Jenny Chamarette that is: 'neither comfortable nor singular. Neither male nor female. Straight nor gay. Is more both/and' (2023, n.pag.).

Watch as both/and tip the balance.

Q: When did you first feel yourself disappear?

Imagine your body is not yet unfurled.

Imagine your existence is in question.

Imagine you are me. You are drawn to watch a video of Marisa Carnesky incising the Star of David onto her skin. The power of the performance lies in the pain you perceive: the affect of her body imagined inside your own. It is the specificity of her body, the jumpy passage of the needle, the shivering energy of her flesh, that makes it possible for your body – your specific body – to imagine it so e(a)ffectively. And it is the specific detail of this writing, invoking the sharp intensity of the blade, the low buzz of the tattoo drill, that I am hoping will make your body – your specific body – imagine how that feels.

This is the paradox of transmission that Palladini was alluding to. The performer's body lives on in our bodies, although our bodies are not her body, have not experienced her body's pain, her body's knowledge, her body's poems, its patterns, its memories, and its marks.

In Jewish tradition, our bodies are not, in one sense, our own bodies, either. Our bodies are on loan from God. Tattoos are not permitted because they violate God's property. In the words of the Torah: 'You shall not make gashes in your flesh for the dead, or incise any marks on yourselves. I am the Lord'. When older-Carnesky introduces *Jewess Tattooess* as being about the conflict between her identities as a Jew and a 'heavily tattooed person', you will remember this ancient edict and imagine it is what she means. But as you watch the Star of David scratch into the borderland of her skin as scar tissue, you will think of a specific, recent, violence. Nazis tattooed numbers onto

Jewish bodies as part of their process to remove Jews from history. In doing so, they rendered us twice un-human: firstly, un-human parts of a machine, on our way to the 'final solution', and secondly, un-human mounds of flesh whose history, whose culture, whose fabric of beliefs could be incised and filled with permanent dye.

The bandaged woman emerges, unsteady, on the stage of the past. She is a figure incised with hidden scars, rendered visible and invisible through the marks she carries. Her body is the border between herself and her history: the inscriptions authored by others that are projected onto her skin, and the inscriptions authored by herself that are carved into it.

Q: What have you lost to obsolete technologies?

The rag doll becomes a person, as a body remembers its past, as a memory transforms in time.

The archives of Europe are loud with silent voices. Our libraries are inscribed with the unwritten histories of Jews who were, for millennia, expelled, imprisoned, and killed. As I write, the magic of words obscures the 'us' I'm really talking about: the us of the libraries (Europeans, knowledge-bearers, truth-seekers) or the us of the Jews. I am the magic of the archive, remember? I am the specific body of the specific archive (live), and I am also the archival desire for becoming (alive): the longing for a future, the paradox of transmission.

I am the scar tissue, struggling to imagine a future to heal the wounds of the past.

'What does it mean to belong to a land?' asks the poet Etal Adnan, and she might also be asking about a (body) (gender) (race). 'For those of us who live away from our private history, the question never heals' (2012: 73).

Dismembered, the archive re-members herself.

Its borders (her borders) (our borders) are an illusion.

Q: What remains hidden when the final layer is removed?

The border is an illusion, conjured into existence with a knife-point pencil on a map whose paper caves beneath its pressure. The border is a trick, a sleight of hand performed by people of unaccountable power whose foreheads, writes John Berger, have 'many horizontal creases. Not furrows ploughed by thought but rather lines of incessant passing information' (2011: 147). The border is invisible without lines of barbed wire, concrete, soldiers wielding rifles. The border is not real until it is transgressed and takes the form of a uniform, a command, a small room, a fist. Violence (restraint), violence (separation), violence (abuse), violence ( ). The border fixes identity, which is to say, it claims or erases identity. The border resists erasure but may be redefined, through negotiation or war. The border prefers war.

'Revolution', writes Jack Halberstam, 'will come in a form we cannot yet imagine' (2013: 11).

Magic cannot end war. Magic cannot end violence or overthrow the kyriarchy. Magic cannot return a man to the womb, or to the moment before fusion. Magic cannot undo, rewind, or erase time.

But magic can disrupt time. Slow time, stop it, make it stretch, blur, loop. Here on the *Ghost Train* (2004), a fairground ride into the past, into shadows, into (herstory) (story) (memory) (fabrication), magic brings lost women back to life, blood-stained, mud-smeared, skeletal. Their bodies, their possibilities, retold, reanimated, restitched, translated. What was missing is almost found. Nowhere becomes somewhere becomes this place, this moment, now.

Magic can invite mystery, give mystery body and presence, imbued not with heft but with lightness. Lightness, writes Sarah Ruhl, can be 'a philosophical choice to temper reality with strangeness, to temper the intellect with emotion, and to temper emotion with humour' (2015: 36). Magic brings levitation, brings levity. In so doing, magic unfixes. And in that unfixing, Ruhl offers (Carnesky offers), magic makes real 'the primary human hope that identity might in fact be fluid ....

And if identity is fluid, then we might actually be free' (2015: 214).

Freedom of. Freedom from. Freedom to. Imagine.

Bibliography

Adnan, E. (2012), *Sea and Fog*, New York: Nightboat Books.

Ahmed, S. (2017), *Living a Feminist Life*, Durham: Duke University Press.

Berger, J. (2011), *Bento's Sketchbook*, London: Verso.

Chamarette, J. (2023), 'Q is for Garden', in *The Nature Chronicles Prize: 1: Winning Entries* with an introduction by K. Aalto and contributions by N. Pitchford, J. Chamarette, L. Coleman., B. Crane, J. Pocock, and N. Sinha.

Federici, S. (2004), *Caliban and the Witch*, New York: Autonomedia.

Grosz, E. (2008), *Chaos, Territory, Art*, New York: Columbia University Press.

Halberstam, J. (2013) 'Introduction' in S. Hardy, and F. Moten, *The Undercommons: Fugitive Planning and Black Study*, New York: Minor Compositions, pp. 2–13.

Lorde, A. (2007), *Sister Outsider*, Berkeley: Crossing Press.

Palladini, G. and Marco, P. (2017), *Lexicon for an Affective Archive*, London: Intellect and the Live Art Development Agency.

Ruhl, S. (2015), *100 Essays I Don't Have Time to Write*, New York: Farrar, Strauss and Giroux.

Schoolman, M. (2019), 'Archive' in H. Paul (ed.), *Critical Terms in Future Studies*, Switzerland: Palgrave MacMillan, pp. 25–28.

Weil, S. (2005), *An Anthology*, London: Penguin.

She closes the circle at the end

She is the Showwoman,
The Showwoman,
The Showwoman

Afterword: The Showwoman's Carriage

Giulia Palladini

What kind of space is the reader invited to enter, venturing into this book, wandering through its pages? I have imagined it as a Showwoman's carriage: one of those sumptuous but decadent compartments where the ladies working in fairgrounds, circuses, and travelling shows, in the nineteenth century, used to sleep, or make love in, or receive their guests, most likely all these things in one space, in between shows: a shelter for living, for creating and for socializing, a carriage poorly furnished, but nevertheless covered in red and purple velvet, with prosecco and whiskey served in half-broken, but majestic flutes.

In this carriage, in this book, Marisa Carnesky's work becomes a dwelling, a site of hospitality for other voices, who progressively appear and crowd the room. First, she has invited another artist and writer, Eirini Kartsaki, to imagine and organize with her the space for this gathering: they carefully open the door to others, engaging them in conversations, either directly or through writings that not only address Carnesky's work but also the authors' own practice.

The experience of reading this book, then, is to sit in the carriage where these conversations are happening, one after the other, maybe overlapping, and to witness the opening of this carriage to even more guests, more Showwomen. The gesture of hospitality that Carnesky and Kartsaki performed in the first place, in fact, is replicated within each chapter, by others: as if every conversation, every article, functions as a Matryoshka Doll, containing, germinating, convoking other figures into a common space, each making their spectacular entrance into Carnesky's carriage. In the writings that ended up shaping this book, other Showwomen are consistently conjured, as if in an imaginary coven: Josephine Baker, ORLAN, Koringa, Kathy Acker, and Penny Arcade, to name just a few. There is a play of resonances and attraction, across the book, growing as a magnet that progressively brings more women in, invites more voices into the carriage.

Carnesky's voice, just like her carriage, is capacious: it resonates in and echoes other voices, brings to the surface the many dialogues that contribute to craft her own, but this voice remains distinctively hers. Her work is multiplied over the years in repeated obsessions, forms, lines of inquiry, overflowing from the stage to the classroom, and back again, but never ceases to be a place of hospitality for others, a place where entertainment is taken joyfully, but also damn seriously. Indeed, reading this book I am reminded of the ancient connection between the words 'hospitality' and 'entertainment': 'entertaining guests' is, after all, an expression summarizing the ancient echo of hospitality into the term and practice of entertainment.

Carnesky's entertainment, however, is one where the names of those women are not only part of an ever-expanding guest list, neither simply tokens for a memory play: they are placed, instead, on an altar ritually staging both a collective impulse to revolt, and an attempt to heal common herstory. In Kartsaki's words: 'all these women carry within them the weight of others, who have been captured, stifled, tortured and destroyed' (Kartsaki, in this volume). The carriage is always alert to their presence, devoted to bring forward the blood of their struggles, not as a relic, but as a form of nourishment: the blood of those who are no longer, who could not be what they wanted, who got lost along the way, who were miscarried, who never made it to a carriage, all of those bodies transform into the bodies of those who will come. This is no horror movie, but rather the reclaiming of women's generative relation with blood, which patriarchy has long intoxicated, by turning it into either a sign of threat or of stigma.

The expression 'Showwomen', proposed by Carnesky, presents itself as a category immediately common, crafted for a multitude, imaginatively handed over to generations of women in the past and the future. 'Showwomen' stems out of, and proudly sits in, a specific genealogy, but is also a concept that can be, on its part, reclaimed and inhabited by others. All of those who have invented forms of social reproduction, in show business, and not simply participated in sheer economic production, all of those who have 'risked it all' blurring the boundaries between their life and their art, all of those who have given birth to themselves through pain and wonder are, in a sense, honorary citizens in the Showwoman's carriage.

This is another key feature that differentiates the Showwoman from a showman: that she fully understands, and embodies, the profound complicity between 'social reproduction' and 'performance production'. While running the show, while graduating to be a doctor, while raising funds for the next show, the Showwoman picks up the pieces and puts them back together again, she mends the costumes and supports her beloved, she invents and celebrates a queer, creative, anarchic praxis of social reproduction, something that in the live art sector is often invisible and disqualified. She does all of that and yet, she never misses a show. Against the *egolalia* of the solo artist, against the spotlight on a solo journey, Carnesky insists to account for, make visible, expose the bonds that have sustained her performance production over the years, informing her politics and poetics. 'Carnesky is not singular', Kartsaki writes, and her practice has opened a space to feel at home for all those subjects Kartsaki calls weird: those who defy, escape, and revolt against proper categories.

I was honored to be the last one invited to enter this Showwoman's carriage and entrusted with the task to close the door behind me, before consigning this book to the future. Before doing so, I want to conjure, on my part, one more ghost, to invite one more woman to this party: Ellen Stewart, founder and life-long defender of the theatre La Mama, in New York. Since I met Ellen, in 2004, and started researching the history of La Mama E.T.C., I have always had a hard time 'defining' Ellen Stewart's role in it, as it escaped all professional categories, and yet encompassed them all, with skills constantly overflowing from art to life. In my writing, I have often called Ellen, La Mama, a 'woman-theatre', someone whose public and private persona embodied and resembled her theatre, not just in terms of production, but also in terms of social reproduction and queer kinship. Today, I was gifted by this book a new word to think about Ellen, a definition she would have wholeheartedly enjoyed for herself: she was indeed a 'Showwoman', someone committed to keep the show going, someone who risked a lot in order to get what she wanted, someone who had no easy way into existing forms of show business, and had to imagine another one, in order to survive. Someone who, furthermore, never looked down on, nor closed the doors of her theatre to, the wonders of popular entertainment. Curiously, the image Ellen chose as the legendary icon of her theatre, from the start, is that of a pushcart. I don't know if Marisa Carnesky and Ellen Stewart ever met, but I like to think of them riding on a common carriage, sharing, and embodying a kindred sense of popular spectacle and queer belonging.

In my fantasy, the Showwoman's carriage locates somehow at the side of *Carnesky's Ghost Train*: a performance I have not encountered live, but I saw described in this book multiple times, words piling one upon the other, painting a multifarious picture in my mind. This is the effect of the peculiar rhythm of repetition punctuating the book: information returns, memories overlap, shows are described again and again from different perspectives, from the stage, and from the audience. Sitting in the Showwoman's carriage, then, the reader listens to conversations between old friends and old witnesses, relating to Carnesky's work through what Gertrude Stein has called a labour of 'insistence': a peculiar form of repetition, not accounting for a finished business, but for what still exists, for what is alive and recognized as such in narration. Insistence, according to Stein, has to do with 'listening and talking at the same time' (1957: 169). It is no wonder that this beautiful dynamic – in which repetition exists in a metabolic relation with Carnesky's own work, with her ageing, with her graduating to adulthood – is the fruit of a collaboration between Eirini Kartsaki (whose work has long explored the clogs and wonders of repetition) and Marisa Carnesky (whose insistence, in performance, has shaped a distinctive style, for herself and for others). In the magic combination of those different inputs, in the echoes of all the voices invited in the carriage, the concept of 'Showwomen' does not crystallize, but keeps transforming, throughout the book, always adding a little piece to its scope of signification, always welcoming new stratifications alongside old scars in Carnesky's body of work, consistently escaping the narrow corset which would entrap it in a stable definition. This concept, just like the Showwoman's carriage, drives on, towards the future.

Bibliography

Stein, G. (1957), 'Portraits and Repetition', *Lectures in America*, Boston: Beacon, pp. 165-208.

Contributors

Liz Aggiss is a Brighton UK-based, award-winning, mature, solo, feminist, dance theatre artist. Her work is framed by extensive contextual research that considers and uses the personal and historical as reference. Her performances have a distinct expressive, grotesque, and British music hall movement style. Her work investigates the shifting nature of presentation, and considers gender politics, feminism, the representation of women, and mature female visibility. Liz Aggiss has, for the past 40 years, been re(de)fining her own brand of British contemporary dance performance, dodging categorization, and ensuring she is classifiably unclassifiable. Her award-winning dance films have been commissioned by and screened on BBC, Channel4, ABC Australia, and Arte TV, and have received numerous international awards. She received the Bonnie Bird Choreography Award 1994, an Arts Council Dance Fellowship 2003, is Professor Emeritus in Visual Performance at the University of Brighton, and has Honorary Doctorates in Interdisciplinary Practice from the University of Gothenburg, Sweden, and Art University of Chichester. She won a Total Theatre Award Edinburgh Festival 2017. *Anarchic Dance*, published by Routledge (Taylor & Francis), is a visual and textual record of her live and screen dance work.

Livia Kojo Alour is an award-winning Nigerian – German-born poet, musician and theatre maker based in London. Her solo show *Black Sheep* rose to critical acclaim at the Edinburgh Fringe Festival in 2022. The show was awarded several rounds of public funding by the Arts Council England and the Birds of Paradise Award for Exceptional Theatre. Livia is the author of *Rising of the Black Sheep*, a daring memoir-style poetry collection that has just been long listed for the Polari First Book Prize 2023. She also has a ten-year touring career as a sword swallower under her belt. During this time, she won several awards with different companies and performed a residency in Las Vegas. Her minimalist art piece the *Female Sword Swallower's Moon Calendar* has been touring museums in Europe since 2019. In 2017, Livia held an inspirational TEDx talk about her life-threatening sword accident and overcoming fear. As a musician, she combines vocals and spoken word in a unique way to address cultural issues and tell her personal stories. She is currently working on her first album. Livia's show *Black Sheep* is scheduled for a second UK tour in autumn 2023 followed by a concert Europe tour as the supporting artist to Anne Clark.

Marisa Carnesky is an Olivier award-winning performer, director, and teacher who is interested in where popular entertainment, contemporary performance, and the important issues of our times collide. In 2004, Carnesky founded Carnesky Productions, a performance and theatre company responsible for original large- and small-scale interactive performance works and interested in the use of spectacle; fairground rides, magic illusions, and grand ritual as a means of creating highly accessible provocative work, rooted in popular culture that promotes cultural and political discourses. Carnesky is best known for her immersive theatre ride *Carnesky's Ghost Train* which toured nationally and internationally for over a decade until 2015. Her experimental group performance work *Dr Carnesky's Incredible Bleeding Woman* toured extensively to wide critical acclaim (2017–20). Most recently, Carnesky created the group theatre piece *Showwomen* and then the large-scale promenade work *Carnesky's Showwomxn Sideshow Spectacular* with a cast of 33 women which was launched at the Bartholemew Fair in 2023. Her work has been funded, commissioned, and programmed by Arts Council England, National Theatre Studios, The City of London, The Arts and Humanities Research Council, and the Attenborough Centre for The Creative Arts amongst many others. She was awarded a Doctorate from Middlesex University in 2019. With experience in creating and teaching a variety of performance practices from performance art and avant-garde cabaret to immersive theatre and contemporary circus, she has been nurturing emerging artists to find their own unique visions and voices for over twenty years. In 2022, she designed and launched BA Contemporary and Popular Performance at Rose Bruford College.

Paloma Faith is a four-times platinum selling, BRIT award-winning musician and has become a household name thanks to her extraordinary talent, creative independence, and chart-topping record sales in the millions. Her global tours and timeless discography have solidified her ongoing relevance in the music industry. But that's not all – Paloma is also an accomplished actress in both film and television, with notable roles in *Pennyworth* and *Dangerous Liaisons*. She launched a documentary *Paloma Faith: As I Am*, where she opened up about the cut-throat world of the music industry while becoming a new mum. She is also an entrepreneur and has her own interior brand called 'Paloma Home' and is considered a style icon pushing the boundaries with her bold fashion. Paloma is now gearing up for another monumental chapter with the release of a brand new single 'How You Leave A Man' from her forthcoming sixth studio album.

Geneva Foster Gluck's work centres on immersive event-production, creative practice, and material storytelling to explore a range of topics and experiences often grounded in decolonizing, feminist, and ecological approaches. In 2006, she founded Sugar Beast Circus, a production platform for interdisciplinary collaborations between circus performers and new technologies. Sugar Beast Circus toured multiple works in the United Kingdom, EU, and the United States, as well as held residencies at the Camden Roundhouse in London, United Kingdom; Blast Theory Creations Space in Hove, United Kingdom; and La Brèche Circus Center in Normandy, France. In 2020, she completed a practice-led Ph.D. dissertation titled *Performing the Electrical or My Heart is an Electromagnetic Chamber: Scenographies of Power, Ecology, and Speculative Practice*. Her research integrates Performance Studies, Spatial Theory, and Energy Humanities to consider the ways that new knowledge is created and shared through artist-led projects. She is currently co-founder of Snakebite Creation Space, a platform for supporting performance, installation, and process-based work in Tucson, Arizona.

Dominic Johnson is a writer and curator and Professor of Performance and Visual Culture in the Department of Drama at Queen Mary University of London. He is the author of four monographs including most recently *Unlimited Action: The Performance of Extremity in the 1970s* (2019). He is also the editor of five books including *Pleading in the Blood: The Art and Performances of Ron Athey* (2013). His essays have been published in *Art History*, *Art Journal*, *Porn Studies*, *Contemporary Theatre Review*, and elsewhere; and he is a frequent contributor to *Art Monthly*.

Eirini Kartsaki is a performance practitioner, writer, and Lecturer in Drama at East15 Acting School, University of Essex. She is the author of *Repetition in Performance: Returns and Invisible Forces* (Palgrave 2017). Her research comprises work around contemporary performance, live art, and feminist practice. Kartsaki has written extensively on repetition, desire, and pleasure in performance. She is currently working on her second monograph *Theatres of the Weird* (MUP). Her performance practice has been presented nationally and internationally (Sadler's Wells, V&A, The Basement, Whitechapel Gallery, Arnolfini, Soho Theatre, Palais de Tokyo, Biennale d'art contemporain de Lyon). Her collaboration with alpha kartsaki as Tante&Tante has received the Audience's Award (2016) and the Champ Libre Award (2017), BE Festival, UK.

Lucifire toured the globe for over twenty years as a speciality act, fire-eater, circus performer, ring-mistress, and flesh-hook suspension artist. After graduating from London Contemporary Dance School, Luci picked up fire torches and power tools, and Lucifire found her place in Sideshow. She cut her teeth on the various circuits of tattoo conventions, fetish clubs, and late-night cabarets as a solo artist before teaming up to create The Fire Tusk Pain Proof Circus with her husband, Dave Tusk. They toured this theatrical stunt show, with motorbikes, chainsaws, whips, darts, beds of nails, broken glass, and lots of fire for many years, from Glastonbury to Tokyo, Moscow, and all across Europe, as a duo and up to an eighteen-person company. Luci retired from touring her own death-defying stunt shows ten years ago upon her twin pregnancy, and now plays baritone saxophone in the rock and roll band The Urban Voodoo Machine. She has been coaxed out of retirement to perform hook suspensions as a cast member of Florentina Holzinger's *Tanz*, an all-female, all-naked, intergenerational dance piece currently selling out theatres in Europe. More recently, Luci has been proud to be a core member of the cast of *Showwomen*, Marisa Carnesky's touring stage show.

Alex Lyons is a queer performance artist, associate lecturer, and Ph.D. researcher in drama and performance at East15 Acting School, University of Essex. She works at the world's first Vagina Museum, London. Her performance and academic work explore gender, sexuality and the representation of vulvas in contemporary performance, and more specifically, how artists expose their vulvas in performance to interrogate sociocultural themes of gender, sexuality, body politics, and beyond.

Josephine Machon is an Associate Professor of Contemporary Performance at Middlesex University, London. She is the author of *The Punchdrunk Encyclopaedia* (Routledge, 2019), *Immersive Theatres: Intimacy and Immediacy in Contemporary Performance* (Palgrave Macmillan, 2013), and *(Syn)aesthetics: Redefining Visceral Performance* (Palgrave Macmillan 2009, 2011). Machon has written about Marisa Carnesky's work since 2000 and continues to publish widely on experiential, immersive and interactive performance, examining the audience experience in this field. She is Joint Editor of the Palgrave Macmillan Series, Palgrave Studies in Performance and Technology, which includes her co-edited collections alongside commissioned titles and on the editorial boards for the *International Journal of Performance Arts & Digital Media* (IJPADM) and *Body, Space & Technology* (BST), a journal of the Online Library of Humanities Library (OLH).

Marawa has been touring the world performing for over fifteen years, her signature style of performance is loved and recognized from the finals of *Arabs Got Talent* to Dita Von Teese's shows, to the Olivier Award winning *La Soiree*. In 2012, she founded her performance troupe: Marawa's Majorettes who perform Busby Berkeley style group routines all over the United Kingdom and EU. In 2022, she was inducted into the Guinness World Record Hall of Fame, with over twelve records broken. She has released three skate collaborations, a rose gold skate, a high-heeled skate, and also a rollerblade – as well as collaborating regularly with shoe designers such as Christian Louboutin on her high-heeled skates for shows. Performance aside, Marawa also likes to write – her 2016 book *The Girl Guide* is the book Marawa wished she could have read when she went through puberty. The book covers the 50 most important questions she had growing up, with factual, visual, and personal information. Available in 22 languages, the book continues to grow, reassure, and inspire young readers around the world.

Roberta Mock is Professor of Performance and Executive Dean of the School of Performing and Digital Arts at Royal Holloway University of London. Most recently, she was the principal investigator for the Transitioning to Sustainable Production across the UK Theatre Sector project (co-commissioned by the Creative Industries Policy and Evidence Centre and Arts Council England, 2022). In addition to a commitment to exploring and celebrating 'green' theatre practices, her research – which takes the form of both performance and writing – tends to focus on sex-gender and bodies, with a specific interest in live art and stand-up comedy by Jewish women. She is the author or editor of six books, and the immediate Past Chair of the Theatre & Performance Research Association (TaPRA). Championing and celebrating embodied knowledge at all stages of a research career, Roberta has written and spoken about and led workshops across the United Kingdom, in Canada, and in Europe on practice-research methodologies. She was the founding co-director of the AHRC-funded 3D3 Centre for Doctoral Training (a partnership between the Universities of Plymouth, Falmouth and West of England Bristol), which supported only practice-led research projects in digital art, design, culture, and performance.

Lalla Morte is a performance artist based in Paris, one of the important figures of the French cabaret, circus, and neo-burlesque scene. After co-founding the Cabaret Dangereux troupe MurderSuicidePresents in 2006, she became a full member of HEY! La Cie. She has collaborated for many years with Cirque Électrique, the Swiss label Voodoo Rhythm Records and more recently with the American sideshow theatre company The No Ring Circus. She creates original numbers in which she develops an aesthetic, the poetry and irrationality of which serve the heritage that inspires her: the cabaret of the early twentieth century played in circus and in music hall. In her work, the intrigue of the gesture prevails, where a hypnotic charm emerges from all of her performances. Each of her acts is a short story populated by characters typical of her universe (the glass walker eating fire, the bird of paradise, the voodoo creature). Fakirism, feather fans, black light, illusion, ballet, body painting are among her means, and her flexible frame allows her to travel in her suitcase to the stage.

Nao Nagai would like to be known as a useful passer-by who got curious. However, she is a London-based lighting designer, technical collaborator, and performer from Japan. After immigrating to the United Kingdom at the age of 15, she has been lighting and collaborating on multigenre performances inter/nationally. Nao also performs regularly with the cult pop performance group, Frank Chickens (winner of Foster's Comedy God Awards). She is a tutor in Lighting Design at Goldsmiths, University of London.

Daniel Oliver is a performance artist and lecturer. He makes raucous, dyspraxic-led participatory performance worlds that have been shown throughout the United Kingdom and overseas for over twenty years. He has published writing on neurodiversity, audience participation, and the value of celebrating awkwardness. This includes *Awkwoods: Daniel Oliver's Dyspraxic Adventures in Participatory Performance*, published by the Live Art Development Agency in 2019.

Giulia Palladini is a researcher and critical theorist. Her work moves between different languages, and fields of knowledge, exploring the politics and erotics of artistic production, as well as social and cultural history from a Marxist and feminist perspective. She has worked as a Senior Lecturer in Drama, Theatre and Performance at the University of Roehampton in London, United Kingdom, and at the Kunsthochschule Berlin-Weissensee in Germany. She is an Alexander von Humboldt alumna and worked as a Visiting Professor at various international universities in Europe and Latin America. She has collaborated as a theorist in a number of critical and artistic projects, in particular with the Colombian artistic laboratory Mapa Teatro. She is the author of *The Scene of Foreplay: Theater, Labor and Leisure in 1960s New York* (2017) and co-editor (with Marco Pustianaz) of *Lexicon for an Affective Archive* (2017). In 2021, she led the international research cluster 'Feminismos Antipatriarcales and Poetic Disobedience', part of the collaborative project 'Queer Feminist Currents'.

Phoebe Patey-Ferguson is a Lecturer at Rose Bruford College (Kent, United Kingdom), teaching Theatre and Social Change, Contemporary and Popular performance and is the Course Director for MA Queer Performance. Their research expertise is in the social context of contemporary performance, primarily festivals and clubs, with a focus on queer and trans practice. Phoebe is the co-editor of a special issue of *Contemporary Theatre Review on Live Art* (2024) and co-convenor of the Queer Futures Working Group of the International Federation of Theatre Research. They frequently collaborate with organizations to deliver public talk programmes, including Buzzcut Festival, the Live Art Development Agency (LADA), and Scottee & Friends. They are on the board for Duckie, and have previously worked as a producer with the London International Festival of Theatre (LIFT), In Between Time (IBT), VFD and are a co-founder of Live Art Club London.

H Plewis is a choreographer and long-time associate artist of Carnesky Productions and Duckie. For many years, as a solo practitioner working at the interstices of cabaret, live art and dance, she explored the extremes of contemporary British feminine identity, make up and emotion, using her own body as a battlefield of sexual and cultural politics. She now brings all that wild provocation to bear as the founder and artistic director of Posh Club Dance Club (PC*DC), the radical older adult dance company based in Hackney. H and her daughter Sula are currently (Autumn 2023) touring with Miss High Leg Kick's latest show *Eau de Memoire*.

Amy Ridler is a writer, Managing Editor of *MIR Online*, and English Teacher in East London, where she runs the LGBT+ society. She has worked with queer, feminist, live art theatre company Carnesky Productions since 2009 and continues to be a member of the company's advisory board. She studied MA Creative Writing at Birkbeck.

Amy Saunders is mostly known as a sword swallower. She has broken the Guinness world record for most swords swallowed by a woman three times. She first broke the record by swallowing five swords in London on 28 April 1999. She then swallowed six swords on the set of *El Show de los Récords* in Madrid on 27 November 2001. On 11 September 2004, she swallowed seven swords in London. Saunders first began sword-swallowing while busking in bars in the West End of London in 1996. She started her performance life in fetish clubs and then moved to freak shows as a sword swallower. Since 2001, Saunders has been performing under the stage name of Miss Behave. She has been compared to Betty Boop and Marlene Dietrich, called 'a live cartoon with a late night attitude'. Industry website 'This Is Cabaret' said that she 'imprints the evening with unapologetic raciness and sardonic mockery. Aggressive and confrontational, she always has a quick riposte to call your bluff'.

Tai Shani's artistic practice, comprising performance, film, photography, and installation, uses experimental writing as a guiding method. Oscillating between theoretical concepts and visceral details, Shani's texts attempt to create poetic coordinates in order to cultivate, by extending into divergent formats and collaborations, fragmentary cosmologies of nonsovereignty. Taking cues from both mournful and undead histories of marginalization and solidarity, her work is invested in recovering feminized aesthetic modes – such as the floral, the trippy, or the gothic – in a register of utopian militancy. Shani's projects examine desire in its (infra-)structural dimension, exploring a realism that materially fantasizes against the patriarchal racial capitalist present. In this vein, the epic, in both its literary long-form and excessive affect, shapes the framework of Shani's artistic practice. Clusters of work like *DC Productions* or *Neon Hieroglyph* take mythical and historical narratives – such as Christine de Pizan's allegorical city of women, or cases of psychedelic ergot poisoning causing social unrest – as a template and retell them, over time, through a range of practices, from watercolours and sculptures to animation in theatrical performance. Collected texts were published in *Our Fatal Magic* (2019) and *The Neon Hieroglyph* (2023). Tai Shani is the joint 2019 Turner Prize winner together with Lawrence Abu Hamdan, Helen Cammock, and Oscar Murillo. Her work has been shown extensively in Britain and internationally.

Annie Sprinkle made porn films and worked in Manhattan 'massage parlors' from 1973 to 1993. She bridged into the art world and toured one-woman theatre pieces, including *Post Porn Modernist* and *Hardcore from the Heart*, from 1989 to 2003 to 20+ countries. The people she met along the way shaped her involvement in social justice, human rights, and freedom of expression and she remains avidly committed to these ideals. Awards include Performance Studies International Artist/Activist/Scholar Award, and four San Francisco Arts Commission grants. Linda M. Montano has been her performance art mentor since 1983.

Beth Stephens is an artist and filmmaker with a Ph.D. in Performance Studies. She grew up in Appalachia, which has had a lasting influence on her work in environmental justice. After making visual and performance art about queer identity during the 1990s culture wars, Stephens left New York for a professorship at the University of California, Santa Cruz. Stephens produced and directed her first feature documentary, *Goodbye Gauley Mountain: An Ecosexual Love Story*, in 2014 and had the filmmaking bug ever since. Stephens has won several awards including from the San Francisco Arts Commission, a Ca$h Theater Grant, a Rydell Fellowship and from Arts Research Institute at UC Santa Cruz.

Beth Stephens and Annie Sprinkle fell in love in 2002 and have worked together collaboratively ever since, doing visual art, performance, theatre, and happenings. They launched the Ecosex Movement in 2008 from their home base in San Francisco. Career highlights include *Wedding to the Sea* at the Venice Biennale, being documenta 14 artists, and a screening of their documentary film *Water Makes Us Wet* at NY MoMA. They received a Guggenheim Grant in 2021 for their current film project *Playing with Fire*. Their book, published by University of Minnesota Press in 2021, *Assuming the Ecosexual Position: Earth as Lover* chronicles their twenty years of adventures in life and art. E.A.R.T.H. Lab SF (Environmental Art, Research, Theory & Happenings) is a non-profit organization started by Beth Stephens and Annie Sprinkle. We build community by creating collaborative, multidisciplinary art projects that re-envision the Earth, all of its beings, and environmental activism with fresh eyes. Our organization expands prevailing notions of environmental art, challenges the mainstream's binary concepts of gender, sexuality, and race, and incorporates inclusive, diverse, and imaginative possibilities for sustainable living.

Empress Stah is an aerial artist, cabaret performer, and show producer, famed for her utterly unique stage shows created with a mash-up signature blend of Circus, Neo Burlesque, and Live Art. As an international headliner, Stah has blown the minds of audiences the world over and inspired a generation of young performers. A glittering career that began in 1995 has spawned many iconic acts including her touring collaboration with cult musician Peaches who wrote the track 'Light in Places' for her *Stargasm*, an aerial act featuring a laser butt plug. *Swinging from the Chandelier* was the recipient of a Jerwood Circus Award and saw the creation of the original aerial chandelier, while her ongoing project to make a performance in outta space led to a commission from the SPILL Festival of Performance for her solo show *Empress Stah in Space* and an experience of weightlessness aboard a zero gravity parabolic flight. Returning to live in Australia during the pandemic, Stah established 'Zero Central Circus', a company that currently teaches aerial skills to young people in the Southern Highlands and on tour around NSW during the school holidays.

Rhyannon Styles is an artist, writer, and performer. Over her established performance career, she has appeared at the Soho Theatre, ICA, Edinburgh Fringe Festival, The Guggenheim Museum NYC, Barbican, Glastonbury Festival, Roundhouse, DOCK11, and the Bethnal Green Working Men's Club. This includes her own solo work and as a company member with Carnesky Productions, Duckie, Mineralwasser, and Eddie Peake. Rhyannon graduated in 2020 from the MA Solo Dance Authorship programme at the Universität der Künste in Berlin. Since 2015, she has been documenting her gender transition and writing on trans issues. Rhyannon was a columnist for ELLE UK (2015–17) which led to the publication of her memoir *The New Girl: A Trans Girl Tells It Like It Is* in 2017 by Headline. Rhyannon's second book *Help! I'm Addicted: A Trans Girl's Self-Discovery and Recovery* was published in September 2021 by Jessica Kingsley Publishers. She also contributes to *Stylist*, *Sunday Times Style*, *Broadly*, and *i-D Magazine*. Alongside her writing and performance work, she has appeared in advertising campaigns for TU clothing, Tatty Devine and recorded make-up tutorials for The Body Shop UK. Rhyannon had a speaking cameo role in the BBC2 drama *Boy Meets Girl*.

The Department of Feminist Conversations (est. 2016) is a collective exploring feminist modes of gathering and exchange. We use publishing, live events, workshops, salons, archives, and interventions to mobilize, share knowledge, and reflect together. Facilitated by Maddy Costa, Diana Damian Martin, and Mary Paterson.

Veronica Thompson/Fancy Chance started performing in the late 1990s and became known as a burlesque clown in London tassel twirling around the big smoke and across Europe and was one of the first UK people to perform hair hang on the cabaret/circus circuit. She then went on to perform in her own work and collaborations with Marisa Carnesky, Fire Tusk Pain Proof Circus, La Clique/La Soiree, Florentina Holzinger, Bernie Dieter, and other productions. Her one-woman show *Flights of Fancy* premiered in 2017 and ran at Soho Theatre and toured across the United Kingdom. She is a founding member of a branch of the activist Stop Shopping Choir in the United Kingdom and continues to be a regular contributor to the cabaret/live art landscape.

Vanessa Toulmin is Professor and Director of City & Culture and Public Engagement at the University of Sheffield, Director of Festival of the Mind and academic lead for the University's Public Engagement and Impact Team. Professor Toulmin is a leading authority on Victorian entertainment and film, and has completed extensive research on travelling show people. She also acts as a leading authority on new variety and circus and has acted as creative advisor to leading festivals in the United Kingdom including the Roundhouse in London and Showzam in Blackpool. Since 2019, she has been Chair of Morecambe Winter Gardens Preservation Trust which owns and operates this Grade II* theatre as a volunteer-led organization.

Rachel Zerihan is a writer and researcher who has taught extensively in higher education and is currently in the final stages of training to become a child and adolescent psychotherapist. Her longstanding interest in catharsis in contemporary female performance led to a curiosity and passion for performances for an audience of one. Her monograph, *The Cultural Politics of One-to-One Performance: Strange Duets* (Palgrave MacMillan) was published in 2022. Rachel has published widely and is co-editor of a Special Edition of *Performing Ethos Journal* on 'Ethics in One-to-One Performance' (2014), *Intimacy Across Visceral and Digital Performance* (Palgrave Macmillan, 2012) and *Interfaces of Performance* (Ashgate, 2009).

Figures

Figure 1: Marisa Carnesky, backstage at The Vauxhall Tavern, 1998. London. © Ruth Bayer, p. 23

Figure 2: Marisa Carnesky, *Lady Muck*, Hackney Marshes, 1995. London. © Ruth Bayer, p. 24

Figure 3: Marisa Carnesky, *Jewess Tattooess*, studio shot, 2000. London. © Manuel Vason, p. 29

Figure 4: Marisa Carnesky, installation inside *Carnesky's Ghost Train*, 2010. Blackpool Promenade. © Jo Duck, p. 32

Figure 5: Marisa Carnesky, lecture from *Dr Carnesky's Incredible Bleeding Woman*, Soho Theatre, 2015. London. © Ruth Bayer. p. 37

Figure 6: Marisa Carnesky, introducing *Carnesky's Showwomxn Sideshow Spectacular*, Smithfield Grand Avenue, 2023. London. © Ruth Bayer, p. 40

Figure 7: Paloma Faith, New York. 2023. © Ryan Muir, p.48

Figure 8: Liz Aggiss, *Slap and Tickle*, 2017. © Jo Murray, p. 53

Figure 9: Marisa Carnesky, excerpts form *Dr Carnesky's Incredible Bleeding Woman*, Cirque Electric, HEY! Festival, 2015. Paris. © Zoe Forget, p. 61

Figure 10 (overleaf): Marisa Carnesky, *Dystopian Wonders*, featuring Marawa The Amazing, Empress Stah, H Plewis, Rasp Thorne, Raphelle Boitel, Duncan De Morgan, Rebel Royale, Amber Topaz, The Roundhouse, 2010. London. © Manuel Vason, pp. 74-75

Figure 11: Chi Chi Revolver, *Carnesky's Tarot Drome*, Old Vic Tunnels, 2012. London. © Sarah Ainslie, p. 79

Figure 12: Rowan Fae, *Carnesky's Tarot Drome*, Old Vic Tunnels, 2012. London. © Sarah Ainslie, p. 79

Figure 13: Marisa Carnesky, *Dr Carnesky's Incredible Bleeding Woman*, Soho Theatre, 2016. London. © Claire Lawrie, p. 84

Figure 14: Annie Sprinkle Polaroid at *Post Porn Modernist* performance, with Marisa Carnesky and Katia Tirado, 1993. San Francisco, p. 96

Figure 15: Marawa live shot at Bal De La Rose for Louboutin, Salle des Etoiles of Sporting Monte-Carlo, 2022. Monaco. © Francois Gautret, p. 107

Figure 16: Marisa Carnesky, publicity shot for Smut Fest, 1994. London. Photographer unknown, p. 117

Figure 17 (left): Marisa Carnesky, *Observer Magazine*, 1997. Photographer unknown, p. 118

Figure 18: David Hoyle and Marisa Carnesky, Queer Up North, 1994. Manchester. © Ruth Bayer, p. 119

Figures 19 and 20: Marisa Carnesky, *Lady Muck and Her Burlesque Revue*, with Jo Jo and Katia Tirado, Nottingham Now, 1995. © Mark Bushnell, pp. 120-121

Figure 21: Marisa Carnesky, *Dolly Blue*, tattooed costume by Amanda Moss, Dragon Ladies Studios King's Cross, 1997. London. © Amanda Moss, p. 122

Figure 22: Marisa Carnesky, *Jewess Tattooess*, Battersea Arts Centre, 1999. London. © Ruth Bayer, p. 123

Figures 23 & 24: Marisa Carnesky, *Carnesky's Ghost Box*, illusion by Paul Kieve, 2000. © Paul Kieve, pp. 124-125

Figures 25 & 26: Marisa Carnesky, *Jewess Tattooess*, studio shot, 2000. London. © Manuel Vason, pp. 126-127

Figure 27 (overleaf): Marisa Carnesky, *Jewess Tattooess*, studio shot, 2000. London. © Manuel Vason, pp. 128-129

Figures 28 & 29: Marisa Carnesky, *Jewess Tattooess*, studio shot, 2000. London. © Manuel Vason, pp. 130-131

Figure 30 (overleaf): Façade of *Carnesky's Ghost Train*, Dagenham Docks, 2004. London. © Jonathan Allen, pp. 132-133

Figure 31: Paloma Faith, *Carnesky's Ghost Train*, Truman's Brewery, 2005. London. © Alastair Muir, p. 134

Figure 32 (right): Marisa Carnesky, *Carnesky's Ghost Train*, Truman's Brewery, 2005. London. © Alastair Muir, p. 135

Figure 33 (left): Geneva Foster Gluck, *Carnesky's Ghost Train*, Truman's Brewery, 2005. London. © Alastair Muir, p. 136

Figure 34: Tai Shani, *Carnesky's Ghost Train*, Truman's Brewery, 2005. London. © Alastair Muir, p. 137

Figure 35: Marisa Carnesky, *Magic War*, studio shot, 2007. © Manuel Vason, p. 138

Figure 36: Marisa Carnesky, *Magic War*, Soho Theatre, 2007. London. © Ruth Bayer, p. 138

Figures 37 (right): Marisa Carnesky, *Magic War*, 2006. © Manuel Vason, p. 139

Figure 38 (overleaf): *Carnesky's Live Archive*, www.carnesky.com/live-archive. 2020. ©Rosie Powell, p. 140

Figure 39: Marisa Carnesky, *The Grotesque Burlesque Revue*, 1996, London. Costume and photo by Amanda Moss. © Amanda Moss, p. 149

Figure 40: Marisa Carnesky, *Portraits of Anarchists*, 1994. © Casey Orr, p. 150

Figure 41: Rocio Boliver, *Needle Striptease*, curator Benjamin Sebastian,]performance space[, 2012. London. © Marco Berandi, p. 153

Figure 42: Rocio Boliver, *My Tail of Hairs with Bells* at Embodiment #3 series, curated by Boris Nieslony and Nadia Ismail, Kunsthalle, Unterer Hardthof, 2022. Giessen, Germany. © Constantin Leonhard & BLACK KIT, p. 154

Figure 43: Narcissister, *Self-Gratifier*, photographed in her studio, 2008. Brooklyn, New York. © Kristy Leibowitz, p. 157

Figure 44: Narcissister, *Winter/Spring Collection*, 2012. Los Angeles. © A.L. Steiner, p. 158

Figure 45: Cosey Fanni Tutti, *Marcel Duchamp's Next Work*, COUM Transmissions, 1974. London. © Courtesy COUM Transmissions and Cabinet, p. 163

Figure 46: Tai Shani, *Carnesky's Ghost Train*, Truman's Brewery, 2005. London. © Alastair Muir, p. 172

Figure 47: Geneva Foster Gluck, *The Magnetic Chamber*, video documentation, 2022. © Geneva Foster Gluck, p. 175

Figure 48: Marisa Carnesky, *Penny Slot Somnambulist*, Visions of Excess, co-curated by Ron Athey and Vaginal Davis, 2003. Birmingham. © Roger Bamber / topfoto, p. 180

Figure 49: Marisa Carnesky, *Carnesky's Tarot Drome* studio shot, 2011. London. © Manuel Vason, p. 189

Figures 50 & 51: Marisa Carnesky, *Carnesky's Tarot Drome*, Cirque Jules Vernes, English Eccentricity Festival, Amiens, 2012. France. © Sarah Ainslie, p 190

Figure 52: Marisa Carnesky as Wheel of Fortune in the set of *Carnesky's Ghost Train*, Spill Tarot, 2009. © Manuel Vason, p. 191

Figures 53 & 54: H Plewis (top), Nao Nagai, and Priya Mistry (above), *Dr Carnesky's Incredible Bleeding Woman*, Soho Theatre, 2016. London. © Claire Lawrie, p. 192

Figure 55 & 56: Rhyannon Styles and Fancy Chance (top) and Marisa Carnesky (above), *Dr Carnesky's Incredible Bleeding Woman*, Soho Theatre, 2016. London. © Claire Lawrie, p. 193

Figure 57 (overleaf): Marisa Carnesky, *Dr Carnesky's Incredible Bleeding Woman*, Menstruant ritual creation workshop, featuring Amy Ridler, Nao Nagai, Rhyannon Styles, Fancy Chance, Livia Kojo Alour, H Plewis, and Marisa Carnesky, 2016. Southend. © Sarah Ainslie, pp. 194-195

Figure 58 (left): Fancy Chance, *Dr Carnesky's Incredible Bleeding Woman*, hair hanging with the menstruant coven, Soho Theatre, 2016. London. © Claire Lawrie, p. 196

Figures 59 & 60: Molly Beth Morossa, Rhyannon Styles, Fancy Chance, H Plewis, Priya Mistry, Livia Kojo Alour, Marisa Carnesky, Nao Nagai (top) and H Plewis and Rhyannon Styles (above), *Dr Carnesky's Incredible Bleeding Woman*, Soho Theatre, 2016. London. © Claire Lawrie, p. 197

Figure 61: Marisa Carnesky, *Dr Carnesky's Incredible Bleeding Woman*, menstrual protest, 2018. Brighton. © Rosie Powell, p. 198

Figure 62: Marisa Carnesky, *Blood Bath Ritual*, disused morgue, 2016. London. © Claire Lawrie, p. 199

Figures 63 & 64: Marisa Carnesky and Lucifire (top) and Livia Kojo Alour and Fancy Chance (above), *Showwomen*, Attenborough Centre for the Creative Arts, 2022. Brighton. © Sarah Hickson, p. 200

Figure 65 (right): Marisa Carnesky, Livia Kojo Alour, Lucifire, and Fancy Chance, *Showwomen*, The Spire, 2021. Brighton. © Manuel Vason, p. 201

Figure 66: Livia Kojo Alour, *Showwomen*, Attenborough Centre for the Creative Arts. 2022. Brighton. © Sarah Hickson, p. 202

Figure 67: Fancy Chance, *Showwomen*, Attenborough Centre for the Creative Arts, 2022. Brighton. © Sarah Hickson, p. 203

Figure 68 (left): Livia Kojo Alour and Fancy Chance, *Showwomen*, Attenborough Centre for the Creative Arts, 2022. Brighton. © Sarah Hickson, p. 204

Figure 69 (top): Livia Kojo Alour, Fancy Chance, Lucifire, and Marisa Carnesky, *Showwomen*, Film shoot, 2022. © Rosie Powell, p. 205

Figure 70 (above): Lucifire, *Showwomen*, Attenborough Centre or the Creative Arts, 2022. Brighton. © Sarah Hickson, p. 205

Figure 71: Marawa, Hilton Hotel, Melbourne, 2023. © Jo Duck, p. 206

Figure 72: Empress Stah, *Stargasm: Light in Places*. © Clive Holland, p. 207

Figure 73: Eirini Kartsaki, *Protrusions*, 2021. Athens. © Spyros Paloukis, p. 207

Figure 74: Fancy Chance, *Carnesky's Showwomxn Sideshow Spectacular*, Smithfield Market, 2023. London. © Holly Revell, p. 208

Figure 75: Claire Heaford and Alex Windsor, *Carnesky's Showwomxn Sideshow Spectacular*, Smithfield Market, 2023. London. © Ruth Bayer, p. 208

Figure 76: Symoné, *Carnesky's Showwomxn Sideshow Spectacular*, Smithfield Market, 2023. London. © Holly Revell, p. 209

Figure 77: Missy Macabre and Jackie Le, *Carnesky's Showwomxn Sideshow Spectacular*, Smithfield Market, 2023. London. © Ruth Bayer, p. 209

Figure 78: Montage by Lee Baxter of *Carnesky's Showwomxn Sideshow Spectacular*, 2023 & 2024. Featuring (from left to right): Tallulah Haddon, Livia Kojo Alour, Katherine Arnold, Claire Heafford, Mysti Vine, Jay Yule, Marisa Carnesky, Meg Hodgson, Lucifire, Fancy Chance, Jackie Le, Molly Beth Morossa, Vicky Butterfly, Kaajel, Livia Kojo Alour. Images © Ruth Bayer and Holly Revell, p. 210

Figure 79: Montage by Lee Baxter of *Carnesky's Showwomxn Sideshow Spectacular*, 2023 & 2024. Featuring (from left to right): Missy Macabre, Suri Sumatra, Ella The Great, Rachel Acham Seagroatt, Claire Heafford, Rhyanon Styles, H Plewis, Kaajel, Vicky Butterfly, Molly Beth Morossa, Lalla Morte, Chi Chi Revolver, Laura London, Tasha Rushbrooke, Hannah Finn. Images © Ruth Bayer and Holly Revell, p. 211

Figure 80: Marisa Carnesky, *Dr Carnesky's Incredible Bleeding Woman*, studio shot, 2016. London. © Sarah Ainslie, p. 212

Figure 81: Fancy Chance. © Jo Duck, p. 221

Figure 82: Rhyannon Styles, *Dr Carnesky's Incredible Bleeding Woman*, Soho Theatre, 2016. London. © Claire Lawrie, p. 222

Figure 83: Livia Kojo Alour, *Dr Carnesky's Incredible Bleeding Woman*, Pleasance Theatre, 2017. Edinburgh. © Roderick Penn, p. 225

Figure 84: Lucifire © Manolo Remiddi, p. 230

Figure 85: Lalla Morte, *The Wild Rose*, Le Divan Japonais, 2019. © Monsieur GAC (Gregory Augendre Cambon), p. 233

Figure 86: Amy Saunders aka Miss Behave, *The Miss Behave Game Show*, 2018. © Matt Crockett, p. 236

Figure 87: Nao Nagai, *Dr Carnesky's Incredible Bleeding Woman*, Attenborough Centre for the Creative Arts, 2018. Brighton. © Reuben and Jay Photography, p. 241

Figure 88: H Plewis, *Dr Carnesky's Incredible Bleeding Woman*, Attenborough Centre for the Creative Arts, 2018. Brighton. © Reuben and Jay Photography, p. 242

Figure 89: Nao Nagai, Amy Ridler, H Plewis, *Bleeding Women Ritual Workshops*, artists' residency, Metal Culture, 2015. Southend. © Sarah Ainslie, p. 256

Figure 90: *Menstruant Action*, Red Riding Hood March, 2017. Soho, London. © Claire Lawrie, p. 259

Figure 91: Signed publicity photo of Koringa, 1943. Photographer unknown, p. 263

Figure 92: Lulu Adams, Bertram Mills Circus, National Circus and Fairground Archive, circa 1937. Photographer unknown, p. 266

Figure 93: Carnesky's Finishing School at the former Foyles Building, 2016. Soho, London. Featuring Claud Palazzo, Oberon White, Scarlett Lassof f, Gwen Delune, Tracey Smith, Tallulah Haddon, Tom Cassani, Marisa Carnesky, Jasmine Shigemura Lee, Fauve Alice, Rene Eyre, Felix Huxtable. © Sarah Ainslie, p. 278

Figure 94: Fancy Chance and Amy Ridler, Metal Culture, artists' residency, 2015. Southend. © Sarah Ainslie, p. 295

Figure 95: Marisa Carnesky, *Showwomen Ritual Action*, The British Library, 2019. London. © Ruth Bayer, p. 304

Acknowledgements

Showwoman show making is often a group effort. You need to build a team, a company, a troupe. In the early days I reached out for collaborators bringing on board a raggle-taggle combination of squatters, performance artists and activists to create events like Smut Fest (Underworld, London,1993) *or Enter the Dragon Ladies* (Raymond Revue Bar, London 1996). I was always serious about my work, it may have been underground and difficult to define, merging with subcultures of its time, but I have always seen my work as an important and vital practice and prioritised it over every other aspect of my life – hence the word *Obsessions* in the title of this book.

Laying between legitimacy and illegitimacy, the work of the 90's tiptoed a well-trodden line in the art world, between art and entertainment, between high and lowbrow culture. Supporting that vision was always a close relationship with a producer, and I learnt about producing as an intern with the wonderful Tuppy Owens and her projects of the Sex Maniacs Ball and The Outsiders Club, amazing multi layered performance events promoting sexual liberation for differently abled people. We went onto producing the Smut Fest together in 1994, inspired by my time in New York, where I met artists like Annie Sprinkle, Jennifer Blowdryer and Kembra Pfahler, who influenced me with their flare and originality, and still do to this day. Attempting to bring a little of the East Villages risqué performance culture to London with cutting edge line-up including early performances from artists including myself, Tuppy Owens and Franko B was London's own Smut Fest of 1994.

A thank you goes to Chisenhale Dance Space who awarded me my first commission to make *Dragon Lady, Tiger Lady* and then to Andrew Caleya Chetty at Nottingham Now festival who helped me make the bigger show *Lady Muck and Her Burlesque Revue* with amazing costumes by Marianna Botey. In forming the collective Dragon Ladies, with the late visual artist Amanda Moss and her partner the electronic musician Adrian Jones, we enquired about hiring the famous Raymond Revue Bar in the heart of Soho, later to become the infamous nightclub The Box. As the first outside programmers of that iconic space, we brought an extraordinary vision that included our work using character, choreography, extreme sculpture-based costume and sound in a show I named *The Grotesque Burlesque Revue*. I thank Amanda and Adrian for working with me and for the great shows we realised. This included legendary guests including David Hoyle, Barry Adamson and an early performance by Anohni as part of the Black Lips Performance Cult who I had encountered in New York.

It was at this point that I started to form my clear ideas for a solo practice and met the fantastic producer Jeremy Goldstein, who helped take my work to the next level. Thanks go to the Live Art Development Agency and Lois Keidan for endorsing *Jewess Tattooess*. Jeremy worked tirelessly on a number of productions with me including *Jewess Tattooess, The Girl From Nowhere* and eventually *Carnesky's Ghost Train* on its London and Manchester outings.

Carnesky's Ghost Train was the biggest project any of us had done, a real ride with moving parts engineered and production managed into life by the late Neil Cooper and then by Simon Macoll and Natacha Poledica, our tireless company and stage manager. The project had a month's residency onsite in The Truman's Brewery on Brick Lane which drew huge crowds. Sincerest thanks go to Paul Kieve for his incredible illusions, Laura Hopkins for her wonderful set designs, Jonathan Allen for his amazing digital artworks and Rohan Kriwaczek for his haunting soundtrack and all the performing and visual artists that were involved, including the ones mentioned in this book. Many thanks also go to Sharon Keane for her great public relations on this run. My gratitude goes out to all of them for their hard work in realising this vision. My dearest friend Alison Murray, founder of Hellhound Productions, came on board as an executive producer and worked to get the project on tour to Glastonbury and Belgium. Deepest thanks go to her and her company, Hellhound, for their extraordinary support. Eventually *Ghost Train* went into a five-year residency managed and presented in partnership with the truly supportive Blackpool Council through the introductions of Professor Vanessa Toulmin. Thanks to Natasha Davies and Rose Sharp, who worked to help run the project in Blackpool, which was presented inside the great heritage site of the Winter Gardens and then on the Golden Mile outdoors, next to the Pleasure Beach. A thank you goes out to the great Blackpool team, including the Sandcastle Waterpark, for their technical management and all the amazing, dedicated Blackpool cast, including Kay Trayford, Harry Clayton Wright and Jason Karl. The ride closed its doors after ten glorious years of life in 2014. A sincere thank you goes to all who made *Carnesky's Ghost Train* possible.

Alongside all of this, I must thank Duckie and Simon Casson and Dicky Eaton for continually letting me try out every new idea at Duckie, all their advice on helping run my company and the warm embrace they shelter me with to this day. Continued thanks go to Dicky Eaton for his producing work on so many of the projects. I had the great opportunity to create courses for the Roundhouse during a residency in 2008-10, which kick started my teaching methods. Huge thanks go to Leila Jones for having the vision to enable me to explore and form this.

With a new idea for a promenade show exploring the symbols of the tarot, and the dedicated and passionate producing of Lara Clifton, we worked to make a spectacular show for the Cultural Olympiad in the Old Vic Tunnels, *Carnesky's Tarot Drome*, with a cast of performance artists in interactive tarot installations, roller skating and wrestling, with costumes by the fabulous Claire Ashley. This then toured to the Cirque De Jules Vernes in Amiens, France. Lara went on to produce *Dr Carnesky's Incredible Bleeding Woman*, which was born from my Practice as a Ph.D. researcher. Sincere thanks also go to Kira O'Reilly and Florence Peake who helped shape that show with their astute outside eyes. With Lara, I also took on a short lease of the disused Foyles building in Soho, and there we ran our school for a few short months prior to its demolition. Lara and I discovered we had grown up in the same neighbourhood and shared close cultural references. Together we ran many classes and courses at the Bethnal Green Working Men's Club for so many great emerging artists, including ones who went on to feature in *Showwomxn Sideshow Spectacular*.

Many thanks also go to Anna Goodman from Abstrakt for her great work in public relations and letting the press know so clearly about the shows in all their complexity. The generous Flora Herberich came on board to take the *Bleeding Woman* to Edinburgh and remount the work, and the kind and patient David Sheppard took over to produce the subsequent tour through a commission from the Attenborough Centre For The Creative Arts in Brighton, under the artistic programme of Laura McDermott.

Thanks go to Andre Pink for introducing me to the Tramshed, where he was curating cabaret courses. With the amazing support of the Tramshed, Artistic Director Jeremy James hosted a number of courses of Carnesky's Radical Cabaret School and suggested a collaboration with Rose Bruford College. Thank you to Jeremy James for this idea. Huge thanks to Professor Brian Lobel at Rose Bruford, with whom I then developed the cutting-edge BA Contemporary and Popular Performance at Rose Bruford College.

David Sheppard encouraged me to focus on *Showwomen* and develop the idea. Together we worked to bring *Showwomen* to fruition as a solo work in progress through Duckie at the Royal Vauxhall Tavern and at The British Library in 2019. The project was born out of an AHRC research grant at the National Circus and Fairground Archive that ran form 2008-11, the idea to make a show from this research had been brewing for a decade. Thanks go to Jon Fawcett and Jonah Albert at the British Library for their continued support of my research. With a pause for Covid, David worked to help make an archival website with filmmaker Rosie Powell and film producer Anne Beresford worked with me to make a short film of the idea. With the continued commitment of the fabulous Artistic Directors Laura McDermott in Brighton, Anthony Roberts from Colchester Arts Centre, Pasco Kevlin from Norwich Arts Centre and Jacksons Lane in London, we went on to make a four-cast version of *Showwomen*. The fantastic Jayne Compton came on board to tour the work to Colchester Arts Centre, Norwich Arts Centre, Jacksons Lane and Latitude Festival. The wonderful Tania Harrison at the City of London commissioned a large-scale promenade version for the revival of The Bartholemew Fair in 2023, *Carnesky's Showwomen Sideshow Spectacular*, working with over 33 performers, producer Jayne Compton and amazing production manager Sam Rush. With original art by the great Dave Pop and costumes by the gorgeous House of Flying Stiches, this went on to be realised as a two-day event for the closing show of the Brighton Festival 2024. A huge thank you to everyone who worked on *Showwomen*, both the stage and street versions. Through the Brighton Festival commission *Carnesky's Showwomxn Sideshow Spectacular* has gone onto to a new phase of artistic development.

This book, which places my practice at the centre, and paints such a thorough and compelling picture, has been visioned in a truly wonderful collaboration with the tireless efforts of Eirini Kartsaki as editor and without whom this book would not exist, and my deepest thanks go to her for her dedication to this process. Sincere gratitude goes to David Caines, designer in chief, who worked so hard to get the beautiful look of this book so right and so detailed. There are lots of people who have helped and worked on projects both paid and voluntarily over the years, who may not have been named in the book or on this page. I am grateful to all of you and send you my thanks.

On the end of the phone and in person with much needed moral support have always been my dearest friends Alison Murray, Kira O'Reilly, Beatrice Brown, Paul Kieve, Mim King, Dicky Eaton and Simon Casson and my sister Philippa, who are always there with love and support, as has my dedicated partner Johnny. Most of all, deepest thanks go to my mother Sybil and my late father Sydney for their tireless patience, time and listening to me on every aspect and every detail of every Showwoman situation. It is only with the support of my community and my family that I have been able to continually make shows and create these wonderful opportunities for myself and others.